Academic Writing

Academic Writing

A Guide for Management Students and Researchers

Mathukutty M. Monippally
and
Badrinarayan Shankar Pawar

 Response
Business books from SAGE
Los Angeles ▪ London ▪ New Delhi ▪ Singapore ▪ Washington DC
www.sagepublications.com

First published in 2010 by

Response Books
Business books from SAGE
B1/I-1 Mohan Cooperative Industrial Area
Mathura Road, New Delhi 110 044, INDIA

SAGE Publications Inc
2455 Teller Road
Thousand Oaks, California 91320, USA

SAGE Publications Ltd
1 Oliver's Yard, 55 City Road
London EC1Y 1SP, United Kingdom

SAGE Publications Asia-Pacific Pte Ltd
33 Pekin Street
#02-01 Far East Square
Singapore 048763

Published by Vivek Mehra for Response Books, typeset in 10/12 pt. Palatino Linotype by Innovative Processes, Delhi and printed at Chaman Enterprises, New Delhi.

Library of Congress Cataloging-in-Publication Data Available

ISBN: 978-81-321-0441-4 (PB)

The SAGE Team: Reema Singhal, Vikas Jain, Amrita Saha and Trinankur Banerjee

Dedication

I dedicate this book to my students, past and present, at Indian Institute of Management Ahmedabad. I have learned from them a great deal more than they will ever suspect.

I dedicate *Muthukutty M. Monippally* this work, with apologies and with prayers for forgiveness, to all those who suffered because of me and, with gratitude, to all those who nourished, taught and helped me. In particular, I dedicate this book to, among others who cannot be identified, my teachers, the families of my brothers and sister, my late father and my mother, and my Gurudevji (spiritual mentor), Sant Shri Asaramji Bapu.

Badrinarayan Shankar Pawar

Contents

PART II: The Anatomy of Academic Writing   63

List of Tables

List of Figures

Preface

Academic Writing is aimed at MBA students, MPhil and PhD scholars, and young faculty in management and behavioural sciences. The nudge for writing this book came from our graduate and doctoral students in the field of management and participants in faculty development programmes—their research papers and other written assignments, to be precise. Some of these students are among the best in the country, perhaps in the world. But their writing often lets them down.

Writing is an integral part of the process of research. It also facilitates success in academics. It is not enough to be smart and knowledgeable; we have to demonstrate our knowledge and insights through writing whether we are students or scholars. Otherwise we would be like wild flowers—perhaps the most beautiful on earth with exquisite scent, but unseen, unsmelt and unsung. That is as bad as being nonexistent. There is a lot of truth in the saying, "Publish or perish." Yet this vital skill required for publishing is not taught in schools and colleges. When attempts are made to teach writing, the focus seems to be more on getting sentences grammatically correct rather than on presenting knowledge in ways that make reading and comprehension easy.

Writing is like singing. Some write well without any special training just as some sing well instinctively. In academics, some manage the transition from creative writing and journalistic writing to academic writing with ease. But many do not, and as a result, they fare less well than they should. Our aim is to help graduate students and researchers, especially in management and behavioural sciences, to refine their writing so that they do well in their studies, publish in national and international journals, and make themselves more useful to society.

Neither scientific knowledge nor its written manifestation is uniform across all disciplines. Even within the same discipline, the degree of rigour varies significantly between what leading journals consider acceptable and what professors are willing to accept in the assignments submitted by their students. *Academic Writing* will help graduate students write better assignments, theses and dissertations; it will help scholars write conceptual and empirical papers for publication in reputable journals. Our objective is to alert all these writers to the broad expectations of readers of academic writing in management and behavioural sciences. It is up to them to figure out the specific expectations of their readers and mould their writing accordingly.

Although academic writing is not taught formally in our schools and colleges, there is plenty of literature on both research methodology and the documentation of the process and fruits of research. That makes it virtually impossible for us to say anything original about either. *Academic Writing* has benefited from the works of several scholars and writers, some of whose contributions we formally acknowledge in the body of the book. We give a list of resources in Appendix 2. We have also learned a great deal informally from our teachers and colleagues who helped us through our own doctoral and postdoctoral research. We are grateful to them. While *Academic Writing* clearly reflects our debt to published and unpublished advice, it is also built on our experiences, observations and reflections in varying degrees.

This book describes the place of academic writing in the broader process of research and scientific knowledge generation, distinguishes academic writing from other forms of writing, describes the process of composing academic papers and reports, and provides guidelines for appropriately acknowledging the use of others' work in one's academic writing. What distinguishes this book from others on similar themes is the extensive use of authentic samples of academic writing from graduate students and the characterization of academic writing as a part of research (knowledge generation process) and science. The student samples illustrate good as well as defective writing. We have refrained from editing the samples except where we feel that leaving some small mistakes in the quoted text might distract the reader without any advantage. Wherever we have edited the samples, we have indicated it. The book also contains a few hypothetical examples of various components of conceptual and empirical papers.

Academic Writing is a joint effort. We conceptualized the contents together, critiqued each other's chapters and revised them. We would like to revise this book to make it even more useful to the academic community. We will be grateful to you—graduate students, researchers, scholars and faculty who teach academic writing—for suggestions. We look forward to hearing from you.

Mathukutty M. Monippally
mpally@iimahd.ernet.in

Badrinarayan Shankar Pawar
pawar@iimk.ac.in

Acknowledgements

Part III of this book is based on *IIMA Citation Style Guide*, which the authors developed in 2004 along with Kaustabh Nande and Babita Deou, both of whom were then working as Academic Associates at Indian Institute of Management Ahmedabad (IIMA). The authors are grateful to them and to the institute for permission to build on that text.

Mathukutty M. Monippally would like to thank students of IIMA (2008–09) for allowing him to use extracts from their written assignments, and Prathyaksh Janardhanan and Divya Bhatnagar (Academic Associates at IIMA) for providing research assistance.

He would like to acknowledge the help he received from his colleagues Smeeta Mishra and Mukul Vasavada, and his former students Sauri Gudlavalleti, Diwakar Puri and Piyush Singhal (Post-Graduate Programme in Management for Executives Class of 2009). These five persons commented on the first draft of the chapters he had written. Their critical comments and suggestions helped him eliminate several defects.

Most of Mathukutty M. Monippally's work on this book was done during his sabbatical leave from IIMA (2008–09). He is grateful to the institute for this luxury.

Badrinarayan Shankar Pawar expresses his gratitude to all those who suffered because of him and those (for example, parents, brothers, teachers, colleagues, students and spiritual mentors) who helped him in various ways to be in a position to render this service to the academic community. He acknowledges his debt to Indian Institute of Management, Kozhikode (IIMK) where the work on this book was completed. He is grateful to his students, teaching whom provided him with the guidance and insights that facilitated the work on this book. He is grateful to all those who have helped him to consider doing this work and to actually complete this work. In particular, the goodness received from various individuals—Dr Kenneth K. Eastman, Dr Wayne Meinhart, Dr Thomas Stone, Dr Steve Barr, Professor Pradip Khandwalla, Professor Vijaya Sherry Chand, Professor Sanjay Bannerjee and Professor S. Krishnamoorthy—is gratefully acknowledged. The blessings of Gurudevji (spiritual mentor), Sant Shri Asaramji Bapu, are gratefully acknowledged. The support received long ago from Sant Dnyaneshwar Vasatigriha is gratefully acknowledged. Support, help, tolerance, acceptance and kindness provided by the families of his brothers and sister—Dattatraya and Tulsa, Ashok and Indulekha, Parshuram and Rajani—and his mother and his late father are gratefully acknowledged. Finally, valuable contributions and inspirations from the virtues in the life and living of his late father and his mother, despite their difficult circumstances, are also gratefully acknowledged.

Both the authors are grateful to *Vikalpa*, the refereed journal published by IIMA, for permission to reproduce extracts for illustrative purposes. They are indebted to Reema Singhal, commissioning editor at SAGE, and Vikas Jain, editor. The book has benefited tremendously from their suggestions.

Introduction

Graduate students and novice researchers trying to write academic papers face problems on three fronts: understanding the process of research or knowledge generation, documenting the process and results of research properly for sharing them with the academic community, and acknowledging the use of others' ideas appropriately. *Academic Writing* addresses all three.

The book is in three parts.

Part I, "The Research Process and the Role of Academic Writing" (Chapters 1 and 2), shows how academic writing is integrally linked to the generation of scientific knowledge (as opposed to other forms of knowledge) and how the structure of academic papers reflects the knowledge generation process adopted.

Chapter 1 describes scientific knowledge and distinguishes it from other forms of knowledge; it also illustrates the process that generates scientific knowledge. It then indicates that academic writing—documenting the process and outcome of research— needs to fulfil certain requirements coming from the features of science and research. There are different types of academic writing. They include conceptual and empirical research papers published in refereed journals, theses and dissertations written for the award of research degrees, and student reports built on field work or review of literature in a particular area. The chapter illustrates how academic writing reflects the essential features of science and research such as objectivity, public verifiability and use of existing knowledge; it also shows how the structuring of the academic paper reflects the structure of the scientific research process. The chapter glosses 19 terms frequently used in academic research. Examples include conceptual research, empirical research, measure, hypothesis, propositions and theory. However, the text in this section focuses only on papers in academic journals.

Chapter 2 describes the structure and illustrates the contents of the two main types of academic research papers, namely, conceptual research paper and empirical research paper. A conceptual paper, for example, typically consists of Abstract, Introduction, Specification of propositions or an integrated theory, Discussion, Closing paragraph and References. An empirical paper is likely to feature Abstract, Introduction, Hypothesis, Methods, Results, Discussion, Closing paragraph and References. The chapter outlines the major stages of the research process and/or outcomes that are included under the various main parts of these papers. Hypothetical examples are provided to illustrate the contents of various parts of conceptual and empirical papers. The chapter also briefly comments on the broad structure and contents of academic papers, theses and dissertations that students write to fulfil course requirements while outlining some of the similarities and differences between these works and conceptual papers and empirical papers.

Thus, the first two chapters cover aspects such as the context of academic writing, its purpose, the requirements that it needs to fulfil, different types of academic reports and papers, and major parts of structure and contents in them.

Part II, "The Anatomy of Academic Writing" (Chapters 3, 4 and 5), focuses on the central characteristics of academic writing and the processes underlying it.

Chapter 3 explains why writing is different from and more challenging in many respects than speaking. The first step towards making our writing better is figuring out what the remote readers expect of us. The chapter illustrates the problems created by writers who do not orient their text towards their readers. The discussion distinguishes academic writing from other forms of writing, especially journalistic and creative. What is common among all classes of academic writing is that ideas take centre stage. The essence of academic writing is making a claim or stating a thesis and supporting it with evidence, which often consists of data or logical propositions. Claims are accepted or rejected because of the evidence presented there, not because of who makes them. The chapter illustrates the style that is appropriate for academic writing. Apart from formality, academic writing displays objectivity, tentativeness and clarity. The broad processes involved in academic writing are narration, description and explanation. Each is illustrated. The chapter also explores the role of grammar and usage in academic writing.

Chapter 4 focuses on the structure and essential qualities of the paragraph, the building block of academic writing, because mastering it helps the writer master the essay. The advantage of focussing on the paragraph is that dissecting it to detect its structure and to verify if it has the qualities of good academic writing becomes more manageable. Unity and cohesion, the two essential qualities of a good paragraph, are explained and illustrated extensively. Other qualities expected in academic writing such as conciseness, logical rigour and clarity also are discussed and illustrated. The major ways of developing the paragraph are dealt with next: defining, exemplification, comparing and contrasting, analysing, explaining and classifying. The objective of this chapter is to equip readers to analyse their own writing to determine its strengths and weaknesses and to help them eliminate the weaknesses.

Chapter 5 describes in detail the process and sub-processes of composing and presenting documents to the reader. Often the fruits of writing become unsatisfactory because writers skip some of those sub-processes either out of ignorance or in the false hope of saving time. After characterizing the academic document as a story, the chapter goes over the stages of telling it: creating an outline of the story, deciding on the beginning, the middle and the end of the story. An academic story is almost like a creative story; the difference is that in a creative story, the writer starts from wherever he fancies while in academic writing the writer joins a conversation that is going on among scholars. Once an outline is created and fleshed out, the next step is polishing the story. The chapter provides a list of important questions an academic writer should ask himself to polish the text and make the document presentable to potential readers. Writing is not complete until the text is revised based on critique by the writer himself and by his peers. The chapter ends with practical advice on how to tidy up the document and make it attractive to the intended readers, especially editors and reviewers of journals.

Part III, "Acknowledging Academic Debts" (Chapter 6), deals with the scholarly convention of meticulously acknowledging the use of other scholars' works which constitute one of the sources of knowledge used in one's academic work. The chapter explains why we should cite these sources, what failure to do so—plagiarism or intellectual theft—entails, and how scrupulous acknowledgement of sources enhances academic reports and papers. It illustrates three kinds of borrowing: borrowing ideas along with the original text it comes packaged in, paraphrasing others' ideas and taking someone's support in general for an idea. It also analyses the anatomy of a citation—both the way a source is cited in the text and presented in the references. The chapter goes on to briefly describe a few popular citation styles (for example, APA, MLA, IEEE, Harvard) and then recommends a style derived from APA (American Psychological Association) style as the most appropriate for academic writing in management and behavioural sciences. The chapter ends with a detailed illustration of the way the most frequently encountered citation tasks, both in the print category and the electronic category, can be dealt with. Also introduced are additional resources where readers can get detailed and authoritative guidance on various aspects of providing citations.

These three parts are interconnected. Each chapter has references to the other chapters in which certain ideas are developed further or supported. It is, however, possible to ignore the sequence and go straight to any part or chapter if a reader wants to.

A note on the writing style adopted in this book

We adopt the standard academic writing style in Part I. In the rest of the book, however, we use a more relaxed, conversational style. This is to demonstrate both the styles and impress on students and researchers that there is nothing wrong with any style as long as it is appropriate to the job at hand and meets the legitimate expectations of the readers.

We have adopted a gender-neutral style. We do not, however, flaunt clumsy expressions such as *he or she, he/she* and *(s)he,* or the eyebrow-raising singular *they* to establish our neutrality. Instead, we use *he* and *she* at random when we refer to nouns such as *student, scholar* and *reader* representing a class. We also use the plural forms such as *students, scholars* and *readers,* when convenient, to refer to members of both the genders.

Note on extracts from student assignments

In Chapters 3, 4 and 5 we use a number of extracts from written assignments submitted by graduate students at the Indian Institute of Management, Ahmedabad, mostly during 2008–09. At the end of each extract we give the title of the assignment it is taken from and the year of submission. We are unable to give more details because we obtained permission to quote from them on condition that we would not reveal the writers' names. As already noted, most of these extracts appear unedited. Where a few minor changes have been made, we indicate it.

Part I

The Research Process and the Role of Academic Writing

1

Academic Writing and Research Process

CHAPTER OVERVIEW

This chapter first indicates that academic writing forms a part of science and research. In order to outline the broader context of academic writing, it then provides a brief description of science and research. It outlines some of the distinctive features of science. It outlines the overall research process and the steps involved in it. As academic writing is aimed at documenting academic research process and outcomes, this chapter provides a brief description of various terms associated with academic research, so as to help the comprehension of the contents of this chapter and subsequent chapters, and to facilitate understanding of the substance that academic writing seeks to document. It then outlines various requirements that academic writing needs to fulfil. These requirements come from the features of science and research, of which academic writing is a part. Thereafter, it briefly outlines the various types of academic writing works. In the end, it outlines the importance of good academic writing.

ACADEMIC WRITING AS A PART OF RESEARCH AND SCIENCE

While writing in general can potentially have various purposes, academic writing seeks to document and communicate knowledge in a written form. Knowledge can be generated through various means such as experience, intuition, tradition and science (for example, Kerlinger, 1988). While science is a means of generating knowledge, it also includes documentation of scientifically generated knowledge. Thus, science can be viewed as a distinctive approach to knowledge generation as well as a collection or body of existing scientific knowledge.

What kind of knowledge does science generate? One view states that science seeks to generate knowledge that is objective, that goes beyond an individual researcher's opinions or preferences, and that is grounded in systematically obtained data (Hempel, 1965, p. 11, quoted in Stone, 1978, p. 7). In this view, there are various distinctive features of the process of generating knowledge that can form a part of science. This process of generating knowledge by adopting practices that have features outlined in the above view of science is referred to as research. Thus, Stone (1978) notes that research involves examination of a phenomenon by using practices that follow certain norms of science. This view suggests that knowledge contained in science has certain features. It also suggests that such knowledge is generated through a process which, because of its compliance with the norms of science, constitutes research.

From this perspective, academic writing, as a means of documenting and communicating scientific knowledge, documents and communicates research process and research outcomes. Documentation of research process describes how the research process was carried out and how the knowledge was generated, and the documentation of the research outcomes describes the knowledge that was generated through the implementation of the documented research process. A few examples described here may illustrate the above outlined role of academic writing in research and science.

Consider an example of academic writing in a journal paper that describes how a researcher carried out a particular study to arrive at certain findings. Here, various steps in the research study constitute the research process and the findings constitute the outcome of research process, that is, knowledge in the form of certain empirical facts. As an example, suppose a researcher studied how employees' commitment to an organization affects their performance of positive behaviours in the organization. Such a paper will first document that it is seeking an answer to the research question as to what is the relationship between employees' commitment to an organization and employees' performance of positive behaviours in the organization. It will then document the existing scientific knowledge on this research question by outlining a review of the relevant existing scientific literature. Then it will conclude that the existing scientific knowledge does not adequately answer this research question and, hence, there is an inadequacy in the existing scientific knowledge about this research question. Based on these descriptions, the paper will outline a conclusion that this research question needs to be studied in order to fill a gap in the existing knowledge. Then the research paper will generate some prediction or conjecture about what relationship seems plausible between employees' commitment to an organization and employees' positive behaviours in the organization. Subsequently, it will describe how this conjecture was tested. Here, it will describe what steps the researcher carried out to generate some data and to conclude from the data the empirically existing nature of the relationship between employees' commitment to an organization and employees' positive behaviours in the organization. This conclusion as to whether or not there actually is a relationship between employees' commitment to an organization and employees' positive behaviours in the organization constitutes addition of knowledge, in the form of an empirical fact, to the existing body of scientific knowledge on this aspect.

While the hypothetical research paper described in this example may include documentation of some other details pertaining to the research process that the researcher adopted and the research outcomes that the researcher generated, the above description indicates that a research paper in an academic journal, as an example of academic writing, contains documentation of the research process and research outcomes associated with science. Science can be seen as a process of generating knowledge and a body of knowledge generated in certain ways. Academic writing can be seen as the documentation of both these aspects of science. First, it can be seen as documentation of various aspects of the research process that forms a part of science as a process of knowledge generation. Second, it can also bee seen as documentation of the outcome of the research process that adds to the existing body of documented scientific knowledge that is contained in science viewed as a repository of documented knowledge. The paper described in this example may be referred to as an empirical paper and represents a category of research referred to as empirical research.

Let us consider another example of a term paper or classroom assignment that a post-graduate management student may complete. This may be an assignment involving a field project (example, a summer project) that the student carried out. Here, the project report will be an example of academic writing. The project report will describe the research question, what knowledge gap the research question could address when the question is answered by the research, how the student collected and analysed data, and what was the answer generated—from the data—to the research question. In this example, the project report also describes the process and outcome of the research that the student carried out. This paper may be referred to as an empirical paper and represents a category of research referred to as empirical research.

Yet another example could be of a journal paper or student report based on the review of literature in a particular area to address a research question. A researcher may review various relevant journal papers, which document the existing knowledge about a phenomenon, and based on the literature reviewed, he will arrive at certain conclusions about the aspect of reality under study. For instance, if the relationship between employees' commitment to an organization and employees' positive behaviours in the organization is being studied, then, based on the review of the literature from the existing journal papers, books, and so on, a researcher may first conclude that the existing literature does not indicate with adequate clarity, whether there is a relationship between employees' commitment to an organization and employees' positive behaviours in the organization. In this example, the journal paper describes the existing knowledge and, based on it, arrives at a conclusion that describes the existing state of scientific knowledge and the gaps in it, if any. Such a paper may be referred to as a conceptual paper of a particular kind—literature review—and represents a category of research referred to as conceptual research.

The above outlined examples are specific forms of academic writing, namely, an empirical paper in a journal, a student project report reporting an empirical research study, and a conceptual paper in a journal. These examples of specific forms of academic writing may help bring out the connection between science, research and academic writing. The above-mentioned examples outline how academic writing documents the process and out-comes of research, and how it forms a part of science as a way of generating knowledge and of science as body of documented knowledge. Because this perspective suggests that academic writing is a part of science and seeks to document the process and outcomes of research, it seems appropriate to understand a few aspects of research and science, so that the nature, requirements and purpose of academic writing can be more adequately understood. Thus, the subsequent parts of this chapter outline a few aspects of research and science with a limited purpose of describing the broader context in which academic writing occurs.

SCIENCE

The above outlined definition of science suggests that science is a particular way of knowledge generation. The view of science outlined above is only one of the views of science, as other views suggesting how knowledge can be generated and what science is, also exist. The view outlined here refers to the positivistic or logical positivistic view or natural science model or quantitative research approach (for example, Daft, 1983; Lee, 1991). Though this is just one of the views of science, it is the view that is extensively used in social science and in organizational studies (Lee, 1991, p. 343). In this view, science seeks to generate knowledge that is objective (for example, Hempel, 1965, as cited by Stone, 1978; Kerlinger, 1988). Individual subjectivities in forms such as opinions and preferences are sought to be restrained. Empirical facts constitute the basis of knowledge. Systematic experimentation and observation is used to obtain empirical facts. This view, reflected in Hempel (1965, as cited by Stone, 1978) and Kerlinger (1988), suggests a specific approach to knowledge generation which seeks empirical facts that are obtained through certain methods. There are other ways of generating knowledge. For instance, Kerlinger (1988, p. 6) notes the various methods of knowledge generation, including those of intuition, authority and science. Science, as a means of knowledge generation, has certain distinctive features. Some of the distinctive features of science are outlined here.

As a preparation for discussing various features of science, it may be useful to consider a few aspects pertaining to the knowledge that science seeks to generate. The reality about which science seeks to generate knowledge resides in the world outside a researcher or human being. For instance, a researcher examining the phenomenon of employees' commitment to an organization does not have employees or their commitment to an organization literally residing inside or with her. What a researcher has or develops is a belief about the phenomenon of employees' commitment to an organization. The reality being examined is represented in the researcher's knowledge as a belief about the reality. In this way, a bit of knowledge about the reality is a belief about the reality. However, as science seeks empirical facts as the basis of knowledge, only those beliefs that are supported by or are correspondent with empirical facts constitute knowledge in a scientific sense. Further, science, as outlined earlier, also requires that the empirical facts used as the basis of knowledge be obtained in a particular manner.

The above discussion suggests that knowledge in science can be seen as beliefs about reality that are correspondent with the reality, as examined through certain processes. These beliefs that are correspondent with the realty and, hence, constitute description of the reality or empirical world, become statements describing empirical facts in science. In this sense, while an individual has beliefs about the reality of a phenomenon or about the empirical world in general, knowledge, as a part of science, is a set of empirically supported statements about the reality or the empirical world. Knowledge, in this view, is a set of beliefs that are correspondent with the empirical reality or a set of statements that describe the empirical reality. Based on this, science can be viewed as a way of forming empirically valid beliefs. From this perspective, science becomes one of the ways of forming beliefs.

Other ways of forming beliefs include tradition, authority, experience and intuition. A person may have various beliefs about reality coming from these ways of generating knowledge. For instance, a person may have a belief that it is harmful not to bow before elderly persons. He may have formed this belief based on one or two experiences where he did not bow before an elderly person and then he suffered harmful consequences. As a result, he has formed a belief through experience as a way of forming beliefs. A person may form such a belief also based on the tradition in the community or society, of which he has been a part. Similarly, an individual may have been told by another person whom he respects that it is harmful not to bow before an elderly person and, therefore, the individual may form a belief by accepting another person as an authority that it is harmful not to bow before an elderly person. This indicates that there are various ways of forming beliefs, and science is one of the ways of forming beliefs. Science, as one of the ways of forming beliefs, has certain distinctive features as outlined here based on various views (for example, Hessler, 1992; Kerlinger, 1988; Murdick & Cooper, 1982).

First, science relies on empirical facts to determine whether a belief can become a piece of knowledge (e.g., Kerlinger, 1988). In the positivistic view of science, observations or empirical facts are regarded as the deciding criterion for determining what constitutes knowledge. For instance, in characterizing positivism, Ritchie and Lewis (2004) note that observation is the guiding criterion on matters of theoretical disputes. This role of observations or empirical facts is reflected in research papers in journals, where the specification of a theoretical model in a conceptual paper is regarded as the specification of conjectures. Such conjectures need to be verified in order to assess whether empirical facts or data support them. Only after the empirical verification supports the conjectures from a conceptual paper do they become a part of statements describing empirical facts and get accepted as a part of scientific knowledge about the empirical world.

Second, science seeks knowledge that is objective and free from individual opinions and preferences (e.g., Hempel, 1965, as cited by Stone, 1978; Kerlinger, 1988). Third, science encourages skepticism (e.g., Murdick & Cooper, 1982), and beliefs are subjected to questions and examination. Beliefs are accepted as statements constituting knowledge only when their examination reveals support for them through their correspondence with empirical reality. Fourth, science subscribes to the norm of public verifiability (e.g., Hessler, 1992). The process and outcomes of science or scientific examination are open to the relevant community for verification. This is reflected in empirical research papers published in academic journals, where a considerable part of the writing in the paper describes the methods that were used by the researcher for carrying out various research steps such as measurement, data collection and data analysis.

Fifth, science uses the existing knowledge to generate new knowledge (e.g., Murdick & Cooper, 1982). New implications are drawn based on the existing body of knowledge. These implications constitute conjectures. Studies are carried out to examine whether empirical facts support these conjectures. Those conjectures that receive support from empirical facts are retained as statements about empirical facts and add to the existing body of knowledge. In this manner, science uses the existing knowledge to generate new knowledge.

Sixth, science aims at accumulation of knowledge (e.g., Murdick & Cooper, 1982). New empirical facts or statements of empirical facts are integrated with the existing body of knowledge. Typically the early part of an empirical research paper describes a research question that reflects a gap in the existing body of knowledge, and the later part of the paper outlines implications of the paper's findings for the existing body of knowledge. In this sense, an empirical research paper identifies where new knowledge needs to be added to the existing body of knowledge and adds some knowledge to the existing body of knowledge, facilitating accumulation of knowledge.

The above description suggests that science, as a way of generating knowledge, has certain features. These features of science are reflected in the academic writing contained in academic research papers.

RESEARCH

Research is a process of generating knowledge through the adoption of science-based approach. A distinctive feature of science-based research is that it seeks to develop, verify and refine theories. Dubin (1969) indicates that one of the objectives of research is to assess whether the existing theories are correspondent with or supported by empirical facts. Dubin (1969) also notes that *research* involves specifying new theories in place of those that have been found to be inadequate for accommodating empirical facts. This view suggests that research involves verifying and improving theories. Thus, a theory is the central feature of research. Consistent with this centrality of theory in research process, the description in Kerlinger (1988) suggests that developing a theory is the main objective of science.

Research adopts a specific procedure to generate knowledge in compliance with the norms of science. There are various assumptions and features associated with science which are reflected in the features of research as a process. For instance, as outlined earlier based on various sources (for example, Hessler, 1992; Kerlinger, 1988; Murdick & Cooper, 1982), science encourages the use of existing knowledge to generate new knowledge; science makes its statements open to scepticism and doubt unless supported by empirical facts; and it regards empirical facts as the criterion for determining whether a belief constitutes a piece of knowledge. These features are reflected in the hypothetico-deductive approach to research. In hypothetico-deductive approach, implications or hypotheses are deduced from existing knowledge or existing observations, but these implications or hypotheses go beyond the existing knowledge and, hence, their subsequent empirical verification can potentially yield new knowledge (for example, Baronov, 2004). In this approach, the research process involves generation of conjectures or hypotheses based on the existing knowledge, and verification of conjectures to assess whether empirical data supports them. Generation of conjectures or hypotheses in the research process typically takes the form of *theory building* exercise whereas verification of conjectures takes the form of *theory testing* exercise. From this perspective, research can be seen as a process consisting of two parts, namely, theory building and theory testing. The theory building part is typically referred to as the conceptual part and the theory testing part as the empirical part of research process. The overall research process consisting of generation of conjectures and their empirical verification contains both conceptual research

Figure 1.1 An Overview of Research Process

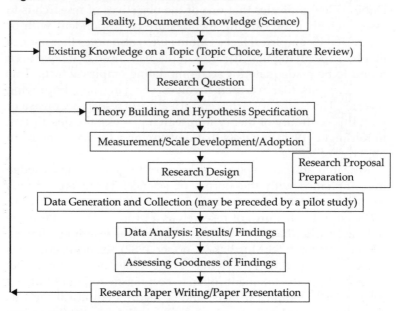

Source: Authors.

and empirical research parts. In particular, the research process involves various steps depicted in Figure 1.1 some of which are briefly described hereunder.

a. One of the early steps is the specification of the aspect of the reality to be examined.

b. A subsequent step is the identification of a knowledge gap and research question on that aspect of the reality. Both these preceding steps, like some of the other steps in research process, would typically require literature review.

c. Generation of conjectures or hypotheses from the existing knowledge to specify plausible predictions about the aspect of reality being examined is the next step. This step involves the process of theory building. The outcome of this step is a set of statements of relationship between concepts. Concepts refer to various aspects of the reality being examined. For instance, the statement that employees' commitment to an organization is positively associated with employees' positive behaviours in the organization is a conjecture. It specifies a positive relationship between two concepts, namely, employees' commitment to an organization and employees' positive behaviours. The concept of 'employees' commitment to an organization' represents a certain aspect of the reality of employees' organizational life being examined. Similarly, the concept of employees' positive behaviours in an organization' represents certain aspect of the reality of employees' organizational life being examined.

d. The step following the preceding ones is designing or adopting measurements for obtaining measures of the concepts in the conjectures to be verified.

e. Specification of the research design for data collection is the next step. This involves specification as to which data will be collected, from whom the data will be collected, what procedures will be used for data collection, how the data will be analysed, and so on.

f. Following the preceding steps, the next step is the actual implementation of the research design steps to collect the data required for assessing whether the conjectural statements receive support from the empirical data.

g. The next step is the analysis of data to examine the pattern in it. For instance, in the example of verifying the conjecture specifying a positive relationship between employees' commitment to an organization and employees' positive behaviours in the organization, the data analysis process will compute the correlation between the values obtained for the measures of these two concepts for a sample of employees. The data analysis will conclude whether or not there is a significant positive correlation between the employees' commitment to an organization and the employees' positive behaviours in the organization in the data obtained from a sample of employees.

h. A subsequent step is drawing a conclusion about whether the conjecture is empirically supported. This conclusion reflects findings of the study. In the current example, if the computed correlation between the measures of employees' commitment to an organization and employees' positive behaviours in the organization is positive and statistically significant in the data obtained from a sample, then the conclusion is that the conjecture is empirically supported. This reflects the correspondence between the conjecture and the empirical reality as contained in the analysed data pattern of correlations. At times, the goodness of conclusion is also assessed.

i. Determining the implications of the conclusion for theory and for knowledge of reality is the next step. If there is empirical support for the conjecture, then the conjecture can be regarded as a statement describing an empirical fact. This adds a piece of knowledge to the existing body of knowledge. This also provides support for the theory from which the conjecture was derived. Generation of new knowledge, verification of conjecture and verification of theory are attained as multiple outcomes of the research process. These contributions of research process are reflected in the feedback arrows from the boxes at the top in Figure 1.1.

A BRIEF DESCRIPTION OF VARIOUS TERMS USED IN ACADEMIC RESEARCH

The depiction of the overall research process in Figure 1.1 and the associated description outlined above uses various terms such as *hypothesis, measurement* and *research design*. The subsequent parts of this chapter and this book would also refer to these terms, as these terms form the various aspects of research that a research paper needs to describe through academic writing. In light of this, these and other related terms associated with research process are briefly described below, so that reading and comprehension of the subsequent parts of this chapter and the rest of the book becomes easier.

Research

Research is a process in which a phenomenon or aspect of reality is examined by following certain norms of science. In the logical positivistic approach, this will be a systematic, objective and empirical (facts-based or data-based) examination of a phenomenon. The various steps in research process are designed to make the process systematic, objective and empirical.

Conceptual Research

This type of research seeks to advance knowledge on a topic without collecting and analysing new data, and without interpreting the patterns in such freshly collected data. It typically relies on the existing published literature and, based on the literature, some of which itself may describe existing data-based studies, it may advance the existing knowledge in various ways such as suggesting conclusions based on the existing literature, synthesizing the existing literature, or pointing out gaps in the existing literature. Thus, only a part of the steps depicted in Figure 1.1 will be typically associated with this type of research.

Empirical Research

This type of research takes up a research question, makes a plausible conjecture pertaining to the matter of the research question, and then examines whether the reality as reflected in the empirical data supports the conjecture. If the conjecture is supported in the empirical reality, then the conjecture statement becomes a statement of empirical fact. Thus, empirical studies are data based and, based on data, they can generate empirical facts. Most of the steps depicted in Figure 1.1 will be associated with this type of research.

Knowledge

While the reality being studied typically exists outside a researcher, it comes to be represented inside a researcher's cognition, and later in the documented body of knowledge as a statement of belief that is correspondent with empirical reality. Thus, in the documented body of knowledge, knowledge is represented as a set of statements, whereas in the mind of a researcher or a reader, it constitutes a statement of belief about an aspect of reality. In research, the existing knowledge about a topic is reflected in the relevant literature on a particular topic. This literature may be in various forms including a research paper or a book. New knowledge generated by a study because of empirical support or data-based support found for a conjecture examined in it, adds a new bit of knowledge to the existing body of knowledge. In this sense, academic writing in an empirical paper describes a bit of knowledge that needs to be added to the existing knowledge, and it also describes how that bit of knowledge was generated.

Theory

A theory is a simplified representation of a limited part of the reality. It typically includes a set of systematically interrelated statements about the part of the reality being represented by it. These statements are of various kinds including statements that serve as premises (assumptions, established principles, and so on), statements specifying definitions for terms (referred to as *concepts*) used to label the different aspects of the reality being represented by the theory, and statements that specify conjectures (referred to as *propositions* and *hypotheses*) about the reality. Theories can be described in a textual form using statements or they can also be documented pictorially by depicting the various aspects of the reality represented through labels (referred to as *concepts*), and the relationships between the various labels indicated through connections (referred to as *propositions*). In research process, for developing additional knowledge about the empirical reality, first a representation of the reality in the form of a theory is developed. From a theory, then, certain conjectures or predictions (referred to as *propositions* and *hypotheses*) can be obtained, either as a part of connections contained in a theory or derived from the theory through further reasoning, about what is likely to be observed in the empirical reality if the theory was a correct representation of the empirical reality. This part of research that develops a representation of the reality and derives conjectures from it for subsequent empirical examination constitutes one kind of conceptual research.

Concepts

Various aspects of the reality that is being studied in research are represented by assigning labels/terms to them and by providing definitions for the labels/terms. These two aspects, namely, a label and a definition, jointly constitute a concept or concept specification. Thus, a concept is a term or label which represents, in a generalized manner, an aspect of the reality. For instance, *leadership* is a concept and represents an aspect of the reality of organizational and social life. The term or label leadership and the associated definition jointly constitute the concept leadership. The definition of a concept is typically specified using other terms. For instance, the concept leadership may be defined as "the process of inspiring others." As another example, the reality of an employee's commitment to an organization is represented in research through the concept *organizational commitment*, wherein the concept specification for this aspect of reality includes the label organizational commitment and an associated definition for it. Similarly, the labels *loyalty, customer loyalty, brand image* and *innovative strategic orientation*, when coupled with their respective definitions, constitute concepts. Thus, in research, various parts of the reality being studied are represented in the form of concepts. An integrated view of the reality in terms of interrelationships between different aspects of the reality is then provided by specifying relationships among these concepts.

Propositions

Propositions are statements specifying relationships between concepts. For example, the statement that a person's need for power is positively associated with a person's leadership is a statement that specifies relationship between the concepts of *need for power* and *leadership*. This is a conjectural statement rather than a statement of fact. Empirical research would be needed to examine whether this conjectural statement is actually supported by the data obtained from the reality. Until empirical research actually concludes the presence or absence of support for a conjectural statement represented by a proposition, it remains a statement of conjecture. Once empirical research supports the conjectural statement specified in a proposition, it represents an empirical fact and becomes a statement of empirical fact.

Variables

Concepts such as loyalty, organizational commitment, customer loyalty, brand image, innovative strategic orientation, and so on, are abstract. As concepts form parts of a proposition, in order to test whether the reality is actually correspondent with the propositions, one has to collect data about the aspects of the reality represented by the concepts. For instance, to assess whether the proposition "need for power is positively associated with leadership" actually corresponds with the reality, one needs to collect data from several individuals on their need for power and on their leadership, and see if there is a positive correlation between the values obtained from several individuals on measures of need for power and leadership. For this empirical verification process to occur, first some measurable indicators need to be associated with concepts. These measurable indicators associated with a concept are referred to as variables.

For instance, one measurable indicator of leadership concept could be the extent to which a person structures other persons' work in terms of setting goals and describing the procedures for attaining goals. In this example, the number of behaviours of a person of setting goals for others, constitutes one measure of a person's leadership behaviour and, in this sense, the number of goal-setting behaviours is a variable that seeks to measure the concept of leadership. Similarly, the concept of an employee's organizational commitment can be measured through the variable of number of years an employee has served the company or through the variable of amount of pay increase the employee would decline from another organization in order to remain with the existing organization. Thus, variables could be seen as measurable indicators that assess the extent of a concept's manifestation in the empirical reality so that concepts become measurable.

Hypotheses

Statements that specify relationships between variables are hypotheses. These are statements of conjecture indicating what relationships are expected or plausible. Only when these conjectural statements are empirically verified and found to be supported by the empirical data, that they become statements of fact; otherwise, they remain as statements of conjecture. There is a similarity between this description of a hypothesis and the one provided earlier for a proposition. This similarity exists because there is a relationship between a proposition and a hypothesis. It was described earlier that conjectural statements of relationships between concepts are propositions. It was also described earlier that the variables are measurable indicators of concepts and, in this sense, there is a correspondence between concepts and variables. In light of this, when concepts in a proposition are replaced with the variables corresponding to these concepts, then the resulting statement will be a hypothesis. For example, a proposition that "employees' organizational commitment is negatively associated with employee withdrawal from an organization" can become a hypothesis that "the number of years spent in an organization by an employee is negatively associated with the number of absence days of an employee." In this statement of hypothesis, the concept employees' organizational commitment is replaced with the variable number of years spent in the organization, and the concept employee withdrawal from an organization is replaced with the variable the number of absence days of an employee. In this example, this statement of hypothesis is derived from a statement of proposition by replacing concepts in the proposition with the corresponding variables.

In practice, however, the distinction between a proposition and a hypothesis is not strictly reflected in the use of labels associated with concepts and variables. This is partly because usually the same label or term is used to refer to both a concept as well as a variable associated with a concept. For instance, the label 'organizational commitment' could refer to the concept of organizational commitment or it could refer to the scores of employees on a scale measuring organizational commitment where the scale score is a variable. Thus, typically in an empirical paper a statement such as "employees' organizational commitment is negatively associated with employee withdrawal from an organization" includes the terms organizational commitment and withdrawal behaviour as concepts which are measured in the empirical verification process, through adoption of corresponding measures described in the subsequent parts of the empirical paper. Typically, such concepts specified in an empirical paper are measurable and are measured in the study reported in the empirical paper, and the statements containing them are typically referred to as a 'hypothesis' rather than a 'proposition' in an empirical paper.

Measures

One of the purposes of associating a variable with a concept is to make the concept measurable. For instance, the concept employees' commitment to an organization is not directly measurable and, hence, a variable number of years spent in an organization by an employee, which can be measured, is associated with this concept and serves as a measurable indicator of this concept. For some concepts, such measurable indicators may be readily available. However, in other cases, it may be necessary to devise a special means for measuring the presence of a concept's attributes in the reality for two reasons. First, readily available indicators may not be adequate measures of the concept. For instance, the indicator number of years spent in an organization may not adequately reflect the concept of employees' commitment to an organization because it may reflect other aspects such as an employee's inactivity in looking for employment opportunities in better organizations. Second, for some concepts, an indicator corresponding to a concept may not be readily available. For instance, the concept of *sense of meaning in work* may not have a readily available indicator or variable through which it can be measured. For such reasons, instead of using a readily available indicator, a special device may need to be designed to measure a concept. Such device is termed as a *measure*.

Typically, in the behavioural areas of management, such a measure would be in the form of a scale that requires a respondent to provide responses, on a predefined response format, to a set of scale items (statements). Each response option within a response format has a distinct score associated with it. The scores associated with the respondent's responses to individual items in the scale are added up to arrive at the total scale score. This score reflects the total score on the variable corresponding to the concept that the measure/scale is seeking to measure. Such scales are developed through a process called *scale development*. A scale would typically contain a set of scale items or statements which describe some aspects that are relevant to the concept being measured; a response format with a set of response options ranging from high magnitude to low magnitude (for example, *strongly agree, agree, neither agree nor disagree, disagree* and *strongly disagree*, carrying scores of 5, 4, 3, 2 and 1, respectively); and directions to help the respondents to make responses to the items on the scale. Such scales, which are devices for obtaining a measure of a concept, are referred to as measures or measurement. The process of developing such scales is typically referred to as *scale development* and, at times, it is also referred to as *measurement design* or *operationalization.*

Research Design

The term research design can have two interpretations. First, it could refer to the plan for collection of data on various aspects being studied in order to assess empirical support for the hypotheses being examined in a study. In this sense of use of the term, research design will include specification of the nature of examination (for example, causal or descriptive) to be done, specification of variables on which data is to be collected, specification of the respondents from whom the data is to be collected (sample profile), procedures (for example, interview or self-report questionnaires) to be used, the timing of data collection on different variables and the number of observations to be obtained. Second, the term research design could also refer to the process actually used to collect data for assessing empirical support for the hypotheses being examined. These two possible interpretations of the term research design suggest that it could refer to a plan of data collection as well as to the actual process carried out for data collection.

Results/Findings

In research process, data is obtained through the use of measures and by implementing the steps in research design. Such data is then analysed to assess the patterns present in the data. This data analysis may yield results in a statistical form. For instance, consider testing a proposition that "employees' organizational commitment is negatively associated with employee withdrawal from an organization." If suitable scales are developed to measure the concepts of organizational commitment and employee withdrawal, then these concepts, through the use of their respective scales, become measurable and, hence, the proposition becomes a testable hypothesis.

To test this hypothesis, data needs to be obtained from a sample of employees on their 'organizational commitment' and 'withdrawal from an organization' through the use of scales measuring these concepts. Then the data on the measures of these two constructs for a reasonably large number of employees would provide two scores: one from each of the two measures for each employee in the sample. In the data analysis stage, when the relationship between these two scores across the sample is assessed through the use of the statistical procedure of correlation assessment, a negative correlation may be found between these scores. The result from the study in the form of an outcome of data analysis, in this example, would be a negative correlation between employees' commitment to an organization and employees' withdrawal from an organization. Based on this result, the finding on hypothesis testing is that this hypothesis is supported by the study results based on the empirical data. In this sense, findings of a study come out in the form of conclusions on hypothesis testing, and indicate the extent to which the empirical reality, as reflected in the results of the analysis of the empirical data obtained, is correspondent with the conjectures (propositions and hypotheses) about the reality that the study was aimed at examining. As shown through an arrow in Figure 1.1, a finding from the results of data analysis relates back to various initial aspects of the study such as the research question and hypothesis.

Goodness of Findings

The findings derived from a study in the form of conclusions on the presence or a lack of empirical support for a hypothesis are an outcome of the implementation of various steps such as measurement design, selection of respondents, use of data collection procedure and use of statistical procedures for data analysis. The strengths and limitations associated with the implementation of these steps are likely to influence the quality of the findings or conclusions derived from a study about the correspondence between the study hypothesis and empirical reality. Thus, empirical research papers will typically also contain a description on the goodness of findings coming from a research study. For instance, a research paper may describe how the study findings may be applicable only to the study sample because of the very specific nature of the respondents (for example, only workers in a particular profession, industry or a region), from whom the study data was collected. This description will reflect the goodness of findings on one aspect, namely, generalizability. Similarly, a research paper may describe how the use of a particular measure or a particular data collection method may have had implications in terms of either enhancing or impairing the goodness of a study's findings.

Implications of Research Study Findings

Conclusions derived from a study may suggest implications for at least four aspects, namely, implications for the theory from which the propositions/hypotheses were derived, implications for the existing knowledge about the phenomenon being examined, implications for practice and implications for future research. Study conclusions indicating the presence of empirical support for hypotheses have implications for the theory from which the hypotheses were derived in that they indicate support for the theory as a reasonable representation of the reality about a phenomenon.

Further, when the research hypotheses are empirically supported, certain pieces of empirical facts get added to the existing knowledge about a phenomenon. As a result, study findings have implications for the existing knowledge about a phenomenon. Moreover, when study conclusions add to the existing knowledge about a phenomenon, they can also provide some guidelines for those who need to act on the reality. These implications are referred to as implications for practice. Further, findings of a study can make the existing knowledge of the reality more complete through various ways such as by adding details to or connections between the various aspects of reality. In light of such new knowledge, new research questions can emerge for which further research may be needed. Such possibilities opened up for future research are referred to as research implications of a study or study findings.

FEATURES OF SCIENCE AND RESEARCH
IN ACADEMIC WRITING

A brief summary of preceding discussion may help comprehend the relationship of academic writing with science and research. As outlined earlier, science seeks to generate knowledge of certain kinds, and research as a science-based approach to knowledge generation needs to follow certain norms of science. Because of this, certain distinctive features are associated with science and research process. As academic writing documents research process and its outcome in the form of the knowledge generated, the earlier outlined features of science and research process result in certain requirements which academic writing needs to fulfil as described below.

The main requirement of academic writing coming from the features of research is that the contents of an academic research paper are required to document the overall research process described above. As a result, the sequence of sections of contents in an academic research paper are somewhat similar to the sequence of the research methods steps in the overall research process as depicted in Figure 1.1. For instance, an empirical research paper will start with literature review on the basis of which a research question is specified. Then theorizing or theory building part is outlined to specify one or more hypotheses pertaining to the research question. These parts of an empirical research paper document the conceptual part of the research process. Subsequently, a separate section outlines the methods adopted for the verification of the hypotheses. This part contains the description of the measurements used to obtain data on the concepts or variables in the hypotheses, the sample of respondents from whom the data is collected, the data collection procedures used (for example, a self-report questionnaire), and the analysis performed. This part is followed by a part that outlines the results where the outcome of data analysis is described. Thereafter, based on the results of data analysis, study findings in terms of the presence or absence or extent of support for the study hypotheses are described. Finally, the last part of an academic research paper describes the implications of the study findings for the theory from which the hypotheses were derived for testing, for the existing knowledge about the phenomenon under examination, and for future research and practice.

The above described brief outline of the contents of a typical empirical research paper describes the correspondence between the sequence of research process steps (Figure 1.1) and the structure of an empirical research paper. This correspondence is there because academic writing documents the process and outcomes of research. Further, some other aspects of the science and research process are also reflected in academic writing, as outlined below, through the discussion of how three of the features of science—objectivity (e.g., Kerlinger, 1988), public verifiability (e.g., Hessler, 1992) and the use of existing knowledge for generating new knowledge (e.g., Murdick & Cooper, 1982)— are reflected in academic writing.

The aspect of objectivity emphasized in science may get reflected in the language of an empirical research paper, where a researcher may distinguish between what is the reality, possibly as reflected in empirical data, and what is the researcher's own view or opinion. As a result, use of specific phrases such as "the data indicates" or "we inferred" have two distinct meanings in an academic research paper, and each conveys a different degree of objectivity. This aspect of the use of specific language allows separation of facts from other subjective aspects such as opinions and views. Further, the feature of science in terms of reliance on data as the criterion for assessment of conjectures is reflected in the language of expression, where a researcher would typically use an expression like "the data suggests or provides support for the hypothesis…," where it is clearly highlighted that the data is the basis of the conclusion.

The public verifiability feature of science is reflected in the practice where academic research papers typically outline the description of the various aspects of the research process adopted. This description can help the readers of academic research papers to see and verify appropriateness of the methods used in a research study. The description of the research methods in a research paper may also provide potential for the readers of a research paper to verify whether similar results can be obtained through the implementation of similar research methods steps.

The use of existing knowledge as a feature of science is reflected in the feature of research papers, where the existing literature is reviewed and summarized in the early part of a research paper to outline the existing state of knowledge in a particular area. The relevant existing literature is also documented in the subsequent parts of a research paper in order to describe how existing knowledge in the literature justifies the research question and facilitates hypotheses specification.

It can be seen from the above description that the contents, structure and language aspects of an academic research paper are shaped by the requirements coming from the features of science and research. Thus, academic writing can benefit from having some understanding of science, research, research process and of the relationship of these with academic writing. The earlier parts of this chapter may facilitate development of such an understanding and, thereby, may facilitate academic writing.

Various features of academic writing are described in greater detail in Chapter 3. A comparison of academic writing with other forms of writing is also provided in Chapter 3.

TYPES OF ACADEMIC WRITING

Academic Research Papers

Academic writing works can be of various types of which a few are briefly described here. First, academic writing could take the form of a research paper that can be submitted to an academic journal for possible publication. Such research papers, consistent with the division of research into two parts pertaining to theory building and theory testing, broadly get divided into two categories, namely, conceptual research papers and empirical research papers. In practice, the word *research* is often skipped from the labels used for these papers and they are referred to as *conceptual papers* and *empirical papers*. Each of these two categories of research papers has its own pattern of structure and content.

Conceptual papers contain documentation of research works of various types. For instance, a conceptual paper may document the outcome of conceptually processing existing research works in forms such as a review or a synthesis of the existing research works. Conceptual papers do not involve testing of specific hypotheses or collection of first-hand and fresh data on empirical reality. Such conceptual papers can take various forms. One form of a conceptual paper can describe a research activity that undertakes theory building process whose outcome is a theoretical model or a set of conjectures termed as propositions and hypotheses. Another form of a conceptual paper can document only the review of the existing literature on a particular topic to outline the existing state of knowledge and the required areas of knowledge development on the topic. Still another form of a conceptual paper can document the review and synthesis of the existing literature on a particular topic. The above described various forms outline just a few possibilities and, in practice, conceptual papers can take various other forms as they document various types of research efforts that do not involve collection and analysis of fresh data about empirical reality.

Empirical papers document the process and outcome of a study aimed at assessing whether there is empirical support for one or more hypotheses. These would typically document brief theory building leading to specification of one or more hypotheses. Then there would be some text under a section title "Methods" or some similar title where various aspects of the research process used in the study are outlined. Typically these would include the description of the sample of respondents from whom the data was collected, the nature of data collection process, the scales used to measure various concepts/variables in the hypotheses and the nature of data analysis performed. This would be followed by sections reporting the results of the data analysis, findings or conclusions in the form of observed presence or absence of empirical support for the hypotheses, and discussions of the implications of the study and study results for theory, existing knowledge, future research and practice.

Theses Reports and Dissertation Reports

Students in certain post-graduate academic programmes may be required to work on a research project as a part of the programme requirements. The process and outcome of research projects carried out for such purposes is documented in project reports. The term *thesis* is used in the present book to refer to such a project report.

Similarly, students pursuing PhD programmes are required to complete research projects as a part of their studies. The processes and outcomes of such research projects is documented in doctoral dissertation reports.

A thesis report or dissertation report typically describes three aspects. First, it describes a research question based on literature review on the topic under consideration. Second, it describes the research process adopted to address the research question. Third, it describes the data analysis performed on the collected data; results, findings and the implications of the findings for the theory and for the existing knowledge on the topic under consideration. In light of these contents of thesis reports and dissertation reports, these academic documents can be viewed as a variation of an empirical paper form of academic documentation described earlier. These two types of reports would typically contain both a conceptual research part leading to hypothesis specification and an empirical research part describing the process and outcomes of the research study as contained in an empirical paper.

It is, however, likely that the amount of details covered and the length of description in a thesis or dissertation is considerably greater than in an empirical research paper written for an academic journal because of the following reasons. First, the purpose of a thesis or dissertation is to facilitate the examiners' assessment of whether the student has acquired adequate research training and whether the student is able to apply the research training in carrying out research. In contrast, the purpose of an empirical research paper is to demonstrate to the journal editor and reviewers that the research question examined in the paper is significant, the research process used is appropriate, and the research outcome is significant. Second, in a thesis report or dissertation, the purpose of the writer would include demonstrating his understanding of a comprehensive body of literature pertaining to the topic of the dissertation or thesis. This may result in the review of very comprehensive literature. In contrast, in an empirical paper the focus will be on reviewing the relevant literature as it pertains to the research question. Third, many journals specify a limit on the length of a typical empirical paper that can be submitted to them, which requires that the descriptions in empirical papers be concise and length of the papers be relatively short.

Academic Papers of Students for Course Requirements

For some courses in post-graduate programmes, writing an academic paper could be one of the assessment components that are required to be completed by a student for fulfilling the course requirements. Such an academic course paper may require students to review literature in a particular area and arrive at some summary and/or conclusions. This will be similar to the conceptual paper category of academic research papers described earlier, though the level of sophistication, rigour and comprehensiveness is likely to be less in it than in a conceptual research paper written for a journal. Academic course papers occasionally may also require students to carry out an empirical study and report its findings in the form of a report. These papers will be similar to an empirical paper category described above though the level of sophistication, rigour and comprehensiveness is likely to be less than in an empirical research paper written for a journal.

IMPORTANCE OF GOOD ACADEMIC WRITING IN VARIOUS ACADEMIC WORKS

As outlined earlier, academic writing seeks to communicate the process and outcome of research. This communication through academic writing needs to fulfil, as outlined earlier, certain requirements coming from the basic features of science and research. Therefore, academic writing needs to fulfil certain requirements such as communicating the significance of research question, adequately describing the research process, describing the research outcome, and describing the implications of the research and research outcome. Because of such various requirements that academic writing needs to fulfil, academic writing itself becomes important in research.

The importance of good academic writing in documenting research process and outcome is reflected in the views of various researchers. For instance, Hinkin (1995) reviewed scale development practices in the area of organizational studies and indicated that for some of the aspects of scale development, the research papers had inadequacies in reporting the required information. Thus, in one instance, Hinkin (1995, p. 971) notes that "the manner in which researchers report the item generation process may do a disservice, due to the omission of important information regarding the origin of measures... This process should be succinctly and clearly reported." Mitchell (1985), while concluding a paper that evaluated correlation-based research in organizations, noted that "more thorough reporting, innovative measurement, and preresearch planning is needed" (p. 205). The aspect "more thorough reporting" seems to pertain to academic writing as a part of research.

Jauch and Wall (1989, p. 162) studied how reviewers approach the task of reviewing academic research papers submitted to journals. In assessing the review process, they included items such as the reviewers' pointing out "problems of conveying meaning" and "how to better focus a manuscript." These items indicating what reviewers focus on while reviewing academic research papers seem to reflect aspects related to academic writing. Whetten (1989, p. 494) drew on his experience as the Editor of the *Academy of Management Review* to outline the list of questions that reviewers raise in assessing conceptual papers and the list includes the question, "Is the paper well written?" Further, the importance of good academic writing is also reflected in the practice that the checklist provided by journals to the reviewers for assessing the goodness of a research paper at times includes a rating dimension related to the writing of the paper and may require reviewers to focus on the various aspects of writing such as organization and clarity.

The expectations of good research reporting are reflected in some of the above outlined views. The above description suggests that good academic writing may help a researcher to convey his research process and outcomes more adequately, and to fulfil the requirements of science and research.

CHAPTER SUMMARY

Academic writing is a part of research process. Academic writing seeks to communicate the process and outcome of academic research carried out by a researcher. Academic research, as an approach to knowledge generation, follows certain norms of science. A set of terms with specific meaning and set of steps are associated with academic research process. The terms and steps associated with academic research constitute the substance which academic writing seeks to document. As the substance of academic writing is research process and outcome, and as research and science have certain distinctive features, academic writing needs to fulfil certain requirements. Academic writing works can take various forms, and various views in the literature highlight the importance of good academic writing. With the documentation of the above aspects in this chapter, Chapter 2 provides more detailed descriptions of various academic writing works. It also describes the structure and contents aspects of two academic writing works, namely, conceptual research paper and empirical research paper.

2

Structure and Contents
of a Research Paper

CHAPTER OVERVIEW

This chapter describes the structure and contents of two main types of academic research papers, namely, conceptual research paper and empirical research paper. The structure of these papers is described by listing the major parts that are contained in them. The content of these two types of papers is described by outlining the major details of the research process and/or the outcomes that are included in the various main parts of these papers. In this chapter, the word 'research' is omitted in referring to conceptual research papers and empirical research papers, and they are referred to as *conceptual papers* and *empirical papers*, respectively. As outlined in Chapter 1, the structure and contents of a dissertation/ thesis report contain elements of both a conceptual paper and an empirical paper and, hence, the description of structure and contents aspects of a dissertation/thesis is not repeated. The structure and contents of academic papers of students for course requirements are described by outlining some of the similarities and differences between these papers, and conceptual papers and empirical papers.

In outlining the contents of conceptual papers and empirical papers, hypothetical examples are provided in order to describe the text that may be contained in various parts of these papers. The contents of the text in these hypothetical examples, including the citations referring to various works, do not refer to any actual research study or to any actual research work. Thus, the citation details referred to in these hypothetical examples do not refer to any real documents. These citations are hypothetical and they are used only for illustrating the likely contents of various parts of conceptual papers and empirical papers. Quite a few terms associated with the research process have been described in Chapter 1 as a part of the description of research process. However, some other technical research-related terms are used in this chapter. A brief description of these additional research-related terms used in this chapter is provided in Appendix 1 at the end of the book. In light of this, whenever a reader encounters in this book a research-related technical term, he can consult the description of research-related terms provided in Chapter 1 or in Appendix 1.

Understanding the structure and contents of the individual components in academic works outlined in this chapter will help in carrying out various steps in the process of doing good academic writing described in Chapter 5. For instance, after reading Chapter 5, a reader will note that the step of preparing a paper outline as suggested in that chapter will, in the context of an academic research paper, involve planning the contents and sequence of various components of a research paper as per the structure outlined in this chapter for an empirical or conceptual paper. Similarly, the tasks in the polishing up step suggested in Chapter 5 include assessing whether all content components of a standard academic paper are included in the paper being written.

CONCEPTUAL PAPER

Conceptual papers report the process and outcome of a research study that does not collect and analyse fresh empirical data. These papers do not test, using freshly collected and analysed empirical data, a set of hypotheses. These papers may undertake conceptual work of various types including those outlined hereunder:

a.   Propose a new set of propositions (or hypotheses).
b.   Propose a new theory or theoretical model containing a
     representation of a theory in pictorial form.
c.   Provide a comprehensive review and summarization of
     literature on a particular topic.
d.   Provide a comprehensive review of literature on a parti-
     cular topic and outline the research issues that need to be
     examined.
e.   Provide a comprehensive review of the research that has
     occurred in a particular period (for example, previous five
     or 10 years) and outline the directions for future research.

Of the various forms such as those outlined above that a
conceptual paper can take, papers proposing a new set of
propositions or a theoretical model may be the most common
form of conceptual papers appearing in academic journals. Hence,
the structure and content aspects of only this form of conceptual
paper will be covered under the conceptual paper category in this
chapter.

Structure and Contents of a Conceptual Paper

A conceptual paper typically contains the following parts:

a.   Abstract,
b.   Introduction,
c.   Specification of a theory or propositions,
d.   Discussion,
e.   Closing paragraph and
f.   References.

The nature of contents covered under each of these parts is
outlined hereunder:

a. Abstract

The abstract of a paper provides an overview of the purpose,
process and outcome of the research work described in the paper.
It is provided as a distinct part of the paper and is separated from
the rest of the paper text. In a printed research paper, the abstract
is provided immediately below the paper title and author details,

and before the main text of the paper. Also, there are no explicit transition statements at the end of the abstract leading to the main paper text that begins below the abstract. As a result, the abstract remains as a standalone and distinct unit of the text separated from the main text of the paper. Journals typically specify a word limit (for example, a maximum of 100 words) or a word range (for example, between 100 to 250 words) for the abstract. On a separate line below the abstract, a few key words related to the paper topic need to be listed and identified with a heading "Key words."

In light of these features, in writing an abstract, it may help to be concise in writing and still describe the purpose, process and outcomes of a study in a manner that provides a standalone and meaningful description of the study. As an abstract includes aspects such as the study process and outcomes, it will be appropriate to write the abstract after the complete documentation of the other parts of a research paper. A hypothetical example of the abstract is provided hereunder:

This paper specifies propositions to explain the occurrence of employees' helping behaviours in organizations. It focuses on one specific category of antecedents—employees' work attitudes—of helping behaviours. It covers seven work-related attitudes of employees as the potential antecedents. These work attitudes are calculative commitment, affective commitment, continuance commitment, job involvement, pay satisfaction, satisfaction with supervision and satisfaction with coworkers. It specifies propositions describing relationships between each of these seven work-related attitudes and helping behaviours. It specifies an integrated model that incorporates the seven propositions in order to provide a comprehensive representation of the posited influences of work attitudes on employee helping behaviours. It also outlines the implications of this integrated model for future research and for practice.

Key words: Commitment, job involvement, job satisfaction, helping behaviours.

b. Introduction

In this part of a conceptual paper, the topic of the paper is specified. Further, the specific research question or issue within the topic that the paper focuses on is also described. The place and significance of the research question in light of the existing research on that particular topic is also documented. What the research paper specifically does in addressing the research question is also outlined. For instance, a conceptual paper might propose new concept definitions, draw on premises from existing literature, apply systematic reasoning to the premises, and specify propositions using the premises and reasoning. This process of conceptual research, which may also be referred to as *theorization* or *theory building*, carried out in the subsequent parts of the paper is also briefly described in the introduction part.

Thus, the introduction part of a conceptual paper will document the purpose of the paper in terms of the research question it focuses on, the significance of addressing the research question and the process adopted for theorizing in the subsequent part of the paper to address the research question. A hypothetical example of the text in the introduction section is provided in the following two paragraphs:

This paper examines employees' helping behaviours in organizations... Researchers (for example, Bavris, 1992; Critford, 1995) have noted that helping behaviours are critical for organizational functioning. While existing research has focussed mostly on studying the consequences of employee helping behaviours in organizations, researchers (for example, Celmist, 1997; McFelt, 1996) have noted that research needs to examine the antecedents of helping behaviour. This paper addresses this gap in the existing research on helping behaviours by specifying the relationship between one category of antecedents—employee work attitudes—and employees' helping behaviours. It covers seven work-related attitudes of employees namely, calculative commitment, affective commitment, continuance commitment, job involvement, pay satisfaction, satisfaction with supervision and satisfaction with coworkers. It specifies seven propositions each depicting the relationship between one of these seven employee work attitudes and employee helping behaviours in organizations. It depicts an integrated model that incorporates the relationships specified in these seven propositions. This paper is organized as follows.

It first provides a review of the existing research on employees' helping behaviours. It then points out the need for further research on antecedents of employees' helping behaviours. It then reviews the existing specifications of the concept of employees' helping behaviours and adopts a particular specification of employees' helping behaviours. Subsequently, it describes the various categories of possible antecedents of employees' helping behaviours and indicates that employees' work attitudes is an important category of antecedents whose relationship with employees' helping behaviours has not been specified in the existing research. Next, drawing on the existing body of literature, it identifies seven work attitudes for specifying their relationships with employees' helping behaviours. Subsequently, drawing on the existing literature, it describes theorizing for specifying relationships between each of these seven antecedents and employees' helping behaviours and for depicting an integrated model incorporating the relationships reflected in these seven propositions. Finally, it describes the limitations of this paper and its implications for future research and practice.

c. Specification of a theory or propositions

This part of a conceptual paper describes the core research process—theory building or theorizing—carried out in the paper. Theory building typically involves identification of premises (for example, assumptions, principles, and so on) from the existing literature and applying some form of logical reasoning to them in order to suggest the resulting conclusions in the form of conjectures. These conclusions are referred to as propositions or hypotheses. For instance, as a hypothetical example, a paragraph in this part of a conceptual paper may read as follows:

> Lewis (2000) indicates that employee commitment can take two forms, namely, affective commitment and calculative commitment. Trabling (2002) suggests that calculative commitment of an employee reflects an employee's concern for the likely rewards for himself from his contributions to the organization. Research (for example, Hermis, 2004; Kelter, 2003) has found a positive relationship between employees' calculative commitment and their concern for rewards. Further, the existing literature (for example, Atwelsh, 2003; Cooper, 2000; Jackerty, 1985; Levenstein, 1977) suggests that when employees are concerned about their own rewards, they are unlikely to perform helping behaviours in an organization. Boortan (1993) has suggested that the more an employee is concerned about his own rewards, the more he will focus on those activities that are rewarded by an organization.

The behaviours that focus on helping coworkers are not rewarded explicitly in organizations (Tumpnil, 2003). The preceding discussion suggests that employees' calculative commitment will reduce the likelihood of their performing helping behaviours. Based on this, it is posited that:

Proposition 1: Employees' calculative commitment will have a negative relationship with employee helping behaviours.

In an actual conceptual paper, the description associated with the specification of a proposition will be different in content because the extent of literature reviewed, the type of literature reviewed (conceptual or empirical literature), the extent of literature review documented and the extent of description pertaining to theorizing would differ from one researcher to another and from one topic area to another. However, in general, usually the text associated with the specification of a proposition is likely to take a form similar to the above description. In a conceptual paper which specifies multiple propositions, as most of the proposition-specifying papers typically do, separate text of the nature described in the above hypothetical example will be associated with the specification of each individual proposition. Thus, in a conceptual paper that specifies a theoretical model containing multiple propositions, the text similar to that in the above example will be associated with each proposition in the theoretical model. A collection of such texts associated with multiple propositions constitutes the core contents of this form of conceptual paper.

d. Discussion

This part of the paper can contain various aspects. First, in this part of the paper, the conclusions emerging from the theorizing done for individual propositions are typically specified. Sometimes, individual propositions can be integrated into an overall theoretical model that contains multiple propositions depicting different connections in the overall theoretical model. In such cases, a description of the resulting overall theoretical model can be contained in the discussion part. Thereafter, there is a section that outlines the research directions that future research can explore, based on the specification of propositions or the theoretical model in the paper. This description can indicate how the concepts contained in the propositions can be measured. For this, it can indicate that scales for measuring the concepts are either available in the existing literature or can be developed without unreasonable difficulty. Then it can document as to how future research can benefit by undertaking empirical research to examine the support for the relationships contained in the propositions. It can also state how future research can benefit by doing conceptual research, coming out as implications from the propositions and/or theory outlined in the paper. It may point out specific research questions that future conceptual research can examine.

Thereafter, the implications for practice are described. Here, the paper provides some description of how the practice in a particular area may benefit from the conceptual inputs coming from the theoretical model developed in the paper and also from the empirical knowledge that may result from the empirical studies that would assess empirical support for the propositions specified in the paper. Limitations, if any, of the research may be discussed in this part either before or after the description of research and practice implications. A hypothetical example of the contents of these various subsections in this part may read as follows:

This paper has specified seven propositions describing relationships between employees' helping behaviours and each of the seven antecedents, namely, employees' calculative commitment, affective commitment, continuance commitment, job involvement, pay satisfaction, satisfaction with supervision and satisfaction with coworkers. All these antecedents reflect employees' work-related attitudes. Thus, the overall theoretical model emerging from the seven propositions specified in this paper indicates the nature of effects of employees' work attitudes on employees' helping behaviours in organizations.

These seven propositions depict a comprehensive set of relationships between employees' work attitudes and employees' helping behaviours in organizations. Through the specification of these relationships, it addresses an important gap in the existing research. The specification of seven propositions in this paper suggests certain directions for future research. First, future research can carry out empirical studies to examine empirical support for the propositions specified in this paper. Second, this paper focussed on only one category of antecedents—employee work attitudes—and posited a set of relationships between these antecedents and employees' helping behaviours. Future research can carry out further conceptual work to specify relationships between other categories of antecedents and employees' helping behaviours. For instance, employee perceptions of organizational features such as procedural justice, distributive justice and organizational support can be another category of antecedents that future research can focus on. Similarly, employee personality-related variables is another category of antecedents that future research could focus on to specify propositions depicting relationships between these antecedents and employees' helping behaviours. Thus, specification of propositions in this paper provides directions for both future conceptual research and empirical research.

Propositions specified in this paper also have some implications for practice. The propositions specified in this paper, if empirically supported in future empirical research, can provide guidelines on how to enhance employees' helping behaviours in organizations. For instance, if the proposition specifying a negative relationship between employees' calculative commitment and helping behaviour receives empirical support in future empirical research, then it could suggest that for enhancing employees' helping behaviours, managers can lower the level of employees' calculative commitment. Thus, a guideline for practice will be that improving employee work attitudes can enhance employees' helping behaviours in organizations. This implication for practice highlights the possibility of predicting and controlling the occurrence of employees' helping behaviours in organizations.

This paper, however, has some limitations. First, it focuses on only one category of antecedents, namely, employee work attitudes. It does not include other categories of antecedents such as employee perceptions of organizational features and employee personality-related factors. Because of its focus on only one category of antecedents, it provides only a partial explanation of the reality of employees' helping behaviours. Second, it adopts a particular definition of the concept of employees' helping behaviours in organizations specified in the stream of research that views helping behaviours as employees' non-reward-receiving activity in organizations. Recently, some researchers (for example, Melros, 2006) have suggested that helping behaviours in organizations could occur for variety of motives such as altruism, expectations of reward, urge to reciprocate past rewards, and urge to enhance one's likeability for others. In light of this, if behaviours that reflect some kind of helping orientation on the surface but emerge from diverse motives such as these, then the present paper's focus on only non-reward-receiving forms of helping behaviours results in representing only a part of the phenomenon of employee helping behaviours. The first of these two limitations can be overcome by the future research that specifies relationships of other categories of antecedents with employees' helping behaviours as suggested earlier in one of the directions for future research.

e. Closing paragraph

A conceptual paper can contain a closing paragraph as the last paragraph. This paragraph can briefly summarize the purpose, process and outcome of the conceptual research described in the paper. A hypothetical example of a closing paragraph is provided here:

> This paper points out that the existing research has indicated the need for explaining the occurrence of employees' helping behaviours. For addressing this research need, it chose to focus on work-related attitudes as a category of potential antecedents of helping behaviours. It focussed on seven work-related attitudes. It specified seven propositions and an integrated model depicting relationships between each of these seven antecedents and employees' helping behaviours. These seven propositions may provide a comprehensive representation of the likely influence of work attitudes on employees' helping behaviours.

f. References

This section lists reference details for all the documents cited in the paper. Journals typically recommend a particular format for listing the references. The details of providing citations for various works and listing references are described in Chapter 6 of this book.

It was indicated earlier that conceptual research and, hence, conceptual papers can take various forms such as doing and reporting a review of the existing literature on a topic, pointing out the knowledge gaps based on the review of literature on a topic, and specifying propositions and/or theories. The above description of contents and structure of a conceptual paper focussed on only one type of conceptual paper, namely, papers specifying propositions and theories. The contents in other forms of conceptual papers, to some extent, vary from those indicated above depending on the specific form of conceptual research it seeks to report. However, the above description indicates the overall structure and contents of one major category of conceptual papers. The structure and contents of each of the different forms of conceptual papers are not described here. The likely changes required in the structure and contents of a conceptual paper of a particular type can possibly be identified from understanding the above description and from studying a sample of published research papers in the specific category of conceptual paper (for example, literature review reporting) that one needs to write.

AN EXERCISE TO STUDY THE STRUCTURE AND CONTENTS OF A CONCEPTUAL PAPER

The preceding section discusses the structure and contents of a conceptual paper by separately focussing on individual parts of it. For each separate part of a conceptual paper, its place in the overall structure of the paper and its typical contents are described and a hypothetical example is provided. After understanding the above section contents, it may help a reader to now see two aspects. First, it may help a reader to see how the various details described within individual parts above occur in various individual parts of a complete conceptual paper. Second, it may also help a reader to see how various individual parts of a conceptual paper coherently fit together in a complete conceptual paper. In light of this, as an exercise to enhance understanding, a reader can now identify a conceptual paper published in a journal and read it while noting how the aspects described above occur in the paper.

EMPIRICAL PAPER

An empirical paper describes the process and outcome of a study that examines whether data collected and analysed provides support for one or more conjectures (that is, the hypotheses) under consideration. An empirical paper's structure and contents seek to describe how the various steps in the empirical research process were carried out and what outcomes were obtained in a study that the paper reports. While contents in individual parts of an empirical paper describe the various aspects of the research process and outcomes, the structure of an empirical paper links the various individual parts to facilitate description of the entire research process as a sequence of steps leading to the findings of the research process. These research process steps and some of the associated outcomes have been shown in Figure 1.1. As a result, the structure and contents of an empirical paper also reflect the sequence of steps in the research process, and the activities and outcomes associated with the various steps in the research process.

Structure and Contents of an Empirical Paper

An empirical paper typically contains the following parts structured in a sequence mostly similar to the one reflected in the following list of content parts:

a. Abstract,
b. Introduction,
c. Hypothesis,
d. Methods,
e. Results,
f. Discussion,
g. Closing paragraph and
h. References.

The nature of contents covered under each of these parts is discussed hereunder.

a. Abstract

The description of abstract provided earlier in this chapter for a conceptual paper also applies to an empirical paper. However, the contents of the abstract will describe the features of an empirical research process rather than that of a conceptual research process. Thus, a brief description of the empirical research process and its outcomes will form the main parts of an empirical paper. Other aspects of the abstract (for example, limit on its length, and its occurrence as a standalone unit) described for a conceptual paper also apply to the abstract of an empirical paper. A hypothetical example of an abstract of an empirical paper is outlined as follows:

This study examined empirical support for the relationship between employees' calculative commitment and employees' helping behaviours. It obtained data from 250 employees in a manufacturing firm. Correlation analysis and regression analysis were performed to assess support for the hypothesis. The results of data analysis provide support for the hypothesized negative relationship between employees' calculative commitment and employees' helping behaviours. The implications of this study's findings for the future research and practice are described.

Key words: Calculative commitment, helping behaviours

b. Introduction

This part describes the topic being examined. It also outlines the specific research question that the empirical study seeks to examine. It typically describes the significance of examining the research question by indicating how the outcome of empirical examination, in terms of support or a lack of support for the hypothesis being examined, will provide relevant information to address a gap in research and provide an input that can guide the practice. A hypothetical example of the introduction part of an empirical paper is outlined as follows:

This paper examines empirical support for the relationship between employees' calculative commitment and employees' helping behaviours. It hypothesizes a relationship between employees' calculative commitment and employees' helping behaviours. It examines empirical support for the hypothesis using a sample of employees from a manufacturing organization in India.

This study is significant for two reasons. First, it empirically examines support for the relationship between employees' calculative commitment and employees' helping behaviours. If the hypothesis examined in this study receives support, then it would facilitate improved prediction and explanation of the occurrence of employees' helping behaviours. Researchers (for example, Harford and Cavin, 2002; Limarg and Mevis, 2004) have indicated that very little is known about the factors influencing the occurrence of employees' helping behaviours. The empirical examination in this study addresses this issue by examining one antecedent variable that could help predict and explain the occurrence of employees' helping behaviours and thereby could contribute to research and practice. Second, this paper can also contribute to research on calculative commitment by assessing its utility in predicting an important form of employees' behaviours—helping behaviour—in organizations. Researchers (for example, Amperdent, 2004; Otbrun, 1996) have noted that calculative commitment is an important work attitude and its behavioural consequences in organizational settings need to be examined. The present study addresses this research requirement by examining whether there is a relationship between employees' calculative commitment and employees' helping behaviours.

c. Hypothesis

This section following the introduction section is about hypothesis specification. It describes theory building leading to the specification of one or more hypotheses. The word *specification* is often omitted from the phrase "hypothesis specification." Hence, this section typically carries the title "Hypothesis," if the study specifies and examines only one hypothesis, and this section is titled "Hypotheses" if the study specifies and examines more than one hypothesis. This section typically describes concepts, concept definitions, premises (for example, assumptions and principles) from the existing literature, reasoning process and the resulting hypotheses. This description will be similar to the earlier outlined description of proposition specification part in a conceptual paper.

As outlined in Chapter 1, both propositions and hypotheses are conjectural statements. The difference between them is that propositions specify relationships between concepts whereas hypotheses specify relationships between variables (for example, Bacharach, 1989). As indicated in Chapter 1, a hypothesis can be derived from a proposition by replacing concepts in a proposition with variables. Further, as in practice, typically a concept (for example, calculative commitment concept as specified through a definition statement) and an associated variable such as calculative commitment scale (a scale that yields the measure of calculative commitment construct) are referred to by using the same label ("calculative commitment" in this example), a proposition and the associated hypothesis would have similar text in the statements specifying them. From the context, one may need to infer whether a conjecture specified is a proposition or a hypothesis. For example, a conjectural statement containing two concepts (for example, calculative commitment and helping behaviour) contained in an empirical paper will constitute a hypothesis. This is because these concepts are measured in the subsequent parts of the paper and, hence, they become variables; as a result of this, the conjectural statement becomes a statement of relationship between two variables, and it is referred to as a *hypothesis*.

In light of the above noted similarity between the description of the text associated with proposition specification in a conceptual paper and with hypothesis specification in an empirical paper, a separate hypothetical example of the text in hypothesis specification is not provided here. However, it is likely that the extent of theorization associated with proposition specification is likely to be greater than that associated with hypothesis specification. This greater extent of theorization for proposition specification may come from the likely greater emphasis on the provision of definitions for concepts than that in hypothesis specification, from the identification of a greater number of premises than those used in hypothesis specification, and from more elaborate reasoning process than that used in hypothesis specification.

d. Methods

This section describes how the research process was carried out to assess empirical support for the hypotheses. It describes the indicators/scales used to obtain the measures of the concepts or variables in the hypotheses being examined and provides information on the goodness of these scales. It then outlines the data collection procedures, covering aspects such as the sample of respondents from whom the data was collected, how the consent of the respondents was obtained, how the data collection instrument (for example, a study questionnaire) was administered (for example, through mail or through in-person distribution by the researcher), and the response rate indicating what percentage of the approached or potentially available respondents actually provided their responses required in the study questionnaire. It also outlines data analysis procedures used. For each of these aspects, the details that are typically covered in describing the methods part of an empirical paper are outlined here.

Measures: This subsection identifies the scales that were used for obtaining the measure of concepts or variables contained in the hypotheses being examined in a study. It also provides a brief description of scales, and outlines past evidence on the goodness (reliability and validity) of scales. The description of the scale would include aspects such as the name of the scale, the number of items in the scale, response format used in the scale and citation details of the past study in which the scale was developed and validated.

In describing the response format, the number of anchor points (a five-point or seven-point response options set) and the set of anchor descriptors (for example, ranging from *strongly disagree* to *strongly agree* or from *never* to *always*) used in the scale need to be indicated. Some description on the nature of the wording of the items (statements) in the scale is also provided and one or two items from the scale are reproduced as examples. Some journals may require that the newly used scales be reproduced completely at the end of an empirical paper, maybe in an appendix, when the scale is being used for the first time in research.

In describing the evidence from past studies on the goodness of an existing scale, typically the following information is provided. Some indication of the extent to which a scale has been used in past research can provide some indirect information about the goodness of the scale. Thus, if a scale has been extensively used in past research, it indicates its acceptance in research as well as its having been good enough to fulfil measurement requirements in several studies. Information on the reliability of the scale from past studies is typically provided. Information on whether the validity of the scale has been examined in past research and the nature of validity evidence obtained in past research is also given.

Sample: The description for the sample provides summary information about the individuals from whom the data for the study was collected. This description contains information on aspects such as the occupation of the respondents (for example, blue collar employees engaged in manual work, clerical staff or professionals), education levels, and the range and average figures for various respondent attributes such as age, number of years spent with the company and number of years spent in the present position. When respondents pertain to different categories within features such as gender, job positions and occupations, percentage of respondents in these categories are mentioned. For instance, the percentages of respondents belonging to male and female gender categories are reported. The objective of including these details in sample description is to provide the information that may help readers to understand the nature of respondents on whom the study results have been obtained and, hence, to be able to assess to which other kinds of respondent samples the study results are likely to be applicable. This applicability of study results, obtained using one respondent sample to another respondent sample, is referred to as generalizability or external validity of study findings.

Data Collection Procedure: The description of the data collection procedure will indicate how the respondents' consent for participating in the study was obtained (for example, by providing some inducement such as a gift, by appealing through a request made by the authority in the respondents' organization(s)), whether participation was voluntary on part of the respondents and whether each respondent filled in his questionnaire separately or the respondents were assembled at a single location where each respondent completed his questionnaire at a common place during a common questionnaire completion session. The response rate of the respondents is also mentioned which indicates what percentage of potentially available respondents actually filled in and returned the completed study questionnaire. Whether the respondents were assured of anonymity (no information on respondent identity is obtained and, hence, the respondent identity cannot be linked to their completed study questionnaires) or confidentiality (respondent identification with the completed study questionnaire is known to the researcher but is not to be revealed to anyone else by the researcher) is also described. These details help the readers to assess the goodness of the data obtained in general and, in particular, whether any aspects of the data collection procedure are likely to have induced a bias in the respondents, causing them to provide information that is not a valid reflection of the reality being assessed. For instance, when respondent anonymity is not assured, the respondents may provide more positive information about positive aspects such as their performance levels, commitment to the organization and involvement in the job.

Data Analysis: This part of the description under the methods section describes the data analysis techniques used for analysing the data. Whether a researcher has used correlations, regression analysis or some more recent data analysis technique such as structural equation modelling is described. Sometimes, the specific steps used in data analysis are also described when the data analysis procedure is technically complex or not common in research. Important decisions made by the researcher in the data analysis process (for example, excluding certain study questionnaires from the analysis, or dividing the respondent sample into two categories based on some study variable level for comparing respondent subgroups) are also described. In published research papers, the location of the description of data analysis part may vary in relation to the methods and results parts. In some papers, data analysis is described as a part of methods section and this description is placed towards the end of the methods section. Some papers provide a section titled "Results" in which, first, data analysis procedure is described, and then the results are described. In published papers, such a section, describing data analysis and results, is found to be labelled as "Data Analysis and Results" or as just "Results."

A hypothetical example of the description in the 'methods' part is outlined as follows:

Calculative commitment was measured in this study using the scale developed by Hernoltz and Arom (1997). This self-report format scale contains seven items, has a five-point response format, and uses anchor points of 'strongly disagree (1)', 'disagree (2)', 'neither agree nor disagree (3)', 'agree (4)' and 'strongly agree (5)'. Detris (2005) reports that this scale has been used in quite a few past studies, and in those studies, its reliability levels have ranged from 0.75 to 0.9 which are quite satisfactory. Hernoltz and Arom (1997) have provided evidence on the validity of the scale based on their assessment of the scale's content validity, convergent validity and discriminant validity. Helping behaviour was measured through the scale developed by Gemolt (2005) who has indicated that the scale reliability in his study was 0.8 and who has also provided reasonable evidence on the scale's validity. This self-report format scale contains 10 items each focussing on a specific form of employees' helping behaviour in organizational settings. For each item, the respondent is required to indicate how frequently he/she has performed the behaviour over a period of past one year. It uses a five-point response format ranging from 'never (1)', 'occasionally (2)', 'sometimes (3)', 'frequently (4)' and 'always (5)'.

Data was collected from 270 blue collar employees from a medium-sized manufacturing organization located in the northern part of India. Respondents came from the departments of machining, assembly, packaging and stores. Eighty-five per cent of the respondents were male, 80% of the respondents had the highest education obtained level of some highschool years, the average respondent age was 42.68 years, the average tenure in the organization was 15.47 years, and the average tenure in the present position was 7.31 years. Respondents held various positions such as machine operator, assembly worker, packaging assistant and stores operator.

Data was collected by researchers at the actual work locations of the respondents in their organizations. The four departments included in this study employed all 500 blue collar employees in the organization. After receiving the data collection permission from the organization, researchers spoke to the employees in groups of 15-20 and explained the study purpose. The researchers indicated to the employees that their responses will be anonymous...and requested their participation. A study questionnaire containing scales measuring calculative commitment and helping behaviours, and containing items pertaining to the demographic and job-related information was distributed to the employees by the researchers. The questionnaire was provided in an envelope to each employee. Employees were requested to complete the questionnaire on their own, place it in the envelope and return it to the researcher the next day. Through this procedure, study questionnaires were distributed to all 500 blue collar employees of this organization. Completed study questionnaires were received from 270 of the 500 employees indicating a response rate of 54 per cent.

e. Results

This part describes the results of the analysis performed on the study data. It typically begins by giving the overall descriptive statistics. Typically, the first table in the results part is the table reporting the descriptive statistics for the data. The mean and standard deviation values for all study variables, values of correlations between each pair of study variables and the reliability levels for each study variable that is measured with a scale having more than two items (reliability can be computed only for scales containing more than two items) are given in the table of descriptive statistics. It typically carries the title such as "Descriptive Statistics and Scale Reliabilities."

After the presentation of descriptive statistics, study results from the statistical analysis conducted for testing each study hypothesis are reported. For each hypothesis, the nature of the statistical test performed, the test statistics obtained and the level of significance of the test statistics are reported. This description constitutes the results of data analysis. As a part of this description, the conclusion, based on the significance level obtained for the test statistics, about the support or lack of support for each study hypothesis under consideration is specified. This description constitutes the findings of the study. It describes, for each hypothesis, whether it was supported or not based on the results of analysis of the study data. Sometimes, the results of statistical analysis and findings in terms of support or a lack of support for a hypothesis are not explicitly distinguished from each other in the description. A hypothetical example of the description in the "Results" part is outlined as follows:

> Descriptive statistics, inter-scale correlations and reliability levels for study scales are presented in Table 1. Hypothesis 1, which specified a negative relationship between calculative commitment and helping behaviour, was tested using correlation analysis and regression analysis. The results of this analysis indicated a correlation of -0.5 between these two variables, which was statistically significant ($p < 0.005$). This result from the correlation analysis supports Hypothesis 1. Further, results of the regression analysis, presented in Table 2, in which helping behaviours was the dependent variable and calculative commitment was the independent variable, indicated significant and negative beta coefficient for calculative commitment ($p < 0.005$). This result of regression analysis also provides support for Hypothesis 1, which specifies a negative relationship between calculative commitment and helping behaviour. Thus, results of both correlation analysis and regression analysis provided support for Hypothesis 1.

f. Discussion

This part contains a description of the implications of the study and study findings, and a description of the limitations of the study. It describes implications of the study findings for the theory from which the hypotheses were derived. For example, if the hypothesis specifying a negative relationship between calculative commitment and helping behaviours was derived using social exchange theory, then the support observed in the present study for this hypothesis will also provide support for the social exchange theory and for its utility in suggesting the relationship between calculative commitment and helping behaviour.

It also provides a description of how the findings from the present study address an important knowledge gap in the existing research. Here, the description links back to the research question and its significance described in the early part of the paper, where the significance of the research question is attempted to be established by describing how the answer to the research question will address a relevant and important gap in the existing knowledge about the topic under study.

Description in this part would also indicate how the findings of the present study can provide some directions for future research through further conceptual and empirical research. For instance, if the hypothesis in the present study is supported, then, using a similar theory to hypothesize additional similar relationships could be another possible direction for future research. On the other hand, if the hypothesis in the present study is not supported, then the researcher can indicate that either the theory from which the hypothesis was derived is not an adequate representation of the phenomenon (for example, the relationship between calculative commitment and employees' helping behaviour) or that there were inadequacies in the research process adopted in the present study, which may have weakened the possibility of obtaining support for the hypothesis. In the former case, a possible direction for future research could be to use a different theoretical perspective to facilitate the specification of a different set of hypotheses to explain the occurrence of employees' helping behaviours in organizations. In the latter case, the researcher would typically suggest directions for future research to examine the same hypothesis using a research process that is free of the inadequacies associated with the research process of the present study.

Contents of this part will also describe how the findings of the present study can provide guidelines for practice. These guidelines typically focus on how practising managers can use the findings from the study to improve some aspects of organizational functioning. For instance, the findings indicating support for the hypothesis that specified a negative relationship between calculative commitment and helping behaviour can provide an input to managers that one of the ways of enhancing employees' helping behaviours is to reduce the level of calculative commitment of employees.

Another aspect described in this part is study limitations. Here, some of the significant inadequacies of the research process used in the study are documented. For instance, if a study used a sample of a particular kind such as only blue collar employees from a single manufacturing organization, then a limitation would be that the findings of the study may not be generalizable to other situations. This description could also indicate how the inadequacies in the research process were unavoidable due to certain genuine constraints associated with the nature of research. Further, some description of how the inadequacies in the research process are unlikely to have distorted the study findings can be relevant in documenting the limitations. These aspects described in the limitations part can help readers understand that the researcher is aware of study limitations and that the limitations have not occurred because of the researcher's ignorance or carelessness but are an outcome of the constraints associated with research setting and research process. These aspects also indicate that despite the limitations, the study findings are unlikely to be distorted and, hence, the research findings are valid. In empirical papers published in journals, in sequencing the limitations part and the part on implications for research and practice, the limitations part can either precede or follow the part on implications of the study findings for future research and practice. Further, in published empirical papers, sometimes the results and associated discussion parts are covered under the single section heading of "Results and Discussion."

A hypothetical example of the discussion part is provided as follows:

> The findings of this study that there is a negative relationship between employees' calculative commitment and employees' helping behaviours are important as they make several contributions. As the hypothesis was derived using social exchange theory, the study findings providing support for the hypothesis also

provide support for the social exchange theory as a representation of the relationship between employees' calculative commitment and employees' helping behaviours in organizations.

Findings of the present study also provide certain directions for future research. The study findings indicate that calculative commitment helps predict and explain employees' helping behaviours in organizations. As a result, a possible direction for future research is to specify additional hypotheses, outlining the relationships between employees' calculative commitment and other forms of employee behaviours in organizations such as employees' deviant behaviours and political behaviours. Another direction for future research is to examine the mediating processes through which employees' calculative commitment has an effect on employees' helping behaviours. In pursuing this direction, research can specify more complex models which would include mediating variables that come between the antecedent variable of calculative commitment and the outcome variable of helping behaviour. Such models will help understand the process through which the effect of calculative commitment on helping behaviours unfolds. Yet another direction for future research comes from the findings of the present study that the observed relationship between calculative commitment and helping behaviours in the present study findings is only of moderate strength (r = -0.5). This finding suggests that there are likely to be other factors that influence the occurrence of employees' helping behaviours. This suggests another direction for future research to examine other antecedents of employees' helping behaviours and to specify more complex models of employees' helping behaviours containing multiple antecedents with a view to enhance the possibility of finding a stronger relationship between the helping behaviours and its multiple antecedents.

The findings of the present study also provide inputs to practice. The findings suggest that employees' helping behaviours in an organization are influenced by employees' calculative commitment. This suggests that reducing the level of employees' calculative commitment could be one way to enhance employees' helping behaviours in organizations.

This study has some limitations. First, the study sample consists of mostly male blue collar employees from a single manufacturing organization. This suggests that there are limitations in extending the study findings to other samples, possibly lowering the generalizability of the findings. Second, the study obtained self-report measures from respondents for both calculative commitment and helping behaviours. As helping behaviours are likely to be socially desirable behaviours, response biases in terms of overestimating the level of one's helping behaviours may have impaired the accuracy of the obtained measures of helping behaviours. In the present study, helping behaviours had to be assessed through self-reports so that each employee could report his helping behaviour along with his calculative commitment in a single study questionnaire and, hence, the need for seeking employee name or other identification details was avoided which allowed to provide anonymity condition to respondents. Seeking the measure of employees' helping behaviours from other sources such as coworkers or the supervisor of an employee would have required each respondent employee to provide his name or other identification detail so that his commitment score could be matched with his helping behaviour score obtained from another source such as a coworker or the supervisor. This would have not allowed maintaining anonymity of the respondents. Thus, the use of self-report measure and the resulting limitation in terms of possibly impaired accuracy in the measure of helping behaviours was necessitated by the provision of anonymity to respondents.

g. Closing paragraph

A separate closing paragraph at the end of an empirical paper is not always provided. However, if such a paragraph is provided, then an overview of some of the study aspects and outcomes can be outlined here. A hypothetical example of a closing paragraph is outlined as follows:

This study drew on social exchange theory (Getorb, 1964) to hypothesize a negative relationship between calculative commitment and helping behaviours. The findings of this study revealed a moderately strong relationship between calculative commitment and helping behaviours, and supported the hypothesis. The study findings suggest a few directions for future research such as specifying more comprehensive models including multiple antecedents of helping behaviours and including mediator variables between calculative commitment and helping behaviours to explain the process through which calculative commitment influences the occurrence of helping behaviours. The study findings also provide a guideline for practice for enhancing employees' helping behaviours in organizations. Though the study has certain limitations, it, through its findings and their implications, adds to the existing knowledge about employee helping behaviours.

h. References

This section lists the reference details for all the documents cited in the paper. Journals typically recommend a particular format for listing the references. The details of listing references are described in Chapter 6 of this book.

AN EXERCISE TO STUDY THE STRUCTURE AND CONTENTS OF AN EMPIRICAL PAPER

The preceding section discusses the structure and contents of an empirical paper by separately focussing on individual parts of it. For each separate part of an empirical paper, its place in the overall structure of the paper and its typical contents are described, and a hypothetical example is provided. After understanding the above section, it may help a reader to now see how various parts of an empirical paper coherently fit in a complete empirical paper, and how the various aspects described in individual parts above occur in a complete empirical paper. In light of this, as an exercise to enhance understanding, a reader can now identify an empirical paper published in a journal and read it while noting how the aspects described above occur in the paper.

THESIS AND DISSERTATIONS

Thesis reports which are required to be completed as part of requirements for a masters degree may involve research works of various types. For example, they could involve specification of a theory (propositions and/or hypotheses), and the description of the process and outcome of an empirical study that was carried out to test the theory. They could also involve specification of just a research question (for example, what types of innovations occur in organizations) and reporting of the description of the process and outcome of the research that was carried out to address this research question. They could also involve only review and synthesis of literature on a particular topic. Depending on the specific form of research work carried out in the thesis work, the description in it will have the structure and contents similar to either a conceptual paper of a particular form or an empirical paper. Thus, the structure and content aspects outlined above for conceptual papers and empirical papers can be applied, with the needed variation in light of the specific form of research that a thesis report seeks to document, to doing academic writing for thesis reports. Some of the differences between a thesis report and a typical published research paper in an academic journal have been outlined in Chapter 1. These differences are likely to be reflected in the differences in the structure and contents of a thesis report and research paper written for a journal.

Many dissertations completed as part of requirements for a doctoral degree involve carrying out and documenting empirical research. As indicated in Chapter 1, the extent of literature review, the extent of description pertaining to theory building and/or specification of propositions and/or hypotheses, and the extent of details in the documentation of the study process and outcomes are likely to be greater in a dissertation than in an empirical paper written for a journal. As outlined in Chapter 1, this is partly because the objective of documentation of research process and outcome in a dissertation is to demonstrate to the examiners that the student has adequately learnt various aspects of carrying out research, and that he has been able to effectively carry out the research process and document the research process and the outcome associated with the research work done for completing a dissertation. While the overall structure and contents of a dissertation are likely to be similar to that in an empirical paper, the above outlined difference between an empirical paper and a dissertation are likely to be reflected in the actual contents of a dissertation.

For the structure and contents of both thesis reports and dissertations, guidelines are likely to be available from the institutes to which students are submitting their thesis reports and dissertations.

ACADEMIC PAPERS OF STUDENTS FOR COURSE REQUIREMENTS

As outlined in Chapter 1, post-graduate students may be required to write academic papers as part of requirements in some of their courses. These papers could describe conceptual research work such as doing a literature review on a particular topic and building a theoretical model. These papers could also describe the empirical research carried out to address one or more specific research questions. These research works are likely to be of rudimentary forms in comparison to the research reported in papers in journals. However, these academic papers can benefit from incorporating the features of structure and contents of conceptual papers and empirical papers in academic journals. The description of the structure and contents of conceptual papers and empirical papers outlined in the earlier part of this chapter can provide inputs for writing conceptual papers and empirical papers of students for course requirements. However, in this type of papers, the extent of technical details of research process reported, precision and formalization of expression, comprehensiveness of the literature covered and the extent of literature-based support provided for various statements is likely to be less in comparison to research papers written for journals. Further, it may be helpful for students to request clear guidelines from the course instructor about the structure and content requirements of the academic papers required for a course.

It would be difficult to provide any universal or general guidelines for academic papers for coursework because the expectations from these papers are likely to vary across instructors, subjects and institutes. Further, even factors such as the extent of the relative share of such coursework paper among the multiple components of course assessment are likely to influence the expectations from and requirements of these papers. For instance, an instructor who is well-versed with the research methods and practice may specify more stringent requirements for such a paper than other instructors. Similarly, a coursework paper that has just 10 to 20 per cent weightage in the overall course assessment is likely to have less demanding requirements than a coursework paper that has a larger percentage weight in the overall course assessment. Aspects such as these do not encourage provision of a set of guidelines for coursework papers. However, some tentative inputs on the structure and contents of this type of paper are outlined below based solely on personal observations and reflections.

Coursework papers are likely to have requirements that are relatively less demanding in comparison to papers in journals. For instance, in a conceptual paper category of a coursework paper, the requirement is likely to be of reviewing and using the existing literature rather than specifying a theory or propositions. As a result, the entire documentation of the process of theory building is not likely to be applicable to these papers. Further, when the coursework paper requirement is to review and use the existing literature, the expectation is likely to be of reviewing and using only some of the relevant and available literature in contrast with the likely requirement in a journal conceptual paper of reviewing and using a comprehensive body of literature. When the coursework paper requirement is to conduct and report an empirical study, the scope of such a study is likely to be narrower than an empirical paper in a journal. These aspects of the requirements of coursework papers are likely to influence the nature of the contents of this paper. In light of this, an important step in writing a coursework paper is to request a clear specification of the paper requirement from an instructor and to understand these requirements.

It may enhance a research paper if it includes a cover page indicating the paper title, course details, student name, instructor name and a statement that the paper is submitted to the instructor for the fulfilment of course requirements (if the paper is the only assessment component in the course) or for the partial fulfilment of course requirement (if the paper is only one of the assessment components in the course). The next page could contain a table of paper contents followed by a page providing a summary or an abstract of the paper. The first content item of the paper can then begin on the next page (for example, the fourth page in this example). Various content items can then be arranged in a sequence. The text should be divided into sections and subsections, each identified by a heading so that the paper could get organized. Different levels of headings and subheadings could be distinguished by using a separate font size and style for each level of heading. An example of a possible option is to document in a sequence the items of introduction, paper objectives (for example, research question examined), description of the process adopted (for example, literature review and synthesis) to attain the paper objectives, documentation of the outcomes of the process (for example, conclusions on the research question issue coming from literature synthesis), and implications and limitations of the outcomes. After the documentation of these items, it would be necessary to give the list of documents cited in the paper. Any content items that have features such as a large volume, complex contents, and only peripheral and illustrative contents that may not coherently fit in the main paper contents can be placed in a separate set of appendices following the page on which the list of references ends.

It needs to be noted that some of the papers of students for course requirements may involve research that is applied and problem-focussed, rather than academic research of the kind reported through empirical in empirical papers in journals that involves empirical examination for the purpose of advancing knowledge on a particular phenomenon. These papers, documenting the applied and problem-focussed research, may be referred to as business research reports. Business research reports are likely to have different orientations as they are written for the use of management practitioners rather than academicians. Books in the specific topic area of business research (for example, Cooper & Schindler, 2003) can provide inputs on the structure and contents of documents such as business research proposal and business research reports.

CHAPTER SUMMARY

Two major categories of academic works are conceptual papers and empirical papers published in academic journals. Conceptual papers report the work of research such as review and synthesis of literature on a topic, review of the existing state of research and indication of directions for future research, and the specification of propositions and theoretical models pertaining to a phenomenon under study. The most common type of conceptual paper is the one that provides specification of propositions and theoretical models. The structure and contents of this type of conceptual paper provide an introduction to the research topic, outline the theorization process and the associated outcomes such as propositions or a theoretical model, describe implications for future research and practice, and list the reference details of the works cited in the paper. Empirical papers report the process and outcome of research aimed at the assessment of whether empirical data supports one or more hypotheses under examination. The structure and contents of an empirical paper include introduction, hypothesis, methods, results, discussion and references as its part. Various details of the structure and contents of conceptual papers and empirical papers are described in this chapter. Thesis and dissertation report and academic papers of students for course requirements can contain some of the parts contained in conceptual papers and empirical papers, but some of the aspects such as comprehensiveness and formalization are likely to be present at a different level in these academic works.

Part II

The Anatomy of Academic Writing

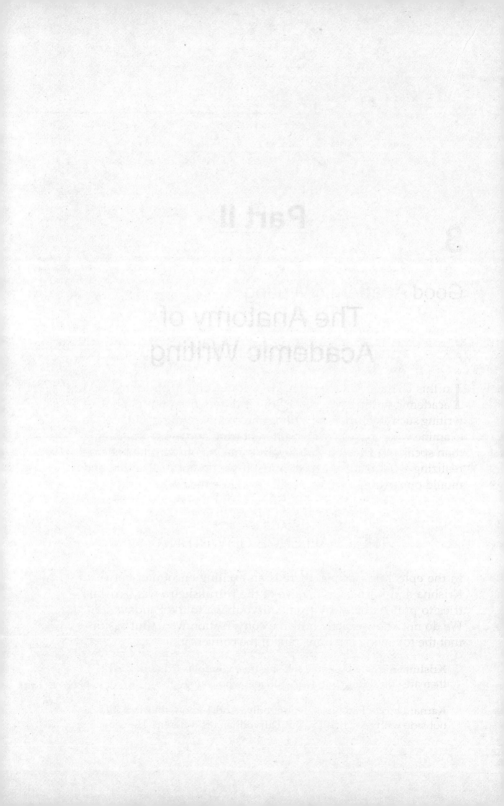

3

Good Academic Writing

CHAPTER OVERVIEW

In this chapter, we focus on the features and qualities of good academic writing. We show how it differs from other kinds of writing such as journalistic writing and creative writing. But first we examine what makes writing different from and more challenging than speaking. The first step towards making our writing better is realizing what readers expect of us. If we do not realize that and mould our writing to it, we are likely to lose them.

THE CHALLENGE OF WRITING

In the epic, *Mahabharata*, there is an exciting encounter between Krishna and Karna. On the eve of the Kurukshetra war, Krishna tries to pull Karna away from Duryodhana to the Pandava fold. We do not know exactly how the conversation went. But assume that the following is a transcript of the conversation.

Krishna: Karna, you know the shastras, you follow dharma. Why then are you siding with Duryodhana, who is ungodly?

Karna: Duryodhana may be ungodly. And I know that I should not side with the ungodly. But Duryodhana is different. He is my friend, and I love him with all my heart. When everyone insulted me because of my low birth, he supported me. He made me Anga's king. What did he want in return? Nothing. Just my friendship. There are only two people I have received love from: my mother Radha and Duryodhana. I live for them. I will die for them too.

Krishna: I appreciate that. But do you know who your real father and mother are?

Karna: Not really. At times I dream that I was born of a princess. Perhaps I was born before she got married and so she abandoned me. What matters is that Adhiratha and Radha brought me up with absolute love. So they are my father and mother. I don't care who gave birth to me. Why should I, if she cared more for her reputation than my survival as an infant?

Krishna: Karna, your dream is true. You are a Kshatriya, born of a princess. You're also right about why you were abandoned. Your real mother now has more sons, but she is still pining for her first born. That is you.

Karna: You mean I am not a Sutaputra? Who *is* my mother? Is she still alive?

Krishna: Yes, very much. Your mother has five other sons. They are the best warriors on earth.

Karna: The best warriors on earth? Then they must be the Pandavas. So you mean…Kunti is my mother and the Pandavas my brothers?

Krishna: You're absolutely right, Karna.

Karna: And my father?

Krishna: Lord Surya!

Karna: Oh! Oh! (*sobbing*) Then I'm the unluckiest man on earth. I am a member of the most illustrious family on earth, and yet the whole world knows me and treats me as a low-born Sutaputra. (*After a pause, and wiping his tears*) If you knew this all along, why did you hide it from me all this while? And why are you telling me this now?

Krishna: Because I want to save you from death. Because I want you to live and reign in glory. By law, you are the eldest of the

Pandavas although you were born before Kunti married Pandu. Therefore, the crown and the beautiful Draupadi are yours. The other five, being younger to you, shall serve you and obey you. You are as good as every one of them in your abilities and better than every one of them because you are the first born. Come, join me. I shall give you a kingdom, a mother, the most desirable woman on earth as wife and five brothers the likes of whom the world has not yet seen.

Karna: Thank you my lord. Everything you say is right. It will be wonderful to have the great Kunti as my mother, the five Pandavas as my younger brothers and the ravishing Draupati as my wife. But Radha and Adhiratha are my mother and father. It was they who brought me up with love. Duryodhana gave me respect, friendship and a reason to live. Even if you bestow on me all the wealth, all the power, all the glory, and all the pleasures in the world, I will not abandon him. I have promised him that I will support him in the war. And that's it. I am a man of honour. I will not go back on my word. I know the Pandavas are under your protection and so I can't beat them. I know I will die in this war. That's fine, but I will not go back on my word.

For the full story, see Subramaniam (2007, pp. 448-454).
The dialogue above is loosely based on it.

Krishna fails to achieve his objective because Karna's love for Duryodhana and his sense of honour are unassailable. They are too strong to be shaken by inducements such as a kingdom, headship of the most illustrious family on earth and liberation from his cursed status as a low-born, which has kept him from living a glorious life. But Krishna does make a fine attempt. He introduces startling facts and powerful arguments in response to Karna's reservations about the suggestion to defect to the Pandavas. He does not, for instance, introduce the idea of Kunti as Karna's biological mother until after the appeal to the sense of dharma fails. Why raise a touchy issue if you can do without it?

Now imagine that Krishna cannot see or hear Karna while speaking to him. The objective is the same: persuade Karna to leave Duryodhana. How should Krishna start? Should he say upfront that he wants Karna to leave Duryodhana? How would Karna respond to it? What if Karna walks out concluding that there is no point in listening on because Krishna is asking him to do what he will never even dream of doing? Or should Krishna present all the facts and arguments, and then finally ask him to join the Pandava fold? What facts should he present, in what order? Would Karna believe those facts? Would he ask for proof, for example, of the claim that Kunti is his mother? How much does he know? What is his attitude to Kunti? Does he love her, respect her or hate her? Would the mention of her name anger him rather than soften his resolve to work with Duryodhana? Would he readily agree to Krishna's request because he recognizes Krishna's divinity? Or does he? What are his most cherished values?

Try talking to someone with your eyes closed and ears plugged. You should not even know if the person you are speaking to is still around and listening to you. Tough to continue, isn't it? This is the challenge you face in writing. We do not know exactly what our potential readers know, what their attitudes are and how they will respond to the ideas we present to them from a distance. At the most, we can make some educated guesses. Those guesses may be reasonably reliable in the case of readers who belong to a group that we also belong to, such as a community of scholars in a particular field. Of course, those guesses can go wrong even under such favourable conditions.

These challenges are the same even when we speak face to face; but we can deal with them by adjusting our moves based on the response we get from the listeners. We can, for example, drop an idea if we find that the listeners already know it. We can postpone an idea if we find that they are not yet ready for it; or we can expand an idea if they do not appear familiar with it. We can produce additional proof if they consider our proof or argument inadequate. Success is not guaranteed — even Krishna failed in his attempt in spite of his divine status and brilliant arguments. But when trying to communicate through writing, the uncertainties and imponderables are even more formidable. We can succeed as writers only when we anticipate the expectations of our readers reasonably accurately and meet them. In other words, we should be able to carry on a conversation with invisible and inaudible listeners.

Some or all the readers may not be familiar with at least some of our assumptions. As a result, they may be unable to make sense of what we write even when our language is grammatically and stylistically correct. At the same time, giving information that they already know can bore them and stop them from paying attention or reading on. Strangely, we often forget this simple truth when

Box 3.1 Much Ado about a Word

Dr Virendra K. Singh, a physics lecturer at Rajasthan University in the 1960s, was deeply impressed by the books written by Richard P. Feynman, who won the Nobel Prize in physics in 1965. On October 17, 1965, Dr Singh wrote to Dr Feynman congratulating him on his books, and stating that they were a landmark that should be treated like the *Ramayana*. He described Feynman as his "ideal lecturer," and asked for an autographed photograph.

Dr Feynman sent him an autographed photograph and thanked him warmly for his "kind and flattering note of congratulations."

If Dr Feynman thought that his gesture would make this enthusiastic physics lecturer in a far-off Indian university happy, he was mistaken. Dr Singh was hurt. He wrote back to Dr Feynman to tell him so. How could the great scientist treat his genuine praise as flattery?

Although Dr Singh ended his letter with a post script that made it clear that he didn't expect a reply from the busy physicist, Dr Feynman did write back, apologizing for his "careless misuse of language." He reassured Dr Singh that he did not treat the words of praise as insincere. He wished he had used "complimentary" instead of "flattering."

He wrote a few more paragraphs to remove any unintentional hurt he might have caused Dr Singh.

You can read the full exchange in Feynman (2003, pp. 204-205).

we write. That is why we do not write as well as we can, even when we know exactly who we are writing to and exactly what we want to communicate. We lose many readers because we are not on the same page with them or we do not provide what they are looking for. As we have no control over them, we will not even know whether they will read the text through or abandon it midway. We cannot know whether the message they reconstruct is even roughly what we think we have put into the text.

Here is the very first paragraph of a report written by a student of management. The title says, "Assignment—Crisis Communication." What can you make of it?

In order to chalk out a plan of action and communication for ROM, we will first analyze the situation and develop the cornerstones of our strategy. Since companies do not always have time to respond in crisis situation, company should have a Crisis Management Plan (CMP) ready for such situations. In the analysis below, the underlying assumption is that the blackmailer has all the information about the credit card using which anyone can do a transaction on the web on behalf of the customer.

(Taken from "Crisis communication," student assignment, 2008)

What or who is ROM? Why is a plan of action and communication needed? Who is the blackmailer with credit card information? Whose credit card information does he have? What does he want? What has all this to do with ROM? The writer has answers to all these questions. But does the reader? To be fair to the writer, we must note here that this report was written in response to an assignment given to her class. In the assignment, the class was told that ROM was an online retailer of movies. A man who claimed to have got hold of the credit card details of nearly 200,000 customers of ROM was blackmailing a senior manager for a large sum of money. The company policy did not allow any manager to negotiate with blackmailers. The assignment asked each student to assume the role of the senior manager, and to develop a plan of action and communication to deal with this crisis.

Now the student's first paragraph makes sense. Perhaps she had assumed that she could skip them because she expected the instructor to remember all these details. Without repeating the entire assignment, the writer ought to have provided enough information inside the report for the reader to make sense of the text. Then readers other than the instructor or an instructor who may have forgotten some of the important details of the assignment can also make sense of the report.

Consider another student's attempt at starting the report, written in response to the same assignment. Here is the very first paragraph:

> We are in the midst of a major crisis, which threatens the very existence of our company. The situation has to be handled with great caution; we have to prepare a comprehensive action plan, based on an effective communication strategy, which will help in mitigating and containing the risk.
>
> The action plan will be based on: ...

(Taken from "Crisis management," student assignment, 2008)

This writer also assumes that the reader knows the details of the "major crisis" that the company is in. The statement is so general that this can be used before writing about any major crisis of which the readers have the details. But if the readers do not recall the details, this introductory paragraph adds little other than bewilderment.

Compare these two attempts with that of a third student. Here is the first paragraph from his report written in response to the same assignment:

> Increase in disposable income among the consumers has interestingly resulted in decrease in time available for spending money. This has changed consumer buying behaviour, as they are looking for easier and faster means of purchasing things. Online retailing is one such purchase option as it offers purchase opportunity via an internet connection from any part of the world. ROM is a company which used online retailing model for movies rentals. ROM is facing a critical situation where both corporate reputation and business model of the company are at stake. Theft of sensitive credit card data would disparage not only ROM's reputation and credibility, but would also question Ecommerce business model deployed by the company. Apart from affecting company's situation, this can leave a serious impact on the whole online retailing industry.
> (*Taken from "Crisis communication," student assignment, 2008*)

There are several problems with this paragraph. But there is enough background information in the paragraph for the reader to make sense of what is coming next.

Here are a few one-sentence examples taken from longer reports. The examples are in quote marks and the questions that arise in the reader's mind while reading them are in parenthesis. The full reports did not provide any answers to these questions.

> "By the end of this year, Ranbaxy estimates to roll back close to 10% of income on R&D." (*Do you mean 'plough back'?*)

> "In today's world, we need to look at rural entrepreneurship from a different perspective where indulgence and investment in it by a corporate can lead to greater returns." (*Returns for whom?*)

> "Affordability is cited as one of the main reasons for the dramatic growth in the number of mobile telephone subscribers in India, as owning a mobile amounted to 93% per capital GDP in 1999 while it was just 29% of per capita GDP in 2003." (*Says who? What is the source of this information?*)

The absence of instant feedback from intended readers makes writing arguably the most difficult communication medium available to us. However, if we figure out reader expectations and meet them when we write, this is the best means to reach out to a large number of people across the barriers of space and time.

Your teachers are among those you need to reach out to while you are a student. Even when you understand a subject very well, if your written assignments do not convince your teachers that you have understood it, you get poor grades. At the graduate level, most of the evaluation of your learning is based on what you write. The failure to master academic writing can, therefore, have major consequences not only for your performance at the university but also for your career.

If you are a scholar or researcher, you have to reach out to fellow scholars through papers in learned journals. Poor writing can lead to editors rejecting your papers that perhaps report good research. The disastrous effect it can have on your academic career needs no elaboration.

There is yet another reason why we should take up the challenge of writing. According to Lewin (2003), after an extensive study, the National Commission on Writing in America's Schools and Colleges asserted in the report they released in April 2003 that "...if students are to learn, they must write." The reason, according to the panel of 18 educators, is that "if students are to make knowledge their own, they must struggle with the details, wrestle with the facts and rework raw information and dimly understood concepts into language they can communicate to someone else..." (Lewin, 2003). In other words, struggling to communicate through writing is an immense learning experience. It is only when we try to write that we realize how unclear we are about many concepts.

DIFFERENT KINDS OF WRITING

Words are like clothes. The context and purpose determine what clothes are appropriate for us to wear. When we are on a picnic or at a fair, we wear informal clothes, generally colourful ones. At a party, we may experiment with new fashions and wear clothes that get us noticed and talked about by others. We tend to avoid clothes that we fear may bring unwelcome attention to us. At home, we are not bothered about fashion or about what others might think of us. We want comfort and choose clothes that are comfortable. What is comfortable may vary from person to person. At work, it is again different. There we have to follow certain norms whether we like them or not. The clothes we wear at work tend to be formal and dignified, their colours subdued and their range limited. Best workplace clothes do not draw attention to themselves.

We cannot say that any one kind of clothes is better than the others. What we can say is that one type of clothes suits an occasion or person better than another type. And that is determined to a large extent by others' expectations. In some contexts, the expectations are so rigid (some employees are, for example, required to wear a uniform at work) that violations are not at all tolerated. In some other contexts, you may be able to get away with minor violations. All this applies to words and writing styles too. You cannot, for example, get your paper published in a scientific journal unless the paper strictly follows all its guidelines, which are substantially different from those of news magazines. If you sent your mother an e-mail in a language you normally use for communicating with your professors, she would wonder what happened to you. As our writing is for others to read and make sense of, we ignore their expectations at our peril.

There are different kinds of writing, each presenting its own special challenges besides those that are common to all forms of writing. In this book, we focus on academic writing, a genre of writing critical for your academic success. In order to master academic writing, we need to distinguish it from two other major approaches to writing, namely, journalistic writing and creative writing. These three genres of writing are like the basic colours. You can mix them to generate other kinds of writing that are suitable for different contexts and readers. Business writing, for example, can be seen as a combination of many features of journalistic writing and academic writing.

All good writing conforms to the anticipated reader's expectations. Fluency in one genre of writing, however, does not necessarily lead to fluency in other kinds of writing. That is why some students who win prizes for short story writing or newspaper articles, struggle hard at the graduate level where they have to write academic papers or submit written assignments. In order to write well, we should figure out what our anticipated readers' expectations are and be guided by them.

JOURNALISTIC WRITING

The objective of journalistic writing, generally found in newspapers and news magazines of the print and digital varieties, is essentially to inform the readers by reporting and commenting on current events. It is targeted at a wide range of people who can spare very little time and yet want to know what is happening around them. The preferred writing style is crisp, lively and attention-grabbing. The sentences and paragraphs are short. The content is people-centred and easy to grasp. There may be photographs and attention-grabbing personal details to support the written text.

Most journalistic writing answers, in as few and simple words as possible, the following questions: Who? What? When? Where? How? Newspaper articles, including editorials, which comment on events and issues, also answer 'why.' Thus, journalistic writing consists of factual reporting (news reporting) and analysis of those events that show the writer's interpretation of those events. There are norms that journalists are required to follow; those norms, however, are not as rigid as the ones academic writers have to follow.

Successful journalistic writing attracts and keeps the casual, even non-committed reader hooked. Writers use many devices including photographs to catch the reader's eyes. Wordplay such as puns, humour and exaggeration are commonplace. Here are some headlines: "Raju beats Obama on web popularity charts!" (*Indian Express*), "Nuns through YouTube" (*The Hindu*), "Satyam, Wipro lose over $4 billion on US bourses in a week" (*The Times of India*), "When Insurance Is Bad for Your Health" (*The New York Times*) and "The scent of a man" (*The Economist*). Once the reader is hooked in through a catchy title, nothing is allowed to hinder the flow of reading because she may leave the story at any point and not come back. So good journalistic writing is lively and quick-paced.

The people-centredness of journalistic writing leads to the generous use of verbs and the active voice. Words that appeal to the different senses are common. They help the reader participate in the event, as it were. He expects the news story to be factual. Short quotes from people connected to the story are generally thrown in too. They give colour and spice, and in a sense, objectivity to the story.

Because of the wide range of readers that a newspaper reaches out to, the reporter has to build up some background information. However, as the writing is generally about current events, the reporter can assume that the readers have quite a lot of background information.

Examine the first two paragraphs of a news report that appeared in the online version of *The Hindu* on Sunday, 25 January 2009:

Two Price Waterhouse auditors held

N. Rahul

HYDERABAD: Two partners of Price Waterhouse, statutory auditors of Satyam Computer Services, were arrested by the Crime Investigation Department (CID) of the Andhra Pradesh police on Saturday on charges of conspiracy, failure to scrutinise records and connivance.

S. Gopalakrishnan and his deputy, Talluri Srinivas, had signed Satyam's annual statements of accounts without performing their statutory duties as external auditors, a senior CID official told *The Hindu*.

Citing a specific charge, he said they had accepted forged fixed deposit receipts and particulars of balances furnished by the company without any verification with bankers.

The writer assumes quite rightly that the newspaper's readers are familiar with the background to this story: the massive fraud perpetrated by the chairman of Satyam Computer Services Ltd and reported widely during the previous weeks. They may not, however, know that PricewaterhouseCoopers is the statutory auditor of the company. Most readers may not know the names of the principal partners of the auditing firm. Interestingly, even the common acronym, CID, has been written out in full because of the possibility that some readers may not know what CID stands for.

While there are five more short paragraphs in the news story, these three initial paragraphs give the readers a reasonably good account of what happened: who did what to whom, when, where, how and why. Even if one reads only the first paragraph, one can get the basic story.

CREATIVE WRITING

Creative writing is expressing oneself—one's experience or imagination or a combination of both—through the written word. It creates something new. It is found in fiction, poetry and plays, collectively referred to as literature. It is the writer's subjective perception of reality that is shared with readers through words. But this subjectivity is acceptable to readers of literature. We do not ask creative writers to tell us the truth. We do not ask creative writers to provide evidence for any assumptions they make or any conclusions they arrive at. We accept what they write because what it says feels right. We reject it when we do not enjoy it. We expect creative writing to entertain us, enlighten us and transport us to aspects of life we have not experienced. We accept the content and the insights because of the way the writers take us along. We willingly suspend our disbelief (to borrow an expression from Samuel Taylor Coleridge) as we enter the world of fiction mediated through creative writing.

Good creative writing displays passion, wit and intuitive knowledge. It is an art. So, one needs the basic creative talent as in music, dance or painting before it can be refined through training. Each creative writer has his own distinctive style. One can often identify the author by examining the style of an extract. In other words, creative writing reflects the personality, attitude and values of the writer's self.

Writers stretch and manipulate the language in different ways in the process of sharing their unusual experiences with the reader. This is often called poetic licence. There are no fixed benchmarks. Rather, a creative writer can ignore such benchmarks to create certain effects. Take, for example, poet e. e. cummings, who does not follow the standard rules about when to use capital letters and when to use lowercase letters. A creative writer can stretch and twist words to create new meanings provided she takes her readers along. That is what Humpty Dumpty says in Chapter VI of Lewis Carroll's *Through the Looking Glass, and What Alice Found there:*

"When *I* use a word," Humpty Dumpty said, in a rather scornful tone, "it means just what I choose it to mean—neither more nor less."

"The question is," said Alice, "whether you *can* make words mean so many different things."

"The question is," said Humpty Dumpty, "which is to be master — that's all."

Source: http://www.sabian.org/Alice/lgchap06.htm

In creative writing, attention is often drawn to the language itself like one's dress at a party. Readers marvel at the way a poet uses words, especially to create unusual metaphors. They may leave a lot to the reader's imagination. In fact, ambiguity adds depth to creative writing by providing for multiple interpretations. If different readers derive different meanings from a poem or a novel, it is welcomed, not merely tolerated.

ACADEMIC WRITING

Academic writing—broadly defined—is for communicating scientific knowledge. It is generally addressed to scholars and other knowledgeable readers who are familiar with that branch of knowledge. The most rigorous academic writing is found in scientific journals and doctoral dissertations in which scholars share with fellow scholars their research findings, leading to advances in knowledge in different disciplines. The content and structure of writing in most of those texts closely reflect the features of knowledge generation that we noted in Chapter 1. (Different but equally acceptable features may be found in some qualitative research, especially in ethnographic studies, field studies and case studies. The papers that present such qualitative research will reflect those differences in content and style. Some of the statements below may not apply to them.)

You also find less sophisticated versions of academic writing in colleges and universities. Most of the assignments that graduate students write and submit to their instructors fall in this category.

What is common among all classes of academic writing is that ideas take centrestage, people are in the background, and the writer's personal feelings have no role in the presentation of ideas or insights. Everything that the reader needs should be explicitly stated in the text; arguments are accepted or rejected because of the logic or evidence presented there, not because of who proposes them. This is in stark contrast to creative writing in which the poet's or writer's personality infuses the text with special meanings. Thus, the meaning of a phrase may vary depending on whether it is from William Shakespeare, John Keats or Emily Dickinson.

Readers of academic writing expect the author to analyse empirical data (collected in many different ways and from different sources depending on the discipline), arrive at a thesis—idea or claim—and support it with evidence. In other words, readers expect to be taken along the path of scientific knowledge, as we have already noted in Chapter 1. Academic writing mirrors the research process that generates scientific knowledge. Mere dumping of data is not welcome.

The basic expectations of readers of academic writing have not changed over the decades. Almost 50 years ago, Klein (1965, p. 2), for example, stated reader expectations roughly the way we would do now:

> We want [academic] writers who manifest orderly thought processes in their writing, who can organize data for analysis, who can be selective, who can distinguish significant detail from just detail, who can measure length in relation to importance, who can analyze, sort out, discern, discriminate, and discard.

This applies equally well to aseptic, double-blind experiments and to ethnographic studies in which the observer may be a participant in the events reported.

Academic Writing: Style

Academic papers—both empirical and conceptual—are to be read carefully and analysed; not just skimmed and tossed away like a newspaper. Naturally sentences and paragraphs tend to be longer and more complex than in journalistic writing.

The language style suitable for academic writing is formal. Conversational contractions such as 'can't,' 'won't' and 'shouldn't' are not welcome. Equally unwelcome are colloquial expressions such as 'grub' for food and 'buck' for dollar.

Academic writing is somewhat subdued like formal workplace clothes. It is not exuberant; it is not supposed to draw attention to itself but to the ideas conveyed through it. Thus, colourful expressions and bold metaphors that populate creative writing are rarely found in academic writing, especially in scholarly papers that scientific journals publish. Fine (1988, cited in Golden-Biddle & Locke, 1997) is among the few scholars who recommend the use of metaphors and literary devices to make scientific writing lively. But the lack of colour in an overwhelming majority of scholarly papers confirms that the advocates of literary devices continue to be in a minority.

Study the following extract from an article written by a graduate student:

> Year 2001! The performance of Indian Railways was at its worst. Revenues were stagnant and costs were escalating. A series of bad years had reduced the fund balance to only Re 149 crores. Operating Ratio (ratio of Total Working Expenses—including depreciation and pension, but excluding dividend to GOI—to Total Earnings) was at 98.34%; and for the first time in nearly two decades, Railways had to defer the dividend payable to Government of India. The Expert Group on Indian Railways (also known as Anand Mohan Committee for Railway Restructuring) had already written the obituary of Indian Railways.
>
> Year 2006! Within five years of the doomsday prophesies, Indian Railways was "back with a bang". With an operating ratio of 78.7%, it was among the most efficient railways in the world. The funds balance had ballooned to Re 12,000 crores—and Railways was finalizing investments to the tune of Re 350,000 crores till 2015 [Raghuram 2007]. This remarkable reversal of fortune and regaining of confidence, for a public sector enterprise, seems a story taken out of fairy-tales.
>
> (*Taken from "Turnaround of Indian Railways," student assignment, 2008*)

This is definitely an interesting, engaging style of writing. But it is a little too dramatic and colourful for an academic report. It is like a flashy, multicoloured shirt under a grey jacket worn at a formal meeting. There is something incongruous about it. Here is an alternative version of the same text, written in a style that is more appropriate for a report of this kind. The original writer's choice of ideas and structure have, however, been retained.

The performance of Indian Railways was at its worst in 2001. A series of financially bad years in which revenues were stagnant and costs rising had reduced its fund balance to Rs 149 crore. The Operating Ratio (that is, ratio of Total Working Expenses — including depreciation and pension, but excluding dividend payable to GOI — to Total Earnings) was 98.34%; and for the first time since 1983, Railways deferred the dividend payable to Government of India. The Expert Group on Indian Railways (2001), also known as Anand Mohan Committee for Railway Restructuring, concluded in the same year that this public sector enterprise was financially unviable.

In the following five years, however, there was a significant turnaround. In 2006, the operating ratio was 78.7%, among the best globally. The balance of funds rose 80 times to Rs 12,000 crore. Buoyed by this, observes Raghuram (2007), Railways decided to invest up to Rs 350,000 crore in the next ten years. This is a remarkable reversal of fortunes for a public sector enterprise.

Compare some expressions from the first version with the corresponding expressions in the second version. "[T]he obituary of Indian Railways" has become "financially unviable." "[B]ack with a bang" is replaced with "a significant turnaround." The expression, "a story taken out of fairy-tales," has been dropped because it appears unnecessary and inappropriate in academic writing.

One of the implications of the formality infusing academic writing is that it closely follows the established conventions of the genre. The most easily noticed convention is the meticulous citing of the sources of data or views borrowed from others, even when it weighs the text down and makes it less readable. The difference it makes is apparent if you compare an article from a scientific journal and an article from a magazine such as *Time* or *The Economist*. The journal article is likely to have a long list of references either at the end or at the bottom of each page while the magazine article may have none, even when the latter is written after considerable research. The detailed referencing we see in academic writing reflects the central characteristic of scientific inquiry, namely, focus on objectivity through reliance on empirical data rather than personal opinions or intuitions.

Depending on which discipline you are writing in, there are different citation conventions; what is common among all such citation styles is the accurate identification of the source of information and the kind of borrowing. For academic writing in management and social sciences, we recommend the citation style developed and popularized by APA (American Psychological Association). Please see Chapter 6 for a detailed discussion of why it is important to acknowledge sources of borrowings and how to do it systematically.

The foregrounding of ideas and the deemphasizing of people and emotions in academic writing are reflected in the way the authors refer to themselves, if required, in their academic papers. In physical and, to some extent, social sciences, writers use the third person to refer to themselves. A hypothetical example: "This paper discusses the challenge of teaching ethics to MBA students and about the author's exploratory attempt at exposing students to managers jailed for corporate fraud." Of course, in some disciplines/genres of social sciences and humanities, the first person is increasingly being used by writers, especially in the plural form ('we,' 'our experience,' 'our hypothesis', and so on). The example given above could be rewritten as: "In this paper, we discuss the challenge of teaching ethics to MBA students and about our exploratory attempt at exposing students to managers jailed for corporate fraud."

Even in those contexts where reference to the author in the first person is accepted, excessive use can give the impression that the author is presenting mere personal views or opinions rather than objective considerations. If, for example, you write, "When I computed the average, I found that…," your personal perspective seems to come to the fore. If, however, you change it to "When the average was computed, it was found that…," the objective tone is restored. So is the focus on the idea. Therefore, even where 'I' and 'we' are permitted, it is a good idea to use them sparingly. The guiding principle should be that academic writing is about empirical data and concepts, and not about the researcher's feelings or opinions.

A fine example of separating the text from the writer can be seen in the practice of blind refereeing followed by academic journals. Before deciding whether to accept or reject a paper received from a scholar, the journal editor sends it to two or more fellow scholars in the field. The paper sent to the referees does not carry the name, affiliation or any information that can help the referee identify the author. When writing a paper, if Lena Pandit quotes from her own paper published in, say, 2008, she has to refer to it as Pandit (2008) rather than "my paper of 2008." The referees have to judge the quality and acceptability of the paper based exclusively on what is found in it, and not on the basis of who wrote it or what institution the author is associated with.

Academic Writing: Characteristics

Academic writing is dispassionate. You may be convinced about something. You may be passionate or excited about it. But in academic writing you have to be like an impartial observer. You must present the pros and cons of the position you hold, rather than just evidence that supports your position. You must not suppress any inconvenient data that you cannot account for or that which block a neat conclusion. The reader may or may not agree with your position or your interpretation. That does not matter. Your credibility as an academic writer goes up when the reader finds you objective and dispassionate.

Here are two extracts from another student article:

The whole world was waiting with bated breath to have a glimpse of the sub $3000 car produced by the Tata Motors. The car was conceptualized and designed indigenously in India. Though the western media reacted with skepticism with regard to the car meeting the safety and pollution control norms, this is seen more as a knee jerk reaction to the threat of India and China overtaking them in the near future in all spheres.

[...]

It is an irrefutable fact that Indians are the one of the most intelligent people on the earth. The world's largest publicly funded CSIR (Council for Scientific and Industrial Research) labs are finding it difficult to recruit scientists due to shortage.

(*Taken from "R & D in Indian industry: Its implications on the human capital," student assignment, 2008*)

Such overenthusiastic and uncritical statements are unacceptable in academic writing.

A related feature of academic writing is that its tone is cautious and tentative rather than categorical. In humanities and social sciences, evidence is extremely unlikely to be so overwhelming that one can arrive at a conclusion with absolute certainty. The sample studied may be inadequate, and there may be factors that one has not controlled. This may be true of some experiments in physical sciences also. We, therefore, come across tentative expressions such as, "This seems to suggest that...," "the cause appears to be" and "this is likely to lead to ... ."

Here is the conclusion that a team of students of Advanced Data Analysis reached in a paper:

> The popular belief among the media and general public is that voting patterns are usually determined by the gender, race or age of the candidates rather than their political ideologies and agenda. The models which we developed above seem to point against these beliefs. Using this, we do not claim that these factors have no role to play in individuals' voting behaviour. Rather, our interpretation of these results is that such features of an individual are overpowered by larger political and socio-economic issues, which, ideally, should be the case in a democracy.
>
> (*Taken from "The trends in US presidential elections," student assignment, 2008*)

Although their analysis is systematic and reasonably comprehensive, the authors are careful not to make a categorical statement based on it. Observe the following clauses or phrases that introduce tentativeness in their conclusion: "the voting patterns are *usually* determined," "the models ... *seem* to point against these beliefs," and "we ... *do not claim* that these factors have no role to play."

They, however, stumble in the last sentence, when they move beyond analysis of data into their socio-political opinion about what *ought to* happen. There is no problem with holding the view that large political and socio-economic issues rather than gender, race or age of the candidates should be the major influences in a democracy. But it is inappropriate here because the paper is an analysis of the trends in US presidential elections, not an evaluation of what trends are good and what bad for the US or for democracy in general. In other words, their analysis does not entitle them to the claim they are making in that clause.

Clarity is arguably the most highly regarded virtue in academic writing. While creative writing is full of ambiguities and multiple layers of meanings that signal the depth, variety and complexity of the human experience, good academic writing has no room for them. The best kind of academic writing is what gives every reader the same meaning. More than half a century ago, writing in *The American Journal of Sociology*, Ogburn (1947) quoted two interesting statements he had heard ("Architecture is life; architecture is you," and "Psychoanalysis is life; psychoanalysis is you.") and said that they were not suitable in scientific writing because it was not clear to the reader what they meant. Or different readers reconstructed different meanings when they encountered such words. Ogburn's statement is as true now as a half century ago.

This is the reason why metaphors—the mainstay of creative writing—are frowned upon in academic writing. When a rich, memorable metaphor is used, the reader may derive a meaning which is different from what is intended by the writer. Take, for example, the expression, "Bengaluru is the Silicon Valley of India." What does it mean? Does it mean that Bengaluru has a heavy concentration of high-tech companies? Does it mean that Bengaluru has generated a large number of creative ideas in information technology? Does it mean that nearly all new ideas in IT in India come from Bengaluru? As the phrase "Silicon Valley of India" is capable of multiple meanings, it is not proper to use it in academic writing, unless, of course, the intended meaning is specified after the metaphor is mentioned.

Cleverly ambiguous expressions and puns are welcome in creative writing, and acceptable to a large extent in journalistic writing too. Once Mark Twain wrote:

> Last week, I stated this woman was the ugliest woman I had ever seen. I have since been visited by her sister, and now wish to withdraw that statement.

Source: http://www.allgreatquotes.com/funny_quotes207.shtml

We generally infer that the second woman is uglier than the first woman. Or we assume that that is Mark Twain's meaning. But strictly speaking, the second sentence does not necessarily mean that the second woman is uglier. The second sentence merely states that his revision of opinion has come after the sister's visit.

Take also Gertrude Stein's celebrated expression, "Rose is a rose is a rose" and E.E. cummings' saying, "The world is mud-luscious and puddle-wonderful." Both are intriguing; they startle you and make you think. But what exactly do the expressions mean? If different readers cannot agree on what an expression means, it has no place in academic writing. Interestingly, while literature thrives on ambiguities and wordplay, literary criticism is not supposed to have them because literary criticism is academic writing.

Words that are more than adequate in ordinary communication such as 'many,' 'quite a few' and 'shortly,' are not welcome in academic writing because they are elastic. What number, for example, would qualify as 'many' or 'quite a few'? Similarly, in academic writing meant for international readers, symbols such as $ and Re are not clear enough because different countries have dollars and rupees as the unit of their currency. Unless the context makes it abundantly clear, you will need to write USD or US$ for US dollar; AUD or A$ for Australian dollar. In the same way, you need to write INR for Indian Rupees, PKR for Pakistan Rupees and NPR for Nepalese Rupees, unless the context defines it for the reader. The idea is that what the writer means should be clear to the reader. Academic writing insists on greater rigour and clarity than is acceptable in ordinary communication.

Observe the way the writer uses 'many' and 'a very small percentage' without sacrificing clarity in a hypothetical report on team formation:

As can be seen in Exhibit 3, a large number of students (39.2%) stated that caste was not a consideration in team formation. This, however, is not borne out by the small percentage of groups (7%) that are socially and ethnically diverse (Table 1).

In order to achieve clarity, the academic writer may have to define the terms used, especially those terms that are loosely used in ordinary conversations.

Take, for example, the following sentence from a paper published in *Vikalpa*, a management journal: "'Effectiveness' for the purpose of this study has been concretized in terms of impact of mobile advertising on the purchase decision of the consumer" (Tripathi & Siddiqui, 2008, p. 48). 'Effectiveness' is a common word that can mean many things. The authors define the term because they want to make sure that the reader gets the specific meaning in which they are using that word.

Here is an example of a more elaborate definition:

Intellectual Property Rights (IPRs) have been defined as, 'ideas, inventions and creative expressions on which there is a public willingness to bestow the status of property' (Hunshyal & Biradar, 2005). Any vital information can have a commercial value and the person who thought of the idea for the first time or the person who created the knowledge work has the right to claim ownership like as any other asset he holds. Its purpose is to prevent unauthorised copying or misuse.

(Taken from "R&D in pharmaceutical industry: Challenges and opportunities from IPR and globalization," student assignment, 2008)

The core definition has been borrowed from a published source. The writer elaborates the definition to help the reader understand how the term 'Intellectual Property Rights' has been used in the paper.

Another way to enhance clarity is to use pictures and charts to illustrate the point you are making, especially when you have to analyse data and compare them. If you display too many numbers one after another, your reader will be overwhelmed. Charts can present complex comparative data in a neat and easily intelligible way. But as Zelazny (2007) shows in his excellent book, *The Say It With Charts Complete Toolkit*, a wrong choice of charts can make the message harder for the reader to figure out. Similarly, if you are not clear about what message you want to present to the reader, your charts are unlikely to create clarity miraculously. So the first step is to become clear about what you want to tell the reader; the second step is to choose the chart form that translates your message most effectively into visuals. Consult Zelazny's book for detailed guidance on how to choose the right chart form and how to make them.

We have looked at several qualities of good academic writing. A coming together of these qualities such as formality, detachment, objectivity, tentativeness, rigour and clarity makes up the style of academic writing. It is this style that distinguishes it from general, journalistic and creative writing. For a more detailed account of academic writing and its requirements, consult Barrass (2002) or Turk and Kirkman (1989). Also, pick up any international journal in your field of research and go through some papers keeping in mind the features of academic writing that we have identified in this section.

Academic Writing: Description and Narration

The broad processes that are observed in academic writing are description, narration and explanation. These processes mirror the research processes that we examined in Chapter 1 (see Figure 1.1: An Overview of Research Process). They are inter-dependent. You cannot explain something—an object, event, process or behaviour—until it has been described or narrated. But a mere narration or description of something does not make it academic until there is an attempt to explain it by analysing it. If you merely list or describe facts, you create a catalogue or a laundry list, and not an analysis. The reader does not know why you have listed them and what you want him to take away from it. If you flood him with facts and descriptive details, you do not enlighten him; instead, you burden him.

Suspenseful narration and vivid description are the stuff of fiction and journalism. In literature, narration and description are generally the fruit of imagination (John Milton's description of hell in *Paradise Lost*, for example); while in journalism, we encounter the narration of actual events and the description of actual things, people and scenes. Imprecise but colourful and highly evocative words and phrases are used in both cases to recreate a life-like experience for the reader.

In academic writing, however, narration and description are factual. When an academic writer narrates an experiment or describes the instruments used, her objective is to give the reader a clear, factual picture, so that the analysis built on it can be evaluated appropriately or the experiment can be replicated. When a writer reviews existing literature, what she does is to briefly describe the existing knowledge as the base on which her argument will be built. In other words, description and narration in academic writing are the factual foundation for the super structure, that is, explanation or theory building.

Study the following paragraph, which describes the ques-tionnaire used by the researchers to gather information on the effectiveness of information technology in government organiza-tions in India:

> The questionnaire was structured along the guidelines given by Franz and Robey (1986), and some other relevant literature. It incorporated questions regarding the independent and dependent

variables—user satisfaction, IT use, organizational structure and information systems performance along with the enablers and inhibitors of IT use. The issues regarding top management and IT management were also included in the questionnaire. The Likert scale was used in formulating the questionnaires, in which the respondents were asked to state their preference on a continuum— 'no effect,' 'low,' 'medium,' 'high,' 'very high,' and 'none,' 'very little,' 'little' and 'moderately.' The answers for the categories were thus mutually exclusive so that the respondent had to state only one choice against an item. An attempt was also made to minimize the bias in the language of the questionnaire. (Gupta, Kanungo, Kumar & Sahu, 2007, p. 11)

There is no colour or drama in this description. It gives the reader enough information to judge how appropriate the questionnaire was.

Description is also commonly used to share with readers the structure of something, including that of the paper they are reading. Here is an example:

This article deals with the issues surrounding the R&D activities in Indian Pharmaceutical Industry and the way it has been shaped by the recent improvements in IPRs as a result of globalization. Section 1 traces the growth of Indian Pharmaceutical Industry over the years and its R&D initiatives. Section 2 evaluates the potential of R&D in aiding the growth of the pharmaceutical industry. Section 3 outlines the guidelines on Intellectual Property Rights in India. Section 4 seeks to focus on implications of patenting and IPRs in the Indian Pharmaceutical Industry. Section 5 deals with the recent problems that have arisen due to TRIPS (WTO) and globalization of the pharmaceutical industry. In conclusion, Section 6 attempts to address what could be done to face the stated challenges and seize the opportunities thereof.

(*Taken from "R&D in pharmaceutical industry: Challenges and opportunities from IPR and globalization," student assignment, 2008*)

Another use of description in academic writing is an extended definition of a thing or process. Here is an example:

Currently the most important worldwide attempt to counter GHG [greenhouse gas] emissions is the Kyoto Protocol. It is an international agreement which can be thought of as a successor to the United Nations Framework Convention on Climate Change

(UNFCCC). The critical distinction between the two is that while the Convention stops at merely encouraging industrialized countries to control greenhouse gas emissions, the Protocol commits them towards achieving specific targets. The Kyoto Protocol sets binding targets for reducing greenhouse gas emissions by its signatories which include 37 developed countries and the European Union. This corresponds to an average of five per cent reduction against 1990 levels over the period 2008-2012 [UNFCC, n.d.].

(Taken from "The EU cap on CO2 emissions by international aviation sector: What to expect?" student assignment, 2008)

We can use narration to give the readers the background to a study or to share with them how the researchers conducted the study. Here, again, the style is factual. Study the two examples below. The first one gives a brief historical sketch of Indian automobile industry in preparation for an analysis of the impact of the current global economic situation on it.

The Indian auto industry made its first appearance in 1898, and exceeded everyone's expectations in terms of the scale and reach that it has achieved. A huge market has developed in two-wheelers, four-wheelers as well as heavy vehicles. The Industry has been around for a long time. However, it got a real kick-start in 1991 when the Indian economy entered its liberalization phase. Policies such as easy finance, price discounts and tax reliefs gave the industry a real boost. The industry grew between 16% and 18% during this period. The government, realising the potential of the industry, formulated liberalization policies which attracted foreign investment into the automobile industry.

(Taken from "Impact of the current global economic situation on Indian automobile industry," student assignment, 2009)

The next one tells us how the Indian biotechnology industry developed from 1995. It is a prelude to identifying certain challenges faced by it and suggesting some measures to promote investment in it.

The Biotech industry saw a major change in 1995 when India signed the Trade Regulated Intellectual Property Rights agreement (TRIPS). In this, India agreed to adhere to the product patent regime from 2005. This ended Indian firms' reliance on reverse-engineering of products and has fostered innovation during the implementation period (1995-2005), evidenced by the huge investments in R&D post 1995 and the number of patents filed by Indian firms. The MNCs now see India as a level playing field where they can compete with their Indian counterparts on equal grounds. This has led to increased FDI flows in the Biotech and Pharmaceutical sectors (Thomas, 2008, pp. 19-22).

(Taken from "Innovations in Indian biopharmaceuticals: Turning the tide," student assignment, 2009)

The following example illustrates how Bhal and Gulati (2007, p. 14) collected data for their research:

Procedural justice was measured using the six-item scale used by the Niehoff and Moorman (1993) which was based on the one used by Moorman (1991). This scale assessed the gathering of accurate and unbiased information, employee voice, and an appeals process in appraisal and pay-related decisions. The respondents were asked to rate the statements in terms of how often were they true for them (1 = equals never, 2 = almost never, 3 = sometimes, 4 = usually, 5 = always).

All these examples show that compared to journalistic and creative writing, the narration in academic writing is colourless, functional, almost boring. But then the academic writer's objective is not to dazzle or entertain the readers but to give them a factual and unbiased report. Such colourlessness is as much part of the general style of academic writing as it is in a *pandit* officiating at a glittering wedding.

You will also have noticed that description and narration generally go together. The second sentence in the first of the last two extracts ("In this India agreed to adhere to the product patent regime from 2005.") is a descriptive comment on the preceding statement. It briefly describes TRIPS for the reader so that he can follow the narrative without any difficulty. In the same way, the second last sentence of the same paragraph ("The MNCs now see India as a level playing field where they can compete with their Indian counterparts on equal grounds.") also is a descriptive sentence. It describes the current condition of India from the perspective of competition. That helps the reader appreciate the consequence, namely, "increased FDI flows in the Biotech and Pharmaceutical sectors."

The second sentence in the second extract ("This scale assessed the gathering of accurate and unbiased information, employee voice, and an appeals process in appraisal and pay-related decisions.") also does a similar job. It briefly describes the six-item scale used by Niehoff and Moorman before the reader is told how it was used in the research project. Such descriptive statements in the midst of a narration help the reader understand the events or steps better.

Now we need to turn to analysis, the staple of academic writing, and distinguish it from data dumping that often spoils students' academic writing.

Academic Writing: Analysis versus Data Dumping

The soul of academic writing is analysis. It is the written manifestation of the core research process, namely, theory building or theorizing, as described in Chapters 1 and 2. The description and narration are to prepare the reader for the writer's analysis, which is nothing but her claim, thesis, logical conclusion or explanation of empirical or conceptual data. Her claim stands or falls depending on the strength of supporting data and the quality of the analysis she subjects the data to.

As Rogers and Rymer (1995, p. 352) remind us, in analytical writing, we expect to be "evaluating ideas, assuming a position, developing reasons and examples, and organizing the material logically." In other words, analytical writing is writing built around analysis.

Study the following example. It is taken from an article written by a team of two graduate students as part of an assignment. The authors claim that India needs to improve its infrastructure urgently and significantly. They present data to support that claim.

Need for Infrastructure

India currently spends 4.5% of its GDP on infrastructure as against China which spends over 10%. There is a broad consensus among political circles that India has to spend at the 10% level by 2010, if it has to sustain the present growth rate (India to surge, 2007). The Indian government estimates that investment of around $320bn is needed by 2012 to upgrade the country's creaking roads, ports and airports (On the road, 2007).

While India has second largest road network in the world spanning over 3.3 million kilometers, the majority of the roads are of two lanes or less and are poorly maintained. With annual growth rates projected at 12-15% for passenger traffic and 15-18% for cargo traffic, an estimated $50bn investment is required over the next five years to improve the road infrastructure (Ministry of Finance, n.d.). Similarly, Indian Railways, which is the world's fourth largest rail network with over 63,000 route kilometers (Railways, 2007), has been growing at over 9% and 7% in freight and passenger traffic respectively during 2004-2006. This is in sharp contrast to the historical trend of 3-4% growth rate (Indian Railways, n.d.). On the aviation front, India is witnessing 15% annual growth in passenger traffic and 20% annual growth in cargo traffic (Ministry of Finance, n.d.) and with more airlines criss-crossing the Indian skies, even the basic ground facilities are not of acceptable standards. These realities expose the glaring gap and urgent need for infrastructure in the Indian transportation arena.

(Taken from "Public-private partnership for bridging the infrastructure gap in India: Lessons from transportation sector," student assignment, 2008)

The authors' claim—that India needs to invest massively and urgently in infrastructure—is given in the last sentence of the second paragraph. The first level of support is the significant gap in infrastructure investment between India and China, the two major economies in Asia, both of which are growing fast. The second level of support comes from the high amount (US$320 billion) which, Indian government estimates, is required in the next five years to upgrade India's infrastructure. The third level of support comes from the substantial and immediate increase projected by the government in Indian road, rail and air traffic.

The data—the difference between Indian investment and Chinese investment in infrastructure, the Indian government's estimate of India's infrastructure requirements and the growth in traffic projected—do not in themselves mean anything in particular. It is when they are arranged in support of a claim that they acquire significance to the reader. If no such claim had been made or if the writers had put in data irrelevant to the claim, it would have been an instance of dumping data on the reader.

There is, indeed, one instance of data dumping in the second paragraph: "an estimated $50bn investment is required over the next five years to improve the road infrastructure." This detail is unnecessary; it also breaks the unity of the second paragraph, which deals with the growth of traffic rather than the amount of money needed to fill the gap in infrastructure. You will notice that such figures are not given for rail and air traffic. It appears that the writers happened to have the information about the investment needed for road infrastructure and they put it in.

Here is an extract from another student paper on a similar theme. This also contains a large amount of data.

Why India needs PPP

Despite being one of the fastest growing economies of the world, public infrastructure in India is in poor shape. Indian ports still average a turn around time of 4.72 days (http://www.indiacore. com/ports.html), long queues at airports are a common sight and the conditions of the road network is functional at best. We lose Rs. 200 billion per annum due to congestion (DEA & ADB, 2007), which can be attributed to poor highway development. While Indian aviation has been growing at about 18% per annum (http:// www.ibef.org/industry/aviation.aspx), there has been little growth in supporting infrastructure. According to Jain et al. (2007), Delhi and Mumbai airports are handling twice as much traffic as they were designed for. India's average power consumption per capita for the period 1996-2000 was 359 kwh, compared to China's 717 kwh and Malaysia's 2378 kwh. The DEA & ADB (2007) report estimates that power shortages cost India about USD68 billion. These shortages and losses have severely limited our prospects on all fronts, especially in the current high growth period.

According to Government of India, Ministry of Finance, Department of Economic Affairs (2007) report on PPP, Planning Commission estimates a requirement of USD320 billion (2005-6 price level) for investment in core infrastructure over five years (2007-12). The Committee on Infrastructure financing, as quoted by the same report, has increased these estimates to USD384 billion (2005-6) in May 2007. This means an average of USD77 billion per year. The only way India can achieve this much investment is making use of private funds via the PPP model.

(Taken from "Importance of public private partnership (PPP) in the Indian context and the roadblocks in its implementation," student assignment, 2008)

The data in the first paragraph support the claim made in the first sentence: "Despite being one of the fastest growing economies of the world, public infrastructure in India is in poor shape." The paragraph does not give enough comparative data except in the case of electricity consumption. We do not know how bad the turnaround time of 4.72 days at Indian ports is, compared to international norms. The financial data in the second paragraph support the claim made in the last sentence: "The only way India can achieve this much investment is by making use of private funds via the PPP model." Again, there is a major weakness in the data. On what basis can the author claim that the Indian government cannot raise that amount? Is it a personal opinion? There should have been some comparative or historical figures to show that the government cannot spare such an amount for infrastructure development. In spite of these defects, the extract illustrates the way data are used to support a claim. If there was no claim which these data supported, this again would be an instance of data dumping.

Now examine the following extract from an article on rural entrepreneurship and biofuels written by another team of two students. The extract comes after the introductory section in which the writers assert that "greener, cheaper and more sustainable alternatives like biofuels" will benefit India's rural entrepreneurs, and they list the environmental, social and economic benefits of biofuels. This extract is followed by a discussion on the technical aspects of generating biofuels and the concluding section in which the writers argue for strong government support for the production of biofuels by rural entrepreneurs. This information about what comes before and after the extract should give us a perspective on the contents of the extract.

The Macroeconomic Picture

Energy Scenario: International primary energy consumption in 2006 stood at 10879 million tonnes as compared to a production of 3914 million tonnes of crude oil and 2851 billion cubic meter of Natural gas (*See Table 4*). As per US data, IEO2007 reference case, total world consumption of marketed energy is projected to increase by 57 percent from 2004 to 2030 (*http://www.eia.doe.gov/oiaf/ ieo/world.html*). On very similar lines, rather more steeply, over the next couple of decades, India's requirement for energy is expected to grow at 4.8 per cent per annum (Gonsalves, October 2006). Our current requirements are met using fossil fuels like coal, petroleum-based products and natural gas. India's consumption of crude oil and petroleum products stands at 266 million tonnes. However, our production is only about 170 million tonnes. (*See Table 5, 6 & 7*). The data also indicates that India currently meets 77% of its crude oil demands through imports. With the ever-escalating crude oil prices, the crude oil import bill for 2006-2007 stood at circa $61.7 billion, which amounts to 10% of our GDP (Gonsalves, October 2006).

Government Initiatives: Given the high consumption of petrol accompanied by the fact that the demand for diesel in India is five times higher than the demand for petrol has led the government to take two major initiatives (Mandal, 2004):

1. The Centre, in January 2003, passed a law mandating the blending of 5% ethanol in gasoline.
2. Promulgation of an ambitious National Biodiesel Mission to meet 20 per cent of the country's diesel requirements by 2011-2012.

The National Biodiesel Mission is being implemented in two stages:

1. A demonstration project to be carried out over 2003-2007 aimed at cultivating 400,000 hectares of Jatropha to yield about 3.75 tonnes oilseed per hectare annually. The project has demonstrated the viability of other aspects like seed collection and oil extraction.
2. A commercialization period during 2007-2012 aimed at Jatropha cultivation and installation of trans-esterification plants which will position India to meet 20 per cent of its diesel needs through biodiesel.

The government is also expected to announce a biofuel policy by February 2008 (Satish, 2008). It is also giving special subsidies to corporates showing interest in Jatropha cultivation in rural areas and encouraging sugar mills to make biofuels out of the molasses they generate.

The government, however, needs to establish minimum support price for Jatropha oilseeds and assuring farmers of timely payments. Since farmers do not consider Jatrropha cultivation to be financially viable, there has been a problem initiating large-scale cultivation (Gonsalves, October 2006). Public-private partnership models or an efficient supply chain maintained by entrepreneurs can resolve the issue to a large extent. There is no excise duty for BioDiesel. However, it attracts State VAT.

Various state governments have also shown interest towards helping Biofuel entrepreneurs. The State Government of Andhra has allocated 120,000 hectares of land for Jatropha cultivation to a firm called Naturol Bioenergy (Satish, 2008).

(*Taken from "Fuelling rural entrepreneurship with biofuels," student assignment, 2008*)

The writers have dumped data on us. We do not know why they have given us these data and where are they taking us. If, for example, the objective of the first paragraph is to show that India needs to spend an unsustainably high percentage of its gross domestic product (GDP) (10 per cent) to import petroleum products in the year 2006–07, the first sentence giving the global production figures for crude oil and natural gas is not relevant; nor is the second sentence about the projected increase in total world consumption of marketed energy till 2030. In other words, these data do not lead us to a conclusion or support the claim. The writers happened to have these data, which they merely dumped on us.

In the second part of the extract, 'Government Initiatives,' the writers do well to mention the two major initiatives the Indian government has taken to deal with the growing gap between production of and demand for petroleum products in the country. But what follows—a detailed description of the implementation of the National Biodiesel Mission—is unnecessary. Because these data do not support any claim nor do they lead us anywhere, we can say that these writers are dumping data on us. They should have analysed the government initiatives to see if they are adequate and, if inadequate, what more should be done.

Study a possible revision of the extract, given below. (No additional information has been introduced. Besides, it is assumed that the information given in the original is correct, although there is a discrepancy between two sets of numbers. We are told that out of the 266 million tonnes of crude oil that we need, we produce 170 million tonnes, that is, 64 per cent. But in the next sentence we are told that we meet 77 per cent of our or oil needs through imports. These cannot both be right.)

With its energy requirements growing steadily at 4.8% per annum (Gonsalves, October 2006), India's oil import bill also is rising. In 2006-07, India spent 10% of its GDP, that is, $61.7 billion, for importing crude oil (Gonsalves, October 2006). This heavy dependence on imported oil is bound to grow because the country's total domestic production of fossil fuels like coal, crude oil, and natural gas is only about 170 million tonnes per annum, leaving a gap of almost 100 million tonnes between demand and local supply in 2006-07.

The government's response to the expensive gap between the consumption and domestic availability of fossil fuels has been to promote the production and use of biofuels. Particularly noteworthy are two initiatives (Mandal, 2004): mandating the blending of 5% ethanol in gasoline from January 2003 and launching an ambitious National Biodiesel Mission to meet 20 per cent of the country's diesel requirements by 2011–12.

However, the government's execution of the National Biodiesel Mission, which depends on extensive cultivation of Jatropha, has been far from satisfactory. It has exempted Biodiesel from excise duty but not managed to get the States to exempt it from VAT. Although it is offering special subsidies to companies cultivating Jatropha in rural areas and encouraging sugar mills to make biofuels out of the molasses they generate, it has not established a minimum support price for Jatropha oilseeds. Nor has it ensured timely payments to farmers cultivating Jatropha. Not surprisingly, they do not consider Jatrropha cultivation to be financially viable. Because of all these, there is still no large-scale cultivation. (Gonsalves, October 2006)

In each of these three paragraphs, the first sentence makes a claim and all the data presented in the rest of the paragraph support it. If we take these three paragraphs together, we can see that the writer is making an overall claim: Indian government's response to its growing oil import bill has been to promote Biodiesel through the cultivation of Jatropha, but the government's execution has been unsatisfactory.

When there is a claim, a reader can check if the data supplied in support are adequate, tenable, and so on. If, however, data are dumped on the reader, he will not know how to respond. It is also possible that the writer has not presented—deliberately or by oversight—data that might be inconvenient for the claim being made. In such cases, a knowledgeable reader is likely to question the claim or conclusion.

THE ROLE OF GRAMMAR AND USAGE

Even when your analysis is excellent, you may lose your readers if your language—grammar, vocabulary, spelling and punctuation—is inadequate, incorrect or too complex to process comfortably. This is one of the consequences of your readers' having to depend exclusively on the clues in the text to reconstruct your meaning. They may not figure out the meaning you have put in the text if your grammar, vocabulary, sentence structure or even punctuation takes them in unwanted directions. Even if they can figure out the meaning, they may abandon the text if those mistakes annoy them or give them the impression that you are too casual and careless. They may read it only if they have to, such as papers they have been asked to study for an examination or for an interview. If your reader is your teacher, there is a good chance that you will get a lower grade than your analysis deserves.

Imagine that you have been offered a cup of tea in a cracked cup. Even if you know that the tea is safe, you may throw it away because the dirty crack in the cup puts you off. You may, of course, drink from that cup if you desperately need tea and you have no other option. Now imagine that you desperately want to drink the tea, but the crack in the cup is so big that tea drains through it by the time you take three or four sips of the hot tea. You want to drink all of it, but you cannot; the cup cannot hold the tea. Language errors are like the crack in the cup. Some annoy you, but do not prevent you from getting the meaning if you choose to read on. Some do not bother you because you instantly recognize them as unintended errors and mentally replace them with their correct counterparts. Perhaps you yourself make some of those errors. Some other mistakes and sentence structures are so bad that even if you want to read on, you cannot figure out the meaning. It is important to avoid all these types of mistakes because you may lose your readers or those who read your writing may rate you lower than you deserve for the work you have put in and the knowledge you have generated.

Let us look at some examples from English. The principles behind this are applicable to writing in other languages also.

Table 3.1 illustrates mistakes (grammar, vocabulary, punctuation) that annoy readers but are not serious enough to prevent them from figuring out the correct meaning from the context.

Table 3.1   Mistakes that Annoy but do not Block Comprehension

Original Sentence	Suggested Revision
A closer look to the consumption pattern of the rural India reveals that not only there is an increase in…	A closer look at the consumption pattern of rural India reveals that not only is there an increase in…
But off late we have seen that rural entrepreneurship opens the gate of…	But of late we have seen that rural entrepreneurship opens the gate of…
…the Telecom Industry with a CAGR of whooping 173% in subscriber base since 2000.	…the telecom industry with a remarkable CAGR of 173% in subscriber base since 2000.
There are lack of funds to manage the system effectively.	There are no funds to manage the system effectively.//There is no money to manage the system effectively.
The government has decided for not charging any entry fee for 3G spectrum.	The government has decided not to charge any entry fee for 3G spectrum.
…the drugs for diseases that are unique to India like malaria.	…the drugs for diseases like malaria that are common in India.
Even though there were 20000 entities only 10 odd companies actually undertake proper R&D.	Even though there were 20,000 entities, fewer than 20 companies actually undertook proper R&D.
One of the most important aspect of any crisis management is communication…	One of the most important aspects of any crisis management is communication…
India is moving fast towards its endeavour of being a developed nation.	India is moving fast towards its goal of being a developed nation.
It may well take anything between 2 to 5 years for the courts to dispose off a case…	It may take two to five years for the courts to dispose of a case… // It may take courts up to five years to dispose of a case…
While foreign companies spend in the tune of about 15 to 20 % of profits for R&D…	While foreign companies spend 15 to 20 per cent of their profits on R&D…
They want to pay as less as possible towards the…	They want to pay as little as possible towards the…
This … growth has translated into increased diversity in the income of rural and urban India.	This … growth has led to increased disparity between the incomes of rural and urban India.

(Continued Table 3.1)

(Continued Table 3.1)

Such a situation not only damage reputation but also shakes the moral of employee.	Such a situation not only damages [the company's] reputation but also shakes the employees' morale.
A single message ... needs to be managed all the more better.	A single message ... needs to be managed better.
...one of the few things that I did as part of my duties were conducting regular client feedback sessions.	...one of the few things that I did as part of my duties was conducting regular client feedback sessions.
The mains segments of the FMCG sector are Personal Care, Household Care, Branded and Packaged Food and Beverages, Spirits and Tobacco.	The main segments of the FMCG sector are personal care, household care, branded and packaged food and beverages, spirits and tobacco. [*Excessive capitalization avoided.*]
It is your duty to communicate the workers regularly.	It is your duty to communicate with the workers regularly.
However in the amount terms there is a net increase of around Rs 450 crore in gross NPA during the half year.	In Rupee terms, however, there has been a net increase of around 450 crores in gross NPA during the half year. // There has been a net increase of around Rs 450 crore in gross NPA during the half year.
Bringing people from other banks will destroy the morals of the Frontier National Bank employees.	Bringing people from other banks will destroy the morale of Frontier National Bank employees.
It contains detail analysis of present situation and legal environment.	It contains a detailed analysis of the present situation and of the legal environment.
This profit will continue till Voltamp can maintain its monopoly status.	This profit will continue as long as Voltamp maintains its monopoly.
The following were the major learning's:	The following were the major learnings:
Train it's workers	Train its workers
A large no of boxes	A large number of boxes
In case if he comes here	If he comes here
10000$	$10,000
In spite of	In spite of // Despite
Till date	To date
They suggested me...	They suggested to me...

Source: Authors (constructed from student assignments).

The original sentences with the annoying mistakes in them have all been taken from formal assignments submitted by graduate students of management. The revision suggested repairs the damage with minimal changes in the original text.

Some errors or awkward sentence structures are such that even after re-reading the text, it is difficult to retrieve the meaning intended by the writer. Some examples, taken from graduate student reports, are given in Table 3.2. The revision attempted may or may not fully capture the original writers' intent.

Table 3.2 Annoying Sentences that are Difficult to Understand

Original Sentence	Suggested Revision
The progress of the telecom industry can be linked to the various policies of the government have been described in Table 1. [*It is not clear whether it is the industry's progress or the government's policies that have been described in the Table. Hence two revised versions.*]	The telecom industry's progress, linked to the various policies of the government, is described in Table 1. // The telecom industry's progress can be linked to the various policies of the government, which are described in Table 1.
There are many challenges in front of corporates to associate with rural entrepreneurship that nullify the advantage of cheap labour availability to an extent.	[*The writer most probably meant:*] The many problems companies face when they associate themselves with rural entrepreneurship nullify to an extent the advantage of cheap labour.
This article begins with the current scenario in the telecom industry, as it stands tainted by weak infrastructure and dissatisfied customers, in spite of which it still remains the among the booming sectors in India followed by the history of the telecom industry and its policies.	This article begins with the current situation in Indian telecom industry, which is booming despite weak infrastructure and dissatisfied customers. It is followed by a brief history of the telecom industry and its policies.
...they had suffered huge financial losses but a proper and well thought out response and actions have not damaged their reputation.	...they had suffered huge financial losses but their well thought-out response and actions have saved their reputation from damage.
The accelerated growth coupled with a stimulating work culture that empowers its people, promotes team building and encourages new ideas, indicates the immense potential of Marico, to grow.	Marico has a stimulating work culture that empowers its people, promotes team building and encourages new ideas. This, coupled with its accelerated growth [*?*], indicates its immense potential to grow.

(Continued Table 3.2)

(Continued Table 3.2)

In nut shell, it has been found that packaged food no doubt has been able to enter indian homes in significant way but still there lies vast opportunity to be explored and ready to eat food market in India which is in high correlation with the traditional food habits.	To summarize: Packaged food has undoubtedly been able to enter Indian homes in a significant manner. There, however, are vast opportunities yet to be explored, particularly in the ready-to-eat food segment that caters to traditional food habits.
The organization having both gender employees and compels constant interaction due to the nature of the job a questionnaire survey was done to identify the existing discourse patterns.	A questionnaire survey was conducted to identify the discourse patterns among the male and female employees of the organization, where the nature of work compels them to interact constantly with members of both the sexes.
There was one new entrant which did not exist in any circle before named Indmobile that participated in bid for one circle.	Indmobile, which had not been present in any circle before, participated in the bid for one circle.
...the Economic growth of India is more reflected in the service sector and ignored the agriculture sector which employs 70% of the population.	...India's economic growth has been mainly in the services sector; it has bypassed the agriculture sector, which accounts for 70% of the population.

Source: Authors (constructed from student assignments).

Even if the words you use are well defined, readers may still have difficulty in understanding your text if you violate their expectations about what to find where. Reading a book or article or even a paragraph is like going into a supermarket. You expect to find shampoos in the hair care section. If they are displayed in the detergents or groceries section, you may get frustrated looking for them in the hair care section. The supermarket manager may have some good reason for putting shampoos in the detergents or groceries section, but you are likely to miss them and get annoyed.

That "information is interpreted more easily and more uniformly if it is placed where most readers expect to find it" is a simple, yet powerful insight provided by George D. Gopen and Judith A. Swan, in "The Science of Scientific Writing," which appeared in *American Scientist* (November-December, 1990).

They say that readers do not read and discover the meaning embedded in the text, but they read and interpret the text. It is a collaboration between the writer and the reader. Therefore, the writer has to figure out reader expectations and provide for them to be understood without difficulty.

Gopen and Swan (1990) illustrate this point with three simple tables, A, B and C, reproduced verbatim below. Table A shows one possible way of presenting the data collected by an investigator who tracked the temperature of a liquid by taking measurements every three minutes.

Table A:

t(time)=15', T(temperature)=32°; t=0', T=25°; t=6', T=29°; t=3', T=27°; t=12', T=32°; t=9', T=31°.

The information presented above is accurate, but we find it very difficult to read and make sense of it because it is not sequenced properly. Table B presents the same information in a different way.

Table B:

time (min.)	temperature (°C)
0	25
3	27
6	29
9	31
12	32
15	32

Table B is easy for readers partly because it is in the tabular form and partly because the structure matches the readers' expectation. Gopen and Swan argue, "Since we read from left to right, we prefer the context [i.e., time] on the left, where it can more effectively familiarize the reader. We prefer the new, important information [i.e., temperature variation] on the right, since its job is to intrigue the reader." In other words, Table B matches reader expectations while Table A does not.

Table B with the same information becomes difficult for readers if the order is reversed as in Table C.

Table C:

temperature (°C)	time (min.)
25	0
27	3
29	6
31	9
32	12
32	15

Here the context (time) comes after the new information (temperature variation) which the writer wants to share with the readers. So, even though this is in the tabular form and far superior to Table A, it is still difficult for readers.

According to Gopen and Swan, the grammatical subject in a sentence should be followed as soon as possible by the verb. The reader expects a "syntactic resolution" which only the verb can perform because the verb tells the reader what the grammatical subject does. If there are many words and phrases separating the two, the reader looks at them as an interruption while waiting for the verb to arrive and settle the issue. She is unlikely to process the interruption adequately while waiting for the verb. Instead, she may treat the intervening words as less important or ignore them. In *Style*, Williams (1990, pp. 23-25) also stresses the need to keep the distance between the subject and the verb as short as possible.

Gopen and Swan (1990) also call the beginning of a sentence its "topic position." New information that deserves emphasis should come in "stress positions," which are normally at points of syntactic closure such as the end of a clause or sentence. If the most important idea appears elsewhere, the reader gets disoriented or distracted. Secondary stress positions can be created in a long sentence with the help of a colon or semi-colon which indicates a syntactic closure almost as good as a period at the end of a sentence.

Being aware of these two most common reader expectations and checking whether your writing meets them will help you generate highly readable academic writing.

CHAPTER SUMMARY

In this chapter, we have seen what makes writing more challenging than speaking. We have noted that the absence of instant feedback from the reader is what makes it tough to write. We have to anticipate the potential readers' expectations and mould our writing to it for written communication to be effective.

We have also looked at the characteristics of academic writing that distinguish it from journalistic and creative writing. Academic writing is centred on knowledge while journalistic writing is built around recent events, and creative writing derives from the writer's imagination. We have also seen that analysis is the soul of academic writing. Dumping data on the reader rather than analysing them to make claims will alienate readers. Another factor that may alienate the reader, even when the analysis is excellent, is the kind of language employed. If there are errors in grammar, vocabulary and punctuation, or if the sentence structure is too complex or strikingly different from reader expectations, readers may be put off.

In Chapter 4, we shall look at the unit of discourse, that is, the paragraph. If we master the paragraph, writing a longer piece is not at all difficult.

4

Mastering the Paragraph

CHAPTER OVERVIEW

We have seen in Chapter 3 that the essence of academic writing is making a claim or stating a thesis and supporting it with evidence, which often consists of data or logical propositions. A writer does this task through a number of paragraphs, each performing a subordinate function within the overall objective of the paper. If we master the paragraph, the building block of academic discourse, we will be well on our way to mastering the essay. In this chapter, therefore, we focus on the paragraph.

The paragraph is like a bonsai tree. Just as a bonsai tree has roots, a trunk, branches and leaves, like a big tree, we can say that a paragraph has everything an essay or report has, but on a small scale. The advantage of focussing on the paragraph is that we can see all parts of the text at one glance and check if it has the qualities of good academic writing. Once we master the paragraph, we will find it easy to put several of them together to form an essay that has the same qualities as we see in good paragraphs.

We shall look at the two essential qualities of a good paragraph: unity and cohesion. We consider these two qualities as essential because a paragraph that does not have them is *not* a paragraph. There are, of course, more qualities that a paragraph should ideally have, qualities such as conciseness, logical rigour and clarity. We shall pay some attention to these as well. We shall also explore the different kinds of paragraphs that make up longer stretches of academic writing such as papers and assignments.

Our illustrations of good and not so good paragraphs are all from student assignments. They could as easily have come from papers published in journals or presented at conferences. At the level of the paragraph, it is immaterial which of these sources of academic writing the samples have come from.

THE STRUCTURE OF A PARAGRAPH

We can easily tell a paragraph when we see one. Paragraphs are blocks of text separated from one another by a line space or an indentation in the first line. But what makes a block of text a paragraph? Let us leave aside those exceptional one-word or one-phrase paragraphs, quite common in journalistic and creative writing, and limit ourselves to standard paragraphs that we encounter in academic texts. We can define such a paragraph as a structured collection of related sentences that together tell a short story about a topic. We find a more elaborate definition in Morris Needleman's (1968) *Handbook for Practical Composition:* "…a group of related sentences expressing and developing a basic idea, or a series of related sentences so arranged as to explicate a single topic, dominant idea, or particular phase of thought" (p. 87).

We observe broadly three types of paragraphs: narrative, descriptive and expository. Narrative paragraphs narrate events, descriptive paragraphs describe things and processes, and expository paragraphs explain phenomena and their relationships. Academic papers are a mixture of all these types. We shall look at each of them but our focus will be on expository paragraphs.

By the structure of a paragraph we mean how the sentences in it are arranged, and the structure depends on the kind of story the paragraph tells. In a narrative paragraph, for example, the sentences appear in the chronological order, that is, the order in which the different steps of an event or process occur. Here is an example:

We generated 6 product concepts using screenshots of the site and five of its competitors (F2H, WD, ML, UV, HZ and CF). For these, we collected pair wise preference data on a five point scale. A total of 97 responses were collected of which 11 were found unfit for use. The remaining data were aggregated to find out the overall preference of the respondents. These were then converted to a dissimilarity scale between 0 (very similar) and 2 (very dissimilar). The symmetric matrix obtained was then analyzed using the multi dimensional unfolding to generate the MDS plots.

(*Taken from "Understanding motivations in ordering food," student assignment, 2008*)

This paragraph tells the reader how the writers collected data and analysed them. The various steps they took are narrated in the order in which they were taken. There can be variations such as starting with the final step and working back, but the chronology is the sequencing principle followed in a standard narrative paragraph.

In a descriptive paragraph, the sentences appear in the spatial order, that is, in the order in which different parts of an object appear to the observer. The writer may choose to move from left to right or from right to left, from top to bottom, from the more prominent to the less prominent, from the shortest to the tallest, and so on. If, for example, you describe a house, then you may want to move from the front door to the lounge, from there perhaps to the dining room and the kitchen, and so on. Or you may start from the back of the house and move to the left or right or to the front. The order you choose depends on your objectives; you should, however, ensure that the order is smooth. It would be difficult for the reader to follow your description if you moved from the front door on the ground floor straight to a room on the first floor and then back to the dining hall on the ground floor.

When describing an abstraction, which we often have to do in academic writing, we use essentially the spatial order. But instead of looking for physical sequence, we look for logical sequence. In other words, it should be easy for the reader to move from one sentence to the next while getting an idea of the whole. Study the following description of Tata Steel:

Tata Steel is the largest integrated private sector steel company in India and fifth largest in the world. Established in 1907, the company manufactures and distributes steel, welded steel tubes, cold rolled strips, bearings and other related products. Chaired by

Mr. Ratan Tata, Tata Steel is held mainly by Tata group companies and affiliates (33.57%), Foreign Institutional Investors (20.55%), Insurance Companies (15.41%) and retail individual investors (19.16%) as on 31st December 2007 (Shareholding Pattern, 2007).

(Taken from "Steel industry report," student assignment, 2008)

Tata Steel is introduced here as the fifth largest integrated steel company in the world. The description goes on to talk about when the company was set up, what it makes, who manages it and who owns what share of the company. As Tata Steel is not a physical object, the order in which the descriptive sentences come may vary without making comprehension difficult for the reader.

Expository paragraphs display different structural patterns, each logical, depending on the kind of explanation or argument presented. You may start with a cause and move to its effect or effects; or start with an effect and move towards its cause or causes. You can compare or contrast two or more things, concepts or processes. You can illustrate an idea. You can present arguments that support an idea or go against it. You can enumerate things starting from the most important to the least important or the other way round. You can also enumerate things that are of equal importance. In other words, you can find a wide range of structures in expository paragraphs.

We will have several sample expository paragraphs analysed later in this chapter. But let us examine one to see a logical structure in action:

It can be safely assumed that the price elasticity of demand for air travel is higher for a flight operating over shorter distances as compared to ones operating over large distances. This can be explained by the fact that a consumer will typically have more alternative transportation options such as cars and railways to substitute shorter duration flights than longer ones. Given that most international flights would be in the bracket of long distance travel, a small increase in ticket price levels can cover the costs due to ETS [Emission Trading Scheme] without resulting in an undesired sharp drop in either air travel activity or airline revenues.

(Taken from "The EU cap on CO_2 emissions by international aviation sector: What to expect?" student assignment, 2008)

This paragraph is part of the writers' argument in favour of the airline industry joining the Emission Trading Scheme (ETS). They want to refute the airlines' position that the additional costs from joining ETS will kill the industry. The writers' claim is in the last sentence of the paragraph reproduced here: a small increase in the price of international air tickets to cover the cost of joining ETS will not adversely affect the industry. How do they come to it? The first sentence of the paragraph states their assumption that demand elasticity affects mainly short distance flights. The second sentence explains why this assumption is right by pointing to readily available data: short distance customers generally have a choice of modes of travel. The implication is that if air fares go up, customers may move to alternative modes of travel. The third sentence articulates the implication of the absence of demand elasticity in long distance travel (which has no reasonable non-aviation competition). As travellers have no choice, they will stick to air travel even if the price goes up a little. Hence, the writers' claim that ticket price increase will not hurt the industry.

In *How to Write a Paragraph: The Art of Substantive Writing*, Richard Paul and Linda Elder (2007) compare writing a paragraph to building a house. Building involves design and construction. Both are important. There has to be a foundation that suits the size and height of the house. There should be at least one entrance, and it should not be difficult for others to find out where the entrance is. We have different kinds of walls for different purposes or in different kinds of buildings. It is good to remember these when we examine the paragraph.

In Chapter 3, we noted Gopen and Swan's (1990) observation that in a sentence, the topic position is generally at the start. Drawing a parallel with the sentence, we can say that in a paragraph also, the topic position is generally at the start. The rest of the paragraph is an expansion of that topic into a story.

This does not mean that the first sentence of a paragraph is always the topic sentence. While the opening of the paragraph is the topic position, the topic sentence can come in the middle or at the end of the paragraph as well. It is possible to have two sentences together forming the topic. It is also possible for the topic to be implied in the paragraph without any particular sentence embodying it. You recognize the topic when you read the paragraph. The most important thing is not where the topic sentence is or whether a particular sentence qualifies to be the topic sentence, but whether the paragraph is about a particular topic. A paragraph is not a paragraph if there is no topic that unifies all the sentences that form it or no story that justifies the presence of all the sentences found in it.

The topic sentence not only introduces the reader to what is coming up in the paragraph but also links back to what has been covered. Through a variety of devices we link each sentence back or forward to the other sentences in a paragraph or to other paragraphs in a document. That is when we have a paragraph that looks like a well-designed and well-built house.

Let us study the impact of paragraph structure on the reader. Here is a paragraph that tells a little story:

> To improve the [railway wagon] turnaround time, bottlenecks in wagon mobility were identified and removed. Round-the-clock loading and unloading was introduced at major terminals. After the discovery that rakes (trains of 58 open or 40 covered wagons) spent most of their time under preventive check-up or waiting for it, the concept of Closed Circuit Rakes was introduced. These rakes would be intensively examined at a designated depot before loading, and would not be stopped for examination till they completed a round trip and returned to the original depot. Rakes that passed the high intensity examination at specific depots were declared fit for the next 7,500 km.

> (*Taken from "Turnaround of Indian Railways," student assignment, 2008; slightly adapted.*)

The story here is about how bottlenecks in wagon mobility were identified and removed to improve the turnaround time of wagons in Indian Railways. The first sentence—the topic sentence—tells us the essence of this story. The rest of the paragraph tells us about the two bottlenecks and how they were removed. The first bottleneck was that loading and unloading were restricted to certain fixed hours even when there was a lot more to be loaded and unloaded at major terminals. This is not stated explicitly but implied in the second sentence, which says that this bottleneck was removed by introducing "round-the-clock loading and unloading." The rest of the paragraph describes the other major bottleneck and what was done to remove it. Excessive inspection was holding wagons from being used optimally. The remedy was intensive inspection followed by fitness certification that was valid for much longer runs.

Another way to characterize the structure of this paragraph is that the first sentence makes a claim: bottlenecks in wagon mobility were identified and removed to improve the turnaround time of wagons in Indian Railways. The rest of the paragraph supplies two illustrations as evidence to support that claim.

We can easily see what the structure of a paragraph does, if we compare that sample paragraph about bottlenecks in wagon mobility with what looks like a paragraph below:

> Rakes that passed the high intensity examination at specific depots were declared fit for the next 7,500 km. After the discovery that rakes (trains of 58 open or 40 covered wagons) spent most of their time under preventive check-up or waiting for it, the concept of Closed Circuit Rakes was introduced. To improve the [railway wagon] turnaround time, bottlenecks in wagon mobility were identified and removed. Round-the-clock loading and unloading was introduced at major terminals. These rakes would be intensively examined at a designated depot before loading, and would not be stopped for examination till they completed a round trip and returned to the original depot.

You find here the same sentences as in the first sample, but together, they do not tell a story. The reason is simple. The first sample is a paragraph while the second is just a collection of sentences. To take Paul and Elder's (2007) metaphor further, the first sample is a brick wall while the second sample is just a heap of bricks. A well-structured paragraph takes the reader gently through the story. If the paragraph is poorly structured, the different sentences in it will drive the reader in different directions.

You should not expect every paragraph in a paper to be perfect. Nor should you expect to find many pure representations of a paragraph type in any text. You have to see each paragraph within the framework of the overall claim made by the paper and the evidence provided in support of the claim. You may, for example, find a few cases where the last sentence of a paragraph does not strictly belong to it, but it draws the reader to the next paragraph, rather like the trailer of a movie. If the flow of a paper is good, and takes you gently from the paragraphs at beginning to those at the end, you can be reasonably sure that the report is written well. Yet, here we focus on the perfect paragraph because we need a benchmark.

There should be enough information or evidence in the paragraph to help the reader understand and accept the main idea presented there. Imagine that the body of an e-mail you received from a friend or colleague consisted of this: "The bank manager did not." You are bound to ask a question: The bank manager did not do what? Did she not come to work? Did she not approve the loan he had asked for? Did she not let him meet her? Did she not recognize him? Unless you and your friend are equally familiar with the background, this cryptic statement leaves you puzzled. It does not communicate your friend's message to you.

Something similar can happen if a paragraph is incomplete or underdeveloped. Some writers announce the topic of a paragraph, but do not develop it enough. In other words, the writer makes a claim but does not elaborate it for the reader to understand it fully or support it with evidence for the reader to consider accepting it. Such underdevelopment can be a serious problem in academic writing because a reader accepts or rejects the writer's claims based on the evidence provided explicitly.

Let us look at the essential and desirable qualities of a paragraph, and then go on to different ways of developing paragraphs. Most of the following discussion applies to all types of paragraphs, and not just to the expository ones.

THE GOOD PARAGRAPH: ESSENTIAL QUALITIES

In this section we shall look at the two essential qualities of good paragraphs: unity and cohesion.

Unity

In a good paragraph there is one main idea or one story, and all the other ideas elaborate it or support it. Such a paragraph displays unity. If ideas that do not elaborate or support the main idea get into a paragraph, they not only destroy its unity but also make comprehension difficult for the reader. This is because the irrelevant ideas take the reader away from the story.

Imagine that someone brings you a twig. If all the leaves on the twig are neem leaves and you recognize that they are neem leaves, you know at once that the twig has come from a neem tree. But imagine further that you also find a couple of mango leaves on the same twig. Now you do not know what tree the twig has come from. The mango leaves confuse you and take your mind away from the neem twig. This is precisely what happens when ideas that do not belong to the topic of a paragraph appear in it. They confuse you and make comprehension difficult.

Study the following paragraph:

> The President is the Head of State and Head of Government of the United States. He is the head of the executive whose role is to enforce national law as given in the constitution and written by the Congress. The President is also the Commander-in-Chief of the armed forces, and has the powers to sign into law or veto any bill passed by both chambers of Congress. The election of the President is held indirectly through the United States Electoral College, for a four-year term (with a limit of two terms for an individual).
>
> *(Taken from "The trends in US presidential elections," student assignment, 2008)*

This paragraph starts telling us a story on the twin positions and powers of the President of the United States of America. After announcing that the US President is "the Head of State and Head of Government," it tells us what it means to be the Head of State and Head of Government of the United States. So far so good. Its unity is, however, spoilt by the last sentence, which is not on the meaning of the two phrases announced; it is on the election of the President, which is a different topic.

If the writer wanted to talk about the presidential election as well, he could have done one of two things. He could have included a reference to the election while introducing the President, such as: "The President, elected indirectly through the United States Electoral College for a four-year term, is the Head of State and Head of Government of the United States," and then continued the story of the two positions the President holds. Or he could have started a new paragraph on how the American President gets elected. Instead, he has chosen to speak about presidential election in a paragraph devoted to the positions and powers of the President. And that breaks the unity of the paragraph.

Here is another example:

With a patent regime that existed only for processes, rigid price control framework, low costs of raw materials and manufacturing, India developed into the world's fifth largest supplier of bulk drugs at cheap rates. Even though there were 20000 entities only 10 odd companies actually undertake proper R&D (Hunshyal & Biradar 2005). Most of these are small scale manufacturers of generics (drugs whose patents have expired). Though small firms are also capable of innovations, for economic viability of the innovation, size does matter.

(*Taken from "R&D in pharmaceutical industry: Challenges and opportunities from IPR and globalization," student assignment, 2008*)

The absence of unity is so pronounced here that it is not clear what the writers are talking about. The first sentence is good. And we expect the paragraph to give us the details of how India became "the world's fifth largest supplier of bulk drugs at cheap rates." Instead, the next sentence tells us that only about ten [pharmaceutical] companies out of 20,000 "entities" undertake research and development (R&D). That is a new topic. The writers then move on to assert that size matters for the economic viability of innovation. Each sentence in the sample paragraph seems to be pulling the reader in a different direction. There is no story here. So, this sample is not a paragraph; it is a mere assortment of sentences.

You will notice that improper use of tense also destroys the unity of the paragraph. The writers start with the past tense and then, within the second sentence, jump into the present tense. We are left wondering whether the writers are talking about the past—how the pharmaceutical industry in India developed—or about the current state of R&D in the industry. If it is about how the industry developed that the writers wanted to tell us, then they should have used the past tense throughout the paragraph.

This sample also illustrates a bad cohesive or connecting device. Although our detailed discussion of cohesive devices comes in the next section, examine the third sentence of the sample. It starts with the phrase, "most of these," which connects the third sentence to the second sentence. But it does that job badly because technically it refers to "10 odd companies" while it is almost certain that the writers wanted to refer to "20,000 entities."

Now, examine a sample that is free from such problems:

> The Indian rural healthcare system has been developed as a three-tier structure on the basis of certain population norms (Exhibit 1). At the bottom of the hierarchy we have the sub centres which are in direct contact with the population. They normally consist of one Auxiliary Nurse Midwife and one Multipurpose Male Worker. They provide basic cures for minor ailments and provide rudimentary healthcare services regarding maternal and child health, nutrition, immunization and control of communicable diseases.
>
> Then we have the Primary Health Centres at the second tier which is controlled by a medical officer supported by fourteen paramedical staff. They provide curative and preventive healthcare as well as…
>
> *(Taken from "Rural empowerment in India through micro-enterprises: A healthcare and Information Technology perspective," student assignment, 2008)*

The first sentence of the first paragraph introduces the idea of the three-tier structure of Indian rural healthcare. The rest of the paragraph describes one of those three tiers, that is, the bottom tier. We are told what the sub centres at that level consist of and what kind of services they provide. Similarly, the second paragraph talks about the second tier of rural healthcare. Thus, we can see that each paragraph has a story.

The reason many paragraphs fail the unity test is that the writer is not clear about the story she wants to tell. If she is clear, she should be able to tell it in a sentence, the topic sentence. Once that is done, she should be able to expand it into a paragraph.

Cohesion

In a cohesive paragraph, all the sentences hang together in a way that makes the reading smooth and comprehension easy. Each sentence is connected to any preceding it and to any following it, like the compartments of a passenger train connected by a vestibule. You can move from one compartment to the next without any difficulty. Cohesion, in other words, is the result of a good structure that has been well cemented.

Examine Sample A and Sample B below:

Sample A

Developing combustion-effective, state-of-the-art power plants is a pro-active approach. Emissions should be reduced. The world's total coal-based power generation capacity is 1000 GW. About 66% of coal-based plants have efficiency of about 29%. Implementation of promising technologies is expected to increase efficiency of coal-based power plants to about 45% (OECD/IEA, 2005). According to an estimate by IEA, efficient plants will reduce GHG [Greenhouse Gas] emissions by about 1.4 billion tonnes. The Kyoto Protocol's target for energy related emission reduction is less than 1.4 billion tonnes.

(*Text based on a paragraph in "Writing a publishable article," student assignment, 2009*)

Each sentence in Sample A makes sense. All the sentences are about developing power plants that have efficient combustion. The movement from the first sentence to the last, however, is neither smooth nor quick; rather, it is choppy. We see just a pile of bricks here. There is no wall emerging.

Now study Sample B:

Sample B

The second and *more pro-active* approach is to develop *more combustion-effective* state-of-the-art power plants. The thrust *here* is on reducing the emissions *in the first place*. The importance of *this initiative* is highlighted by the fact that *the world's* total coal-based power generation capacity is 1000 GW. About 66% of the plants *worldwide* have efficiency of about 29%. Implementation of promising technologies is expected to increase *this figure* to about 45% (OECD/IEA, 2005). According to an estimate by IEA, *this alone* can reduce GHG [Greenhouse Gas] emissions by about 1.4 billion tonnes, which is even *higher than* the target set by Kyoto Protocol as far as energy related emission reduction is concerned.

(*Taken from "The trends in US presidential elections," student assignment, 2008; slightly adapted, italics added*)

In Sample B, the sentences appear in the same sequence but the movement from the claim in the first sentence to the evidence that follows is smooth. The reason is the cohesive devices shown in italics. They link the ideas to one another and to the topic of the paragraph. They act like cement that fills the gaps between bricks which are arranged in a good sequence.

Common cohesive devices include linking words and phrases such as 'but,' 'however,' 'besides,' 'first,' 'second,' 'finally,' 'on the other hand' and 'on the contrary.' Repeating words or their synonyms (for example, "...that *the world's* total coal-based power generation capacity is 1000 GW. About 66% of the plants *worldwide...*") and using pronouns to refer back to a noun in an earlier sentence (for example, "...efficiency of about 29%. Implementation of promising technologies is expected to increase *this figure* to...") are yet more ways to link them. With the help of such devices, the different sentences in a paragraph are held together.

It is also interesting to note the subject of the first sentence of Sample B: "The second and more pro-active approach." This device couples the entire paragraph to the one preceding it. Although that paragraph is not given here, we can infer that it will have talked about another approach to reducing emissions. The word 'second' links this paragraph to the 'first.' Similarly, the comparative expression, "more pro-active," also invites the reader to compare the new idea with the one already discussed.

Study one more example of the way cohesive devices work within and between paragraphs. The relevant words and phrases have been italicized:

(a) The pharmaceutical industry offers *another* classic case-study of the link between (anticipated) market power and *R&D* spending. Fundamentally, *R&D* in the pharmaceutical and biotechnology industries is different from that in telecommunications and software because *it* is more uncertain and risky, in part due to the regulatory framework that mandates extensive testing and trials (FTC, 2003). *On the other hand*, innovation in hardware or software tends to be incremental in nature. *Moreover, the cost* of research in telecommunications is far lower than that in pharmaceuticals because *it* relies primarily on mathematics and computational resources.

(b) The result of *these differences* is readily apparent when we examine the structure of R&D activity in the pharmaceutical industry...

(*Taken from "The linkages between market power and R&D in industry," student assignment, 2008; italics added*)

The word 'another' in paragraph (a) hooks it to the previous paragraph and signals to the reader that this paragraph is a continuation of the same line of argument or same kind of evidence built around a classic case study. The phrase, "these differences," in the first sentence of paragraph (b) connects the new paragraph to the earlier one which talked about some differences.

It is not necessary that every sentence should have a physical hook to achieve coherence. The hooks can be invisible. Study the following sample:

Many commercial banks cut their interest rates as a response to RBI's decision to slash repo, reverse repo rates and cash reserve ratio. State Bank of India and Central bank of India reduced their benchmark prime lending rate (BPLR) by 0.75 per cent. ICICI Bank and Vijaya Bank reduced their BPLR by 0.5 per cent. These four banks also cut their deposit rates by 0.25 to 1.00 per cent. Other banks that have recently reduced their interest rates include Bank of Baroda, Bank of India, Union Bank of India, HDFC Bank and Bank of Rajasthan.

(*Adapted from "Impact of the current global economic situation on Indian Banking Industry," student assignment, 2009*)

There are just two visible cohesive devices: *these banks* and *other banks*. The cohesion in the paragraph is achieved by the way the topic sentence—the first sentence of the paragraph—is framed. It states that "many commercial banks cut their interest rates." The rest of the paragraph consists of examples of different banks cutting interest rates on loans and deposits. The parallel structure acts as the cohesive device.

Before we close this section, let us revisit the sample on rural healthcare system. The cohesive devices have been italicized:

The Indian rural healthcare system has been developed as *a three-tier structure* on the basis of certain population norms (Exhibit 1). At the bottom of *the hierarchy* we have the *sub centres* which are in direct contact with the population. *They* normally consist of one Auxiliary Nurse Midwife and one Multipurpose Male Worker. *They* provide basic cures for minor ailments and provide rudimentary healthcare services regarding maternal and child health, nutrition, immunization and control of communicable diseases.

Then we have the Primary Health Centres at *the second tier* which is controlled by a medical officer supported by fourteen paramedical staff. *They* provide curative and preventive healthcare as well as...

(*Taken from "Rural empowerment in India through micro-enterprises: A healthcare and Information Technology perspective," student assignment, 2008*)

"The hierarchy" connects the second sentence to the first because it announces "a three-tier structure," which implies hierarchy or is synonymous with it. The next two sentences start with the pronoun 'they,' which connect with "sub centres" in the second sentence. "Then" and "the second tier" in the first sentence of the second paragraph firmly link it to the first paragraph which talks about the bottom tier of the three-tier structure. "They," the first word in the second sentence, links it to the first by referring to "a medical officer supported by fourteen paramedical staff" in it.

At the beginning of this chapter we talked about the structure of a paragraph. A paragraph cannot have a good structure if there is no cohesion among the sentences. Each sentence may be correct and meaningful. But if the sentences do not hang together, there will be no structure. If there is no structure, there is no paragraph. A pile of excellent bricks does not make a wall.

THE GOOD PARAGRAPH: DESIRABLE QUALITIES

If your paragraphs have unity and cohesion, your writing will be acceptable to most readers. If, however, you want your academic writing to be a pleasure to read, you need to strive for a few more qualities. We shall turn to them now. We will take up conciseness, logical rigour and clarity. These also apply to all kinds of paragraphs, and not just the expository ones.

Conciseness

Examine the following paragraph. In 97 words, the writer summarizes his 1,000-word report:

The report analyzes the problem of selecting the right team to assist Ross Abernathy in reviving Frontier National Bank. It evaluates three alternatives, namely, selecting a team from within, building a team out of new hires and building one that mixes both. The criteria used for evaluation are ability to develop new business practices by leveraging existing resources, effect on organization morale, and ability to enjoy the CEO's trust. The report concludes that a team having a blend of people from within the bank and new hires with relevant prior experience will have the best overall impact.

(*Taken from "Ross Abernathy and the Frontier National Bank," student assignment, 2003; slightly edited*)

This paragraph is concise. It defines the problem, mentions the three alternative solutions evaluated, lists the criteria used for evaluation, and states the conclusion or the decision recommended. The writing is concise because you cannot easily drop any words from it without reducing the content or changing the meaning.

Compare it with the following sample, extracted from another decision report dealing with the same issue:

[...] The Frontier National Bank has had a glorious past having been the biggest and the most profitable bank in the region of its location. It has, however, come to a situation where it has fallen behind the newer banks that have come up in the region in terms of profitability, assets and number of employees per dollar of assets etc. [...]

(*Taken from "Ross Abernathy and the Frontier National Bank," student assignment, 2003*)

This is wordy. We can easily delete several words and phrases without harming the meaning or reducing the content:

[...] The Frontier National Bank has ~~had a glorious past having~~ been the biggest and the most profitable bank in the region ~~of its location~~. It has, however, ~~come to a situation where it has~~ fallen behind the newer banks ~~that have come up~~ in the region in ~~terms of~~ profitability, assets, and number of employees per dollar of assets ~~etc.~~

Revised text:

The Frontier National Bank has been the biggest and the most profitable bank in the region. It has, however, fallen behind the newer banks in the region in profitability, assets, and number of employees per dollar of assets.

With the unnecessary words and phrases cut out, the extract now has 38 words compared to 60 in the original. That is almost 40 per cent less, but the word order and the meaning are both preserved. With the flab cut out, the text is now easier to read and understand.

Here is one more example of wasteful writing, taken from another student report:

> Presently, the penetration of alkaline batteries in the Indian battery market is very less due the high price of alkaline batteries and due to low penetration of high drain products, which use alkaline batteries.

(Taken from "Indian battery market," student assignment, 2004)

This also can be recast with fewer words and without any reduction in the meaning. Here is one possibility:

> Alkaline batteries have not penetrated the Indian market significantly because of their high price and the country's low adoption of high drain products that use them.

The original sentence uses 34 words while the alternative makes do with 26 words. Between the two versions, the shorter one is definitely clearer and easier to comprehend.

There is another important difference between the two versions. The original uses a verbal noun 'penetration' where the corresponding verb 'penetrate' would have been crisp. Here, it is useful to go back to the notion of storytelling to understand why we should generally prefer the verb to its noun form. A sentence is a story where the verb tells us what the subject does or what happens to the subject. That completes the story. When we use verbal nouns in place of verbs, that closure may not come easily. If a sentence uses empty verbs (such as, 'is,' 'was') to connect verbal nouns, it is unlikely to be a concise sentence.

Let us look at one more example:

Original Version:

> India's biggest pure science based industry today is Pharmaceuticals. It is one of the fastest growing (approximately 9% per annum) and has a current net worth of about five billion dollars. Though the growth is rapid at this point of time, the percentage

of profits allocated towards research and development by Indian pharmaceutical companies has been low. While foreign companies spend in the tune of about 15 to 20% of profits for R&D, average Indian spending until very recently has been only about 2% (*Indian pharmaceutical industry: an overview, 2007*). One of the main reasons for this risk averse nature of the Indian manufacturer is the high degree of fragmentation within the Indian market, which is indicative of a lack of clear-cut market rulers. By recent estimates, the market leader only held about 7% of the entire market share ('How R&D Is Changing Indian Pharma', 2005).

(*Taken from "Biotechnology research and development in India," student assignment, 2008*) (*146 words*)

Let us accept the first sentence assuming that it connects this paragraph to the earlier ones in the original report in which the role of or the need for R&D in science-based industries may have been talked about. Let us assume that the writers' main idea is that although the Indian pharmaceutical industry is growing fast and is rich, it spends very little on R&D as compared to foreign companies because the Indian market is highly fragmented; as there are no clear leaders, it is risky for any company to invest a lot in R&D. Let us also assume that the references and inferences are acceptable. Now, let us ask ourselves: have the writers wasted words? Can we make the paragraph more concise?

Before looking at the revised version below, which is not a model but one possibility, try to rewrite the paragraph on your own, cutting out any flab you notice:

Revised Version:

Although pharmaceuticals is India's biggest science-based industry with a net worth of about US$5 billion and among the fastest growing (about 9% p.a.) industries, it has until recently been spending just about 2% of its profits on research and development compared to 15 to 20% that foreign companies do (Indian pharmaceutical industry: an overview, 2007). One of the main reasons for this low investment in R&D may be that the Indian market being highly fragmented with no company's share exceeding 7%, it may be risky for any player to invest heavily in research (How R&D Is Changing Indian Pharma, 2005).

(*Based on "Biotechnology research and development in India," student assignment, 2008*) (*101 words*)

The revised version conveys the writers' ideas with 30 per cent fewer words than the original. The third sentence of the original paragraph ("Though the growth is rapid at this point of time, the percentage of profits allocated towards research and development by Indian pharmaceutical companies has been low.") has been dropped because the meaning is repeated in the following sentence. The last two sentences of the original ("One of the main reasons for this risk averse nature of the Indian manufacturer is the high degree of fragmentation within the Indian market, which is indicative of a lack of clear-cut market rulers. By recent estimates, the market leader only held about 7% of the entire market share.") have been collapsed into one for two reasons. First, the second sentence repeats the ideas of the first. Second, by appearing as an independent unit, the second sentence takes our attention away from the topic of the paragraph.

The way to ensure conciseness is to revisit what you write and ruthlessly cut out any word or phrase that you think you can drop without weakening the story you are telling in each paragraph (see Chapter 5 for more on how to do this). If you have used verbal nouns, see if you can convert some of them to verbs. You may need to rearrange the sentences to get the right fit. This is somewhat like the way a mason builds a wall with irregularly shaped granite pieces. He turns the pieces around and rearranges them until they fit well and the wall appears beautiful.

Logical Rigour and Supporting Evidence

You have every right to hold any personal views. You may, for example, believe that the earth is 78,206 years old; that eating yogurt after dinner is bad for health; that capitalism is superior to communism in creating an equitable world; or that by 2019, India will be the world's biggest economy. You may know several others who hold identical or similar views. However, if you are making any such claim in academic writing, you must provide evidence to support it. You must build on logic. If your logic is weak or if the supporting data is shaky, then the reader is likely to disagree with you. As you cannot respond to a reader's silent objections or reservations that arise as she reads, you may lose her midway. While logic should pervade the entire report, each paragraph should display logical rigour to take the reader along.

As logic is the hallmark of expository paragraphs, we should expect logical rigour and supporting evidence mainly in them, rather than in descriptive and narrative paragraphs.

Study the following sample from a student report on the growth of telecommunications in India:

Unit for Bidding:

[Department of Telecommunications] chose 'circles' as the unit for bidding for administrative convenience, hence India was divided into 21 circles. There was consolidation of 2 or smaller states under a circle and larger states were divided into 2–3 circles. Bids from operators for each of the circles were invited. The circles were further classified as A, B or C depending on the revenue potential of the areas. The allocation of different states into these categories has been shown in the Exhibit 1. Similar spectrum allocation in UK was based on geographical proximity where instead of the circles and the spectrum is divided into blocks of A, B, C, D, E & F.

(*Taken from "Licensing for spectrum allocation in telecom sector," student assignment, 2008*)

The very first sentence of the paragraph provokes the reader's objection. It suggests that 'circle' was a pre-existing unit like 'State' or 'district' and that because the Department of Telecommunications chose that unit, it divided India into 21 circles. The fact is that the Department of Telecommunications divided India into 21 units (some the same as a state, some a part of a large state, and some a combination of two or more small states) for administrative convenience and chose to call them "circles" because they did not match any of the existing geographical divisions.

The last sentence of the paragraph is also problematic. It is not clear why a reference has been made in this paragraph to spectrum allocation in the United Kingdom (UK). Is it that there was no bidding in the UK? Was spectrum allocated there on some other basis? Does the writer want to show the contrast? What does the writer mean when he says that spectrum was allocated on the basis of "geographical proximity?" Does the writer merely want to indicate that in the UK, they call their administrative units 'blocks' as opposed to 'circles' in India? If that is all that he wants to do, is it worth drawing the reader's attention to it?

Here is a revised version of the paragraph:

[Department of Telecommunications] divided India into 21 'circles' for administrative convenience. A circle consisted of [a State], a part of a large State, or two or more small States. These circles were further classified as A, B or C depending on their revenue potential (Exhibit 1). Telecom operators were invited to bid for [spectrum in] each of these circles. In the UK, however, spectrum was divided into six blocks and allocated on the basis of geographical proximity.

This revision assumes that in the UK there was no bidding for spectrum but it was allocated on the basis of something else. The lack of clarity in the original extract regarding the allocation of spectrum on the basis of "geographical proximity" has been retained. If, however, this interpretation is not right, it is best to drop that sentence. It has little to do with the main topic of the paragraph, which is about spectrum allocation in India. All it does is to destroy the unity of the paragraph.

The revision has also shortened the extract by 30 per cent, that is, from 113 words to 77.

Examine the following extract from a student paper on public private partnership for construction of airports in India. After making a case for a Model Concession Agreement (MCA) for Public Private Partnership (PPP) in airport construction like the MCA in road construction, the writers critique the bidding process currently adopted by the government:

Technical Bid Specifications:

In the case of roads, output service level requirements can be easily translated into technical specifications regarding lane width and the like. Moreover, there is uniformity in the requirements for different roads in terms of these basic quality standards. Such clear terms cannot be laid down for airports which vary widely in their passenger traffic and size. Therefore, the current system requires all potential bidders to have had a minimum of five years of experience in the construction industry to be deemed technically competent (Ministry of Finance, Dec 2007). They are also expected to have a track record of profitable projects in recent years. This condition is viewed as a proxy for the output service level, the belief being that a hitherto successful company will continue to deliver good results in future as well.

However, we believe that such reasoning has two inherent flaws. The first is the problem of the moral hazard involved in selection. Once a contract has been awarded to any one party, it enjoys a monopoly power (especially in the case of airports) over the delivery of services. As a result, there is no incentive for it to maintain its past level of service. Therefore, the track record of a company in the past is no guarantee of its performance in the future. Secondly, such an approach encourages the automatic favouring of a few players over all others. Under the present system, once a player can claim to have been awarded one project on the strength of its credentials, it automatically lays a much stronger claim on all subsequent projects that it bids for. This makes it extremely difficult for a technically sound but new entrant to successfully bid for a project. Moreover, over time, such a system can foster the growth of close relations between the consistently successful player and government officials. Such relations are unhealthy and have the potential to destroy the free and open nature of the selection process.

(*Taken from "Public private partnership for bridging the infrastructure gap in India: Airports," student assignment, 2008*)

The writers make three claims in the first paragraph, which are, (1) Output service level requirements cannot be specified clearly in airport construction as in road construction; (2) it is because of this difficulty that the Ministry of Finance requires all potential bidders for airport construction projects to have been in the construction industry for at least five years to become eligible to bid; and (3) the Ministry believes that a company with a successful track record of profitable projects will continue to be successful.

In the second paragraph the writers criticize the Ministry's approach by showing two "inherent flaws" in it. They assert that a company's good track record does not guarantee performance in the future because once a company signs a contract, it has no incentive to maintain its past level of service. The Ministry's insistence that bidders should have successful experience of at least five years in the construction industry shuts out technically sound new parties from bidding. They also state that relying on a few regular successful bidders will lead to corruption.

Thus, the writers attempt to analyse the situation and make inferences from the facts available. The attempt is good but what they have achieved is a case of giving a dog a bad name and shooting it. The inherent flaws that the writers talk about in the second paragraph are their own creation. They assume that the three claims they make in the first paragraph are tenable. However, none of them is tenable because all three of them are the writers' opinions, not fact-based inferences. Why can't the output service level requirements be specified clearly in airport construction projects? How did the writers jump to the conclusion that the Ministry's eligibility conditions regarding bidders' prior experience are due to its difficulty in specifying service level requirements? Does the Ministry believe that a company with a successful track record of profitable projects will continue to be successful? Is that why the Ministry looks for bidders with a good track record? The writers provide no evidence to support their claims. Instead, they treat their assumptions as facts and then go on to fault the Ministry's approach to the bidding process for airport construction contracts.

Even in the second paragraph, the writers present their views as facts. While a reader can readily agree with them that a company's good track record does not guarantee performance in the future, he may balk at their claim that once a party signs a contract, it has no incentive to maintain quality because of its monopoly status. Evidence contradicts this claim. If only companies with a successful track record are allowed to bid, is it not reasonable to assume that a company would want to maintain a good record so that it can continue to get business? In any case, is it because of the belief that a company's good track record guarantees performance in the future that the Ministry insists on successful execution of past projects? Isn't there a simpler explanation for this standard practice of insisting on bidders' prior experience and good track record? Can the Ministry be faulted for preferring bidders who have demonstrated their capability, to untested bidders?

The writers may be right in claiming that doing business repeatedly with a few contractors is likely to lead to corruption. But allowing parties without a track record does not solve the problem of potential corruption. On the contrary, such a move may lead to greater corruption because parties without experience of success or ability to deliver the goods might attempt to win contracts through bribing.

When we make claims, we need to supply evidence in support of the claims. Empirical facts, results of scientifically conducted studies, unbiased opinions of experts, legal documents and logic (deductive and inductive) may all qualify as evidence. Let us see what kind of evidence the writers of the extract on the bidding process could have supplied in support of their claims.

Claim 1:

"Output service level requirements" cannot be specified clearly in airport construction. A quote from the Ministry of Finance or an international airport construction expert on how difficult it is to specify the "Output service level requirements" in airport construction would have been useful. In the absence of any such support, we are likely to think that even if airport construction is more complex than road construction, it is not impossible to specify "output service level requirements."

Claim 2:

It is because the Ministry of Finance is unable to specify clearly the technical requirements of airport construction that it insists on bidders to have had at least five years' experience in construction. A quote from the Ministry to this effect would be needed for us to accept it. Or if the writers show that for road construction (where specification of technical details is relatively easy, according to the writers), the Ministry does not insist on bidders' prior experience or good track record, we can go along with the writers' claim.

Claim 3:

The Ministry believes that a company with a successful track record of profitable projects will continue to be successful. Again, a quote from the Ministry stating or implying this would have helped us accept the writers' interpretation. A quote in support of the writers' view from any other major domestic or international agency that awards large and/or complex contracts exclusively to bidders with experience and a good track record would also have helped.

What is acceptable as evidence varies considerably from discipline to discipline.

The quality of evidence required in physical sciences is of a much higher order than what is acceptable in social sciences. Quotes from scientists are not evidence in physical sciences; but considered views expressed in conceptual research papers by highly regarded experts are often treated as evidence in social sciences. Hard data obtained through observation and controlled experiments may, however, override them.

Evidence accepted in art and literature is at the other extreme. Here is a statement from the thirteenth century poet Jalaluddin Rumi (1207–73):

> I died as a mineral and became a plant, I died as plant and rose to animal, I died as animal and I was Man. Why should I fear? When was I less by dying?'
>
> —http://www.answers.com/topic/rumi-jalal-al-din

This is indeed an inspiring, uplifting statement. The logic (if A leads to B, B leads to C and C leads to D, D will lead to E even if we have never seen E) is built partly on the hierarchy observed in the mineral, plant and animal world, and partly on the scientific fact that plants, animals and human beings are all made up of minerals. Rumi's logic, however, is faulty. First of all, there is no proof that I have emerged from minerals to human being. That, upon death, my body will change to minerals does not necessarily mean that I have emerged from minerals. Even if I have emerged from minerals, it does not imply that upon death, I will move on to a higher level of existence. But then Rumi is not a logician; he is a poet. If he inspires us to strive for something bigger and not be disheartened by our weaknesses including death and disease, his objective has been achieved.

In a religious discourse, statements taken from the holy scriptures of a particular religion or its prominent leaders may be treated as evidence by followers of that religion. They may not, however, be accepted by followers of other religions. Something similar happens in political discourses too. Followers of a particular political party may readily accept certain data and certain interpretations while those who oppose that political party may reject them.

Your skill as a writer lies in figuring out reasonably accurately the kind of evidence that will satisfy your anticipated readers. What is not acceptable in any kind of academic writing is making claims without supporting evidence.

Clarity

If a paragraph is clear, every reader takes out the same meaning from it. And that meaning is what the writer has put into it. If a paragraph is not clear, different readers may get different meanings from it or meanings that are different from what the writer has put in. Therefore, it is easy to see why clarity is an important feature of good academic writing.

Lack of clarity often comes from muddled thinking. We cannot communicate an idea clearly to a reader if we are not clear about it ourselves. When we are not clear about our idea, we may be tempted to use jargon to hide our problem. We must resist the temptation.

Examine the following extract from a student report:

The following are the criteria in the descending order of priority:

1. **Riddance of the inert market share and making an inertial motion towards profitability.** Without this happening, the institution *can only move in a horizontal reform, not vertically ensnare their lost hold in the region.*
2. **Bringing a sea-change in the mentality of the workforce** that meets eye-to-eye with Ross Abernathy's objective. *'Horses don't win races, jockeys do'* and the planning and subsequent implementation must be at the same wavelength. [...]

(*Taken from "Ross Abernathy and the Frontier National Bank," student assignment, 2003*)

If these are the criteria the writer uses to evaluate the various options that he mentions in his report, he obviously has some meaning in his mind. We cannot, however, figure it out from the text that he has given us. Unfortunately, the text is the only resource available to us to decipher what he means.

Let us guess what the writer means:

These are the two criteria, in the order of importance:

1. The proposal should not only increase the bank's market share but also make it profitable.
2. It should align the employees' mentality with Ross Abernathy's objective.

It is not at all certain that this is what the writer means. If, however, this is roughly what he has in mind, should he not write something like it? The revised version is much clearer than the original, although it uses less than half as many words. By adopting jargon—using technical words where they are not needed or are inappropriate—the student merely manages to turn his potential readers away. It is unlikely that readers, especially teachers, would invest their time to tease out meaning from such murky writing. It is certain that editors of journals will reject it.

Here is another extract from the same report. It is easier to understand but still clouded by an unnecessary display of unusual words. Why would we invest our time and effort to extract the writer's meaning from this morass?

> The bank was in need of a protagonist who could absolve them from the quagmire of defeatism of being in a gridlocked state of immobility as a cash cow which if persisted would lead to it going become '**doggone**' in terms of Boston Consulting Group matrix (See **EXHIBIT 1**).

> (*Taken from "Ross Abernathy and the Frontier National Bank," student assignment, 2003*)

Jargon does not impress readers; it puts them off. They will not struggle with difficult text when they suspect that nothing new or insightful will come out of it. One may dip one's hand into the drains to retrieve a gold coin, but not a dime.

There are many instances where you have to use technical terms. While most of your readers such as the scholars who read the journals you publish in, and your professors who set your assignments, know the meanings of the technical words you use, it is a good practice to define such words. There are three reasons for this suggestion. First, your readers may include well-educated people who are not familiar with the terminology you use or cannot immediately recall its meaning. Second, as we have already seen in Chapter 3, defining any technical or critical terms you employ will help you inform your reader unambiguously about what you mean by them. Third, in the context of an educational institution, the teacher (who probably knows the meaning) may want to know whether the student-writer is familiar with the meaning.

Examine the following sample from a student report on telecommunications:

> Spectrum is a range of electromagnetic radio frequencies used in transmission of voice, data and television. India's Global System for Mobile communication (GSM) operators get 4.4 MHz of spectrum initially while Code Division Multiple Access (CDMA)

operators get 2.5 MHz of spectrum. GSM operators are allocated up to 10 GHz of frequency when their subscriber base crosses the 1 million mark while the CDMA is given up to 5 GHz in that case. The difference lies in the more efficient technology of CDMA which can accommodate 5 times more traffic in the same band as compared to the GSM technology.

(*Taken from "Licensing for spectrum allocation in telecom sector," student assignment, 2008*)

The writer gives the full forms of the common expressions 'GSM' and 'CDMA.' This particular report was not written for experts in telecommunications or information technology. It was written for highly educated general readers. We can say that the writer has done a good job of introducing some of the technical terms.

The writer's objective should be to make his meaning as clear as possible. As we have noted in Chapter 3, clear and unambiguous expression is the hallmark of good academic writing.

HOW TO DEVELOP PARAGRAPHS

Depending on the nucleus of the story in the topic sentence, a paragraph can develop in a number of ways. We have already examined paragraphs that narrate and those that describe. We have also looked for different qualities. We shall now analyse a few more from the perspective of developing them.

Defining is a way of specifying a concept or a claim. In a paragraph built around a definition, the writer specifies what she means by a concept, a thing or a process. In "Man is a rational animal," man is defined by specifying the general class (*animal*) and the distinguishing feature (*rationality*). We can build a paragraph or indeed a whole essay on this definition by elaborating on what it means to be an animal and what it means to be rational.

Here is a paragraph that loosely defines the form of microfinance pioneered by the Nobel Prize winner, Dr Muhammad Yunus:

In this model of microfinance, pioneered by Dr Yunus, groups of five to seven members are formed. This is the key unit which interacts with the lending institution. Initially loans are sanctioned to only two members and contingent upon their timely repayment, loans are extended to the other members. The pressure from the other members reduces the chances of default. Loans are repaid on a weekly basis at an interest rate of 20% per annum. The prompt repayment by the members is rewarded through a gradual increase in their borrowing limits. Thus the system has mutual accountability and high repayment built into it.

(*Taken from "Microfinance: A boon or a bane for rural entrepreneurship?" student assignment, 2008; slightly adapted*)

As the definition is not tight, this paragraph can also be seen as a brief description of the kind of microfinance developed by Dr Yunus. Yet another way to see it is as illustrating how "mutual accountability and high repayment" are at the core of Dr Yunus's microfinance.

Exemplification is one of the common ways of supporting a claim or making the claim easy to understand. In the following example, the first sentence is the topic sentence. It claims that there may be a backlash if a company withholds information from investors. The rest of the paragraph gives an example of a backlash from investors at Starbucks, a company that withheld information from them.

Withholding information from investors can cause backlash. For instance, Starbucks, in January 2008, decided to stop disclosing same store sales (around the same time that its same store sales began a declining trend). This decision haunted the company as analysts and investors continued to grill the company and beat down the stock. As a result, the company was forced to begin disclosing same store sales again in late 2008.

(*Taken from "Communicating with investors," student assignment, 2008*)

The Starbucks example helps the reader accept the writer's claim that companies withholding relevant information from their investors are likely to suffer investor fury. While this is a very useful example, we should not ignore the lack of logical rigour in it. There could be factors other than the decision to withhold information that beat down the company's stock. After all, the company's sales, and presumably, profits had been declining. Thus there can be several causes contributing to an effect. Identifying an effect (erosion of stock price) exclusively with one cause (withholding of information) without adequate evidence is likely to lead to false conclusions. A critical reader may be unwilling to go along with the writer.

Comparing and contrasting two or more things is another way to develop a paragraph. When you compare and contrast, you look for similarities and differences between two or more things or ideas.

Study the example given below:

Exceptions do exist, but overall there is a great asymmetry in the pace at which development is taking place in urban and rural India. According to the census of 2001, 742 million people, that is, 74% of the Indian population, live in the rural areas. But while the household electrification rate in urban areas in India has reached 88%, in rural areas it is only 44% as of 2001. At the same time rural tele-density in India is 2% as opposed to urban tele-density at 31% (Bhandari and Dutta, 2007). Rural India has also been almost untouched by broadband connectivity which is, anyway, at infancy at 3% in India. Similar scenarios exist in all other basic sectors like agriculture and healthcare etc.

(Taken from "Rural empowerment in India through micro-enterprises: A healthcare and Information Technology perspective," student assignment, 2008; slightly adapted)

In this paragraph, the writer claims that there is considerable asymmetry in the pace of development between urban India and rural India. He then goes on to quote statistics related to electrification, tele-density and broadband connectivity in urban and rural areas. In each of these three categories, the writer compares the numbers from both rural and urban areas to demonstrate the asymmetry that he claims at the start of the paragraph.

It is also worth noting the way comparative facts have been quoted to buttress the claim that "there is a great asymmetry in the pace at which development is taking place in urban and rural India." Without such factual support, the comparison might appear to be subjective and impressionistic.

Analysis, as we have already seen in Chapter 3, is the mainstay of academic writing. When you analyse something, you break it into its parts, look for the relationships or functions, and the interconnections. It is not surprising to find many analytical paragraphs in academic writing.

Study the following sample:

> What contributed most to the turnaround of Indian Railways (IR) was the decision to increase the axle load (the maximum weight the wagon axle and rails are allowed to carry). It was raised from 20.3 to 22.9 tons on selected routes and for selected commodities in 2004-05, allowing a 4-axle wagon to carry 10.4 tons more. As 160,000 wagons were declared fit to carry the extra load and as each wagon could be loaded up to 60 times a year (the average turn-around time was 6 days), IR's carrying capacity went up by 76.8 million tons a year. With each ton carried earning Rs 500, this enhanced the revenue potential by Rs 384,000 million a year.

> (*Adapted from "Turnaround of Indian Railways," student assignment, 2008*)

In this paragraph, the claim, which comes in the first sentence, is that the decision to increase the axle load contributed more than anything else to the turnaround of Indian Railways. The writer looks closely at the relevant numbers and finds some vital connections between them. His analysis leads to a link being established between the decision to increase the axle load and potential revenue of Rs 384,000 million a year. The beauty of the analysis is that by the time you come to the end of the paragraph, you are willing to accept the claim made in the beginning.

We can consider the same sample as an illustration of developing a paragraph through demonstrating the cause and effect relationship between two things or events. The effect here is the enhancement of Indian Railways' revenue potential by Rs 384,000 million a year. The cause is the decision to raise the axle load of railway wagons. The reader may not readily accept a causal relationship between the two. That is why the writer presents a series of numbers which establish it.

Explanation is an equally common way to develop paragraphs. When you explain a concept or a process, you make it simpler for the reader to understand your claim. You give a reason why something happened or will happen.

In the following sample, the entire paragraph explains why the writers decided to study the interaction between non-governmental organizations (NGOs) and the government.

> The effectiveness and efficiency of an NGO depends to a very large extent on building and managing its reputation, more so probably

than a private enterprise. An NGO's reputation not only helps it to garner public funds and volunteers but also government grants and change in policies. The relationship between NGOs and the government is a complex one involving collaboration on certain issues and confrontation on some other. The key issue in this relationship is a certain amount of fear and mistrust of each other. It was in this context that we thought it would be very interesting to study the interaction between these two parties.

(*Taken from "Communicating with the government," student assignment, 2008*)

In this paragraph, the topic sentence comes at the very end. It is preceded by statements about why reputation is important for NGOs and how complex the relationship between NGOs and the government is. As you come to the topic sentence at the end of the paragraph, you realize that the earlier statements explain the reason why the writers chose to study the interaction between NGOs and the government.

Listing or *classification* is another common method of paragraph development. Here is an example:

There are varied types of risks that are associated with the implementation of a PPP project. These may arise out of delay in getting various clearances, default by the private player, damage to the environment or due to incorrect projections of market demand leading to a scenario of insufficient demand and perhaps infeasible user levies (Planning Commission 2004). The project may also have to face financing problems if there are considerable changes in inflation rates, exchange rates, interest rates and or tax rates. Operations can be stalled if there are problems with labour or with the technology. There can be legal hassles owing to changes in laws, lease rights, security structure or due to insolvency of private player.

(*Taken from "Airport modernization through PPP route in India," student assignment, 2008*)

The first sentence is the topic sentence. It states that there are different types of risks associated with the implementation of a PPP project. The rest of the paragraph is a list of the main risks as perceived by the writer. The risks are varied. What connects them all and make them part of the category called 'risks,' is the topic sentence.

This section has illustrated a few ways of developing a paragraph. These are by no means the only ones. Needleman (1968, p. 95), for example, identifies 15 methods of developing effective paragraphs, none mutually exclusive, under four broad categories: "order (time order or chronology, climax), illustration (exemplification, comparison and contrast, analogy, restatement, summary), the whole and its component parts (definition, analysis, classification, explanation), and logical analysis (evidence and proof, cause and effect, enumeration, elimination)." The next time you read a well-written paper in an academic journal, look carefully at paragraphs that impress you. They will illustrate various ways of developing good paragraphs. See what you can learn from them.

CHAPTER SUMMARY

In this chapter we examined the structure and qualities of a good paragraph. The two essential qualities are unity and cohesion. Desirable qualities include conciseness, logical rigour and clarity. We also discussed the various ways of developing paragraphs, especially expository ones.

This chapter may give you the impression that there are so many things to look out for while writing that you will never be able to write well. That, however, is not our intention. This discussion is to make you aware of the different aspects that make up a good paragraph. It is like a description of how to drive. One has to talk about how to accelerate, how to change the gears, how to look out for traffic on the road, how to brake, and so on.

This discussion will help you in two ways. First, when you read others' writing, you will be able to analyse it systematically to see what is good about it and what is not so good about it. That will help you write better. After all, it is while watching others closely that we learn many skills. Second, you will be able to review your own writing to check if your paragraphs pass these minimum tests.

5

The Writing Process

CHAPTER OVERVIEW

A few decades ago many south Indian families had big stone grinders. Soaked rice and *urad dal* (black gram or lentils) were ground manually in them to make the batter that ended up as *dosa* (thin, flat, often crisp pancake) and *idli* (fluffy, steamed cake). The grinding process was so slow that a family of four or five would easily need two to three hours to make enough batter for two days. Then came small electrical mixer-grinders that could make the same amount of batter in less than half an hour. The new time-saving machines with steel blades were welcomed enthusiastically, especially by working couples. The texture and flavour of the *idli*s made with the machine-made batter, however, left connoisseurs disappointed. The heat generated by the blades of the electrical mixer-grinders running at high speeds reduced aeration as well as fermentation that were essential for creating the soft, fluffy *idli*s that they were used to and expected from the wonder machines.

Academic writing is a similar process with several sub-processes as we shall see later in this chapter. If we skip some of those either because of ignorance or in the false hope of saving time, we are likely to end up with an unsatisfactory product. In Chapter 2, we looked at the structure and components of research papers. In this chapter we will focus on the process and sub-processes of composing and presenting the document to the reader.

We will divide the writing process into three phases:

create an outline —► *flesh it out* —► *polish it*

THE ACADEMIC DOCUMENT AS A STORY

In Chapters 3 and 4 we noted that a sentence is a story about its grammatical subject, and a paragraph is a short story about a topic. We can extend that metaphor further and say that a report or a dissertation is a bigger story. As Golden-Biddle and Locke (1997, p. 49) argue, the research paper can be seen as a story "composed of a complication, a development, and a resolution," just as in a short story. A reading of the relevant literature throws up a gap, an anomaly, a problem or a complication; through research, which may involve data collection and analysis or meta-analysis, the researcher fills the gap, explains the anomaly, resolves the problem or unravels a complication. They treat the writing up of research as "Crafting the storyline," "Developing the storyline," "Characterising the storyteller" and "Rewriting the story."

If we look at a report or a dissertation as a story about a topic, how do we go about writing it? We must have a story to tell in the first place. Let us see what is involved in creating a story.

Here is a story from Aesop's Fables:

A tortoise got tired of his home and wanted to move to a new, far-off place. So he asked an eagle if she could take him to some far-off place. The eagle agreed, and flew up and away holding the tortoise by the shell with her talons. On their way a crow flew along and told the eagle that tortoise flesh was great to eat.

"But the shell is too hard," sighed the eagle.

"Oh, just drop him on a rock; the shell will crack open," suggested the crow. And the eagle did precisely that as soon as she saw a huge boulder on the ground. Then the two birds had a delicious meal of tortoise meat.

Moral: Never depend on the generosity of your enemies.

adapted from http://www.aesops-fables.org.uk

This story, like every good story, has a beginning, a middle and an end. We can say that the beginning of this story is: "A tortoise got tired of his home and wanted to move to a new, far-off place." It sets the background by introducing the central character about whom we are going to hear the story. The last sentence of the story, "Then the two birds had a delicious meal of tortoise meat," is the end. The text in between makes up the middle of the story, which tells us what the tortoise and the other characters in the story did before the eagle and the crow enjoyed tortoise meat. The moral is not really a part of the story, but a comment on it.

Academic writing also should have a beginning, a middle and an end as in a creative story. The difference is that in a creative story the writer starts from wherever he fancies while in academic writing the writer joins a conversation that is going on among scholars. Also, as we have noted in Chapter 3, the academic writer's style choices are restricted.

CREATING AN OUTLINE OF THE STORY

Creating an outline of our story is one of the first and most important processes in writing it up. If we cannot create an outline with a beginning, a middle and an end, perhaps our thinking is muddled and we have no story to tell. We may have amassed data but are unable to string them into a coherent, meaningful and interesting story. As Wayne Booth says, "the accumulation of accurately observed detail cannot satisfy us for long" (quoted by Golden-Biddle & Locke, 1997, p. 58); the reader is looking for meaning, for significance, for a story. The outline helps us see if we have a story and if we are ready to share it with others.

Let us go back to the story of the tortoise. What is the core of the story? What kind of minimal outline can we start with? Here is a possibility:

A tortoise wanted to move to a new place to live.

An eagle agreed to help.

While the eagle was flying the tortoise off, a crow suggested that she drop the tortoise to the ground. The eagle did so.

The tortoise's shell broke and exposed the meat; the two birds ate it.

Once we have an outline like this, we can expand it and make it more detailed. Take, for example, the first idea or the beginning of the story: "A tortoise wanted to move to a new place to live." We can add details to each of the major words in that piece and expand the beginning of the story:

tortoise — young, daydreaming, alone, slow...

bored — same food again and again, same surroundings, same neighbours, nothing interesting to see or do...

surroundings — trees, pond, wall...

months pass by without any exciting events or sights...

some new place — glittering world beyond, plenty to eat, plenty to see...

Your outline will have been gradually forming itself in the process of doing research, which, as we have seen in Chapter 1, is fairly structured. As you were reviewing the literature in your field, you were struck by a gap in existing knowledge or a phenomenon that could not be readily explained. You then had a hypothesis about why something worked or did not work; you gathered evidence to prove or disprove the hypotheses; and thus arrived at a conclusion, at least a tentative one. In other words, a story was emerging as you did your research. Now, you need to develop a detailed outline to start the process of writing.

We should not look at the outline as a straitjacket. It is more like a skeleton. It determines what kind of flesh and how much flesh should go where. The advantage of working with an outline is that we do not lose track of the story. We know where to start and what place we need to reach. Whether we have one sentence, one page or a whole chapter on where the tortoise lived, how he got tired of his surroundings, and how he was constantly dreaming of getting to an exciting new place, we know we are still setting the stage for the body of the story.

Developing the outline of a story in academics is different from developing one in fiction. When developing a creative story, there are no restrictions other than those imposed by the writer's imagination. The writer can freely create settings, characters and actions. The only condition is that he should be able to take the reader along. Kalidasa's *Abhijnanasakuntalam*, Leo Tolstoy's

War and Peace, Herman Melville's *Moby Dick or the Whale* and Lewis Carroll's *Alice's Adventures in Wonderland* are all such creations, each substantially different from the rest. Yet, they have managed to take along numerous readers from different generations.

Academic writers, however, have to build their story with data or evidence that has been gathered systematically and in ways that are approved by the relevant scholarly community. They have to branch off from an existing conversation among scholars in the field, mainly by confirming, disproving or extending what others have discovered or developed. As we have seen in Chapter 2, there are well-established norms about what should appear in what order in conceptual and empirical research papers. They will shape your outline when you write for publication. For a wide range of academic papers that you submit as part of your coursework, you may have to create your own outlines unless you have already been asked to follow a certain structure. The discussion here should help you more with those written assignments than research papers for publication, which are covered in Chapter 2.

If you are writing a paper for publication in a journal, you must go through several papers published in it and figure out the expectations of that scholarly community so that you structure your paper and shape your style accordingly. Most journals set aside a page (usually titled notes/instructions/guidelines for contributors/authors) in each issue to formalize their expectations about the content, style, length and even formatting. Failure to comply with them might lead to the rejection of your contribution. If, however, you are writing an assignment for submission to an instructor, make sure that you know what his expectations are. What is acceptable to one instructor may not be acceptable to others. There are, of course, a few general guidelines that are likely to be acceptable to all. We will focus on them.

The Beginning of the Story

The beginning of the story, like the introduction in any discourse, is to create a framework that helps the reader understand what to expect in the article or essay that you are writing. If doing research is like joining a conversation, think of the introduction or the beginning as greeting others at a party. You want to indicate to the readers what aspect of the conversation you want to take off from and how you intend to proceed. This helps them understand and possibly accept your contribution better.

There are many options. A common beginning is to give the reader the background to the issue or problem you are going to deal with. Related to this is giving the reader connections to work already done in the relevant field. You may support, extend or reject what others in the field have found, as we have noted in Chapter 1 while discussing the features of science. You may tell the reader why have you written the paper, that is, your justification or your objective. You may want to evaluate a proposal or question the conclusion of another study. Another simple introduction is to describe the structure of the paper. This helps the reader make sense of what is coming in the rest of the paper. Therefore, the kind of introduction you attempt depends on what you are going to say in the article or paper.

The beginning should be brief. Give the minimum background to help your readers place, understand and appreciate your thesis or argument. Unnecessarily long background information can annoy readers and dissuade them from reading on and getting the insights you offer in the paper.

The Middle of the Story

The middle is where you present your hypotheses, methods, data and analysis. This makes up the bulk of your paper. When you prepare the outline, you can decide what kind of information should be presented to your readers and in what order.

The End of the Story

The end of your story is nothing but saying goodbye to your readers. But you do not want to just say goodbye and leave. How you say it depends on what your objective is and how well you have achieved that objective. You may, by summarizing the main points, want to remind the readers of the journey you have taken together with them. You may want to show the reader that you have done the task you set out to do, or fulfilled your promise. You may also want to indicate questions you have not attempted to answer or have left unanswered. In theses or in research articles, this is where you indicate limitations of your current research and directions for future research.

A Sample Outline

Here is a possible initial outline of a story on microfinance in India. (We shall revisit an abstract of the story later in this chapter, in the section "Self-critiquing.")

The beginning/Background:

Microfinance = giving small scale financial services to small-time entrepreneurs with no access to banks/financial institutions. Supposed to support self-sustainability and promote rural entrepreneurs. But does it?

The middle/Development:

Two Models: Grameen Bank (Dr Yunus, Bangladesh) & Self Help Group (SHG, popular in India). ⟶ Critical analysis of the operation of microfinance.

Advantages: But for microfinance, most small entrepreneurs, especially rural ones, will have no access to funds except those of exploitative moneylenders; data supporting the benefits derived from microfinance by rural entrepreneurs in different regions of India/abroad.

Disadvantages: Microfinance not as entrepreneur friendly as is often made out; interest rate too high; repayment schedules inflexible (linked with the rest of one's group); some entrepreneurs have to borrow from moneylenders at exorbitant rates to pay back microfinance loans on schedule; almost two-thirds of those who join drop out by the third year; despite all this, microfinance not reaching the bottom 20% of entrepreneurs.

The end/Conclusion:

To benefit small-time entrepreneurs, make repayment schedule far more flexible. Reach out to the poorest of the poor through combining microfinance institutions' resources with the government's poverty alleviation initiatives. Introduce differential interest rates linked to the entrepreneurs' income. In general, introduce more flexibility in interest rates and payment schedules.

(Outline built from "Microfinance: A boon or a bane for rural entrepreneurship?" Student assignment, 2008)

Once you have a basic storyline like this in place, you can make the outline more detailed. Take, for example, the two models of microfinance. You can provide more details of both the models. You can perhaps supply some relevant statistics from Bangladesh, where the *Grameen* model was developed, or from South India, where SHG is very popular. There could be comparisons with Indian chit-funds, a kind of SHG, which have been popular for decades in different parts of India.

Even if you have a lot of data on both these models, you should not put them all into the outline. The reason is simple. The main part of the story is a critical analysis of microfinance's advantages and disadvantages. There is no point in giving a detailed account of the two microfinance models focussing on the differences and similarities between the two. You should stop when you have provided enough information for the reader to make sense of the critical evaluation of the advantages and disadvantages of microfinance for small-time entrepreneurs, especially rural ones.

FLESHING OUT THE OUTLINE

Once you have developed a reasonably detailed outline, the next step is to flesh it out or write the first draft. Here you have to move fast. Do not worry about spelling, grammar or punctuation. Do not waste time waiting for the right word. Your objective should be to tell the story fast. The advantage of moving fast is that the story you want to tell will be constantly in your mind guiding you. If you are unsure of a word or phrase, put a question mark in brackets after whatever you have written down and move on. Do not let it slow you down.

The fleshing out also should be in cycles. Once you come to the end of your story, go back to the beginning and ask what more should be put in where in order to make it easy for your reader to understand and accept your story. This is the stage at which you might consider providing visual support for the reader. You may want to compress some of your data into reader-friendly tables or graphs. This is also the time when you may want to refer more specifically to the scholarly conversation your paper is going to be part of. Perhaps you have not shown enough of the existing conversation, that is, the relevant literature, to place your own story firmly in it. Perhaps you need to explore the literature a bit more to make sure that you have not missed out any significant strands of scholarly conversation relevant to your topic.

During the fleshing out process you may discover some gaps in your outline. You can fill in those gaps by introducing new details. You may discover that some of the details you have provided originally are unnecessary. You can cut them out. Even at this stage it is not a good idea to focus on grammar or vocabulary. Your aim should be to get the first draft of your story out. You can refine, edit and polish it at the next stage.

POLISHING THE STORY

There may be a tiny minority of writers, especially creative writers, whose first draft is so well crafted that it can go straight to the reader without any revision. Most writers, however, need to fill many gaps and polish the draft before they can present their story to their potential readers. This is particularly true of academic writing, where expectations can be somewhat rigid. If you doubt it, ask the editors of any good peer-reviewed journal and they will tell you that even those who publish regularly in such journals are asked to revise and resubmit their papers. If you are asked to revise a paper, it is obvious that it has not met all the expectations of the editors or reviewers about the content or style or both. If this is the fate of the final version of papers that authors submit to journals, what about their first drafts? What about the first draft of your assignments?

Polishing your draft is essential because writing is a conversation with an invisible, inaudible reader. You have to ensure that your reader can make sense of and interpret what you have put in. You cannot deposit meaning in texts and expect readers to just pick it up; meaning is created by the writer and the reader working together. Your job is to help the reader in that process. If your writing does not help her interpret and create meaning, she is likely to skip the text and move on or create meanings that are different from what you have in mind. It is good to note Gopen and Swan's (1990) remark: "We cannot succeed in making even a single sentence mean one and only one thing; we can only increase the odds that a large majority of readers will tend to interpret our discourse according to our intentions." Increasing the odds depends on revising and fine-tuning the draft.

There are two ways to check whether your readers can interpret your text along the lines you have in mind: (1) put on the reader's hat and read it critically, and then (2) get at least a couple of peers to read it critically. Remove from the text any hurdles that you can identify before you hand the text to your peers for their review. This is the minimum courtesy you should show your peers who offer to read and critique your paper. We shall now look at these two stages of critiquing in the order in which they should be done. Both these steps are essential before you present your document to the ultimate readers.

Self-Critiquing

Put aside your first draft for a few days; at least for a day if the deadline for submission is very close. You need this temporal distance from the text to critique it like a consumer rather than as the producer. Self-critiquing is not at all easy because you already know the story you want to tell and feel that it can be retrieved by others from the document you have created. It is extremely difficult to see gaps and inconsistencies in one's story, almost as difficult as recognizing one's own body odour.

Here is a set of questions you can ask to help you critique the first draft reasonably thoroughly:

Have you given the report a title?

If you have not given a title, give it one. *Report, Paper* or *Assignment* is not a useful title. Imagine going to a classroom and finding row after row of pupils without any name or all named 'boy' or 'girl.' If your child is one of them, there is a good chance that he or she will not be remembered or referred to by anyone. By not giving your child a name or by giving her a generic name like 'girl', you are discouraging her from standing out from the crowd. This applies equally well to your reports.

Is the title crisp, appropriate, informative and attractive?

A title that reads like tabloid headlines may be eye-catching but no more appropriate in an academic report than a bikini in a boardroom. On the other hand, a long, sentence-like title may be boring; it may prompt the reader to move on. He may conclude that the yawn-inducing title reflects the style of the entire article. In under a dozen words you should be able to write an attractive title that also tells the reader what the area of inquiry is and how have you approached it. If you are writing for publication in a journal, you will do well to incorporate in the title at least one of your key words, that is, words or phrases which reflect the theme or central ideas you explore in your paper.

Here are a few examples from graduate student reports:

a. "A Comprehensive Communication Strategy for XX XX Pvt Ltd"
b. "Communicating with Investors: An Entrepreneur's Perspective"
c. "Communicating with the Government – XX India Limited"
d. "Rural Entrepreneurship: An Answer to Naxalism in India"

These four titles are brief, to the point, and clear. The reader knows what the report is about. Now examine the following titles, also from similar graduate student reports.

e. "Communicating With The Government Officials"

(*Not good enough; although we know the broad area — communicating with government officials — covered by the report, the focus of the report is not clear; unsatisfactory grammar.*)

f. "Building and Managing Corporate Reputation: Project Report"

(*Highly inadequate;* "Building and Managing Corporate Reputation" *is the title of the course for which this report was prepared. The students' title does not tell the reader what to expect. All we can figure out from the title is that it is a project report submitted in connection with the course,* "Building and Managing Corporate Reputation." *That is not saying much to the course instructor, is it? As this report happened to be on how a particular steel company in India built and managed its reputation, a more appropriate title would have been:* "How XX Steel Ltd Built and Managed its Reputation" *or* "How XX Steel Ltd Builds and Manages its Reputation," *or* "Building and Managing Corporate Reputation: The XX Steel Ltd story.")

g. "Advantages for Corporate of Indulging in Development of Rural Entrepreneurship"

(*Highly inadequate, unclear and ungrammatical.* "Promoting Rural Entrepreneurship: How it Benefits Companies," *or* "Promoting Rural Entrepreneurship: How Companies Benefit," *or* "Corporate Profits through Supporting Rural Entrepreneurship" *would probably have captured the student's intention better.*)

Have you written an abstract?

If you have not written an abstract, write one. The best time to write the abstract is of course after you have finished writing the paper. But this is the first thing—after the title—that a reader is likely to process. It pays to invest in an abstract even if the recipient does not insist on one.

Does the abstract give the reader a clear idea of what to expect in the paper?

As we have noted in Chapter 2, the abstract is a standalone unit. One should be able to make sense of it without reading any part of the article or report. The abstract is all that is often read. It nearly always determines whether the reader will go on to the body of the paper. A journal editor may form a poor impression of a good paper sent in for publication if the abstract is inadequate or unexciting. A poor abstract may bias your instructor also against reports you submit to him.

Here is an abstract written by a team of two graduate students. It gives the reader a good idea of their paper ("Microfinance: A Boon or a Bane for Rural Entrepreneurship?") while employing just 7 per cent of the words (147/2100, excluding exhibits and references):

> The concept of microfinance is not new to India. But with the increasing availability of credit and development of new frameworks for microfinance, it has gained immense popularity as a contributor to self-sustainability and development at the grass-roots level. This article critically evaluates the claim of microfinance as a leading means of fuelling rural entrepreneurship in India. The essential characteristics of microfinance are outlined and the recent developments in this sector are discussed in the Indian context. The two most widely used microfinance models, the *Grameen* model

and the Self-Help Group model, are explained. Based on data from several sources, the article analyzes in detail the pros and cons of the microfinance lending framework for rural entrepreneurs in India. The article reconciles these contradicting views and based on the various issues uncovered from the analysis it recommends what needs to be done to make microfinance more entrepreneur-friendly.

(*Taken from "Microfinance: A boon or a bane for rural entrepreneurship?" student assignment, 2008; 147 words*)

There is, however, a problem. This is largely an indicative abstract. Although it mentions the paper's objective and structure, it does not share with the reader any of the ideas that the writers have put into the paper. It merely tells the reader what kind of ideas he will find in the paper: an explanation of the differences between the *Grameen* model and the Self-Help Group model of microfinance; an analysis of the pros and cons of microfinance for rural poor; a way that "reconciles these contradicting views," and a few recommendations "to make microfinance more entrepreneur-friendly." But what are those ideas? The reader has to read the article to find out. He can neither agree nor disagree with any of these ideas because the abstract does not tell him what those ideas are.

While such indicative abstracts are useful and are provided in some journals to help readers decide whether a paper dealt with topics that interested them, an abstract that captures the main ideas of the paper would be generally more useful and appropriate. The reader may be encouraged to read the paper either because the ideas confirm what he believes in or question them.

Here is a different way to write an abstract for the same paper:

This paper critically evaluates microfinance, which has been hailed as a major contributor to rural entrepreneurship in India. Dr Yunus's *Grameen* model of microfinance depends on group accountability that prevents default; the Self Help Group (SHG) model, popular in India, leverages the members' savings. Despite its very high interest rates, microfinance appears to benefit poor rural entrepreneurs who would otherwise get no institutional credit at all. But evidence shows that little credit reaches the poorest entrepreneurs; besides, more than half of those who join microfinance schemes drop out signalling systemic weaknesses. Flexible repayment schedules and differential interest rates are recommended as a solution. (*103 words*)

This abstract captures the main ideas in 103 words (less than 5 per cent of the paper). It tells the reader what claims have been made by the writers. Of course, he has to read the full paper or relevant sections to find out the kind of support the authors provide for the claims they make. What, for example, is the evidence for the claim that "little credit reaches the poorest entrepreneurs" or that "more than half of those who join microfinance schemes drop out"? How would "flexible repayment schedules and differential interest rates" solve the problems that have been identified? One has to read the paper. But this abstract shares the writers' story with the reader and challenges his thinking in a way the original abstract does not. This is the preferred way to write abstracts. Write an indicative abstract only if there is a severe limit on the number of words you can use (for example, 50 words for a 3000- or 4000-word paper).

Is the abstract short enough?

The abstract should not generally exceed 10 per cent of the report. A journal or an instructor may set lower limits as we have noted in Chapter 2. Some journals, for example, want the abstract to be under 100 or 150 words even when the full paper exceeds 5,000 words. Some indicative abstracts found in journals use fewer than 50 words. Similarly, an instructor may announce the maximum acceptable length of the abstract. It is important that you abide by such guidelines.

Compressing a paper to one-tenth of its size is not at all easy. But this is a skill you must master because of the enormous importance of abstracts and executive summaries in reaching out to readers. Your audience may not bother to watch your marvellous film if the trailer does not excite them through a good preview.

Have you chosen appropriate key words?

Most journals ask you to indicate four or five key words or phrases that help others reach your paper without difficulty when they search databases, looking for research done on the topic of your paper. Some journals specify the number of key words you can give. Choose them carefully. Avoid making them too broad or too narrow. Study the key words given, usually at the end of the abstract, in a few international journal articles to get a clear picture of their role and relevance.

Key words are not required when you submit a paper to your instructor. Looking for the right key words, however, might give you useful practice that will help you when you write to publish. It will also help you summarize in half a dozen words the story that you are telling in your paper.

Does the paper have all the essential components?

In Chapter 2, we examined the standard components of empirical and conceptual papers. Ask yourself if your paper has those components. If you have missed out any, ask why. Unless you have a very good reason, do not drop any of those standard components. If you need additional reading or additional thinking, do so.

If you are writing an assignment for an instructor, find out if she expects any particular structure. If yes, make sure that you adopt it. If she does not insist on any special structure, choose one that comes closest to the standard structure of an empirical or a conceptual paper. It is likely to present your ideas most acceptably.

Does each component do its job well?

Each major component has a specific and important role to play in the paper. The introduction, for example, should give the reader an overview of what to expect in terms of content and structure. The literature review should acquaint the reader with the relevant literature and the argument or conversation so far around the topic. Ask yourself if your literature review prepares the reader adequately for placing and making sense of your contribution and your insights. Ask similar questions of the other components as well. Chapter 2 will help you ask the right questions.

Are the components well balanced?

The arms of a young man may be well developed and good to look at, but if they are longer or fatter than his legs, there is a problem. His body is not well balanced. In the same way, if any component of a paper is disproportionately big or small, the paper is not well balanced. There are no hard and fast rules about the right proportion in academic papers. You need to figure it out by becoming familiar with good papers in your discipline.

What you should avoid is padding a particular section merely because you happen to have a lot of data or leaving a particular section underdeveloped because you have not done enough research. Imagine, for example, that you are writing a paper on the advantages and disadvantages of microfinance based on the outline we have seen earlier in this chapter. Imagine also that you happen to have substantial data on Dr Yunus and microfinance in Bangladesh. Do not burden the paper with that because the focus of the paper is on the advantages and disadvantages of microfinance. If, however, the paper is a comparative study of the two main models of microfinance, a detailed account of the way both these models work or have emerged in different countries over the years might be useful.

Is the structure of the paper clear and transition smooth?

In other words, is your thesis—your story—clear? Are there suitable subheads within the major components to help the reader navigate smoothly through the report? If you think subheads will enhance clarity and transition, provide them. They generally help because they are like signposts. They keep the reader on track. Long stretches of text with no subheads can be difficult for the reader to process.

Some journals provide guidelines on the different levels of subheads and their formats (for example, all letters in upper case, title case, italics) expected. In the absence of such guidelines from a journal or an instructor, a researcher needs to decide on the number of levels and appropriate format for each. Word processors such as Microsoft Word illustrate different formats. You can choose one that suits your purpose.

Is the evidence provided adequate?

Take special care to adopt a neutral and impartial approach. When you are convinced of something, even inadequate data and weak arguments in favour of it may appear strong and indisputable. This is quite natural; but you must guard against this tendency with special vigour. You may be tempted to suppress or downplay any evidence that goes against your argument or data that cannot be explained within your framework. Resist it. It is in trying to explain inconvenient data or evidence that you create new and unexpected theories that are more powerful than the ones you are working with. If you suppress any counter-evidence, you behave dishonestly and do yourself and the scholarly community a major disservice. You should adopt a healthy sceptical attitude to the point you are making. If your evidence satisfies the sceptic in you, you can be reasonably sure that it will be acceptable to your intended readers.

When you critique your first draft, you may discover that some parts are underdeveloped. You may require additional research, additional data or additional support from relevant literature to buttress your claim. Never cook up data. It is as bad as stealing data.

Is the writing style appropriate?

This is a tricky question to answer. There are different styles all of which may be equally good and yet not appropriate to the given readers, as we have seen in Chapter 3. If you are writing for publication in a journal, you must check out the writing style adopted by it in its recent issues. There are practitioner-oriented journals such as *Academy of Management Executive, Organizational Dynamics* and *Harvard Business Review*, and purely academic journals such as *Academy of Management Review* and *Journal of Applied Psychology*. A quick glance at a few papers published in these journals is enough for you to notice major differences in writing styles. Your paper will not be processed for publication if its language deviates significantly from the journal's norms.

If you are writing for an instructor, find out her preferences. Some instructors are annoyed, for example, by the use of the first person in your paper. Some others are equally deeply annoyed by the impersonal and roundabout use of the third person where a straightforward first person account would be more interesting and more effective. Our advice: play by ear. When in doubt, be conservative. It should be possible to write clearly and beautifully, but if you have to choose between clarity and beauty, choose clarity.

Examine each paragraph. Does it display qualities such as unity and cohesion that we have identified in Chapter 4? If a paragraph appears to be very long, ask if you can split it into two. If a paragraph appears to be too short, ask if its topic is developed adequately. Does it need further fleshing out?

Is the text free from biased expressions?

Down the centuries English (and other languages as well) has picked up many words and expressions that unjustly glorify the male members of the human race at the expense of the other half. There is a strong move to redress the imbalance. Detailed guidelines are available. See, for example, UNESCO's (1999) *Guidelines on Gender-Neutral Language.*

Check your draft specifically for any gender biased expressions that may have crept in unnoticed. There are several online checklists available (including UNESCO's); use them.

Is the text free from language errors?

It is amazing how many language errors we fail to recognize when we meet them in our own documents. Because we know what we have written, we often read what we wanted to write rather than what we have written. Spotting language errors is harder for most people when they read documents on the computer screen rather than on a printed page. The least we should do is to enable the spell checker and the grammar checker of the word processor we use. They are not yet fully reliable; but they are generally better than our unaided eyes when we read our own texts. Seek someone's help if you are not sure of your grammar and usage.

You will find in Appendix 2 some excellent resources that you can use to help you improve your English grammar, usage and punctuation. Have at least a couple of them ready on your desk when you go through your draft looking for any errors in grammar, usage and punctuation.

Is the punctuation appropriate?

Punctuation plays an important role in making your text easy to read. A missing comma or a wrongly placed comma can change the meaning of a sentence or confuse the reader. If you find that there are too many punctuation marks in a long sentence, you must ask whether you can reduce some of them by splitting the sentence into two or three.

There are well established norms about when to use capital letters, italics and boldface. Follow them. If you are writing a paper for publication in a journal, you should ensure also that you follow any special instructions it has on punctuation. Do not use italics or boldface indiscriminately. If you find yourself using punctuation marks at random, consult a suitable reference book.

Is the text free from factual errors?

When you write the first draft, you should not stop to check whether the figures you quote are correct. And yet it is imperative to avoid factual errors in our reports. The time to check them is when you do the self-critiquing. A couple of factual errors can destroy the credibility of an entire report like the way a couple of dead flies floating on the surface can spoil a cauldron of soup.

Have you acknowledged everything you have borrowed?

Acknowledging sources meticulously is so central to academic writing that we have devoted a whole chapter (Chapter 6) to this issue. Please read it thoroughly to find out about the different kinds of borrowing and how to acknowledge them appropriately in your academic writing. You should avoid plagiarism of all shades.

Is the visual support clear, attractive, appropriate?

The old saying that a picture is worth a thousand words is true, especially when it comes to writing. Tables, graphs and charts can compress and present in a reader-friendly fashion the data that you may want to share with your reader. Graphical representations also help you tell the story better because the thread that strings the data is more easily seen in them. As you go through your draft, ask whether the data that you present will benefit from conversion to graphics. If the answer is yes, the next step should be to choose the most appropriate graphic representation for the data. The Internet offers many websites which help you convert different kinds of data to attractive and useful graphs and charts. Zelazny's (2007) *The say it with charts complete toolkit* is a useful resource.

Have you numbered and labelled your exhibits?

Label your exhibits. The title of each exhibit should tell the reader what to expect in it. If you have two or more exhibits, number them. If you have borrowed the exhibit or the information that you have put into the exhibit, acknowledge the source.

Here is a sample exhibit from a graduate student assignment entitled "Rural Empowerment in India through Micro-Enterprises: A Healthcare and Information Technology Perspective."

Exhibit 2   Status of Health Infrastructure in Villages

Infrastructure/Services	% of villages
Connected with Roads	73.9
Having any health provider	95.3
Having trained birth attendant	37.5
Having Anganwadi worker	74.2
Having a doctor (private and visiting)	43.5
Having a private doctor	30.5
Having a visiting doctor	25.0

Source: Bhandari & Dutta (2007).

Here, the source Bhandari & Dutta (2007), has been indicated without the full bibliographical details because they appear in the references section of the paper. The writers may have referred to the same source for other information as well. If the source of an exhibit is not mentioned elsewhere, you can give the full source right at the bottom of the exhibit. Example: Bhandari, L., & Dutta, S. (2007). Health infrastructure in rural India. In Kalra, P., & Rastogi, A. (Eds.), *India Infrastructure Report 2007* (pp. 265-285). New Delhi: Oxford. How these bibliographical details are presented will of course vary depending on the citation style being followed. Please see Chapter 6 for details.

Are the exhibits introduced properly in the body of the document?

If you have tables, graphs, charts and other visual support for the point you are making, have you referred to these exhibits in the text? You should not present an exhibit unless it has been introduced in the body of the paper. Check to make sure that any exhibit that you provide either in the body or at the end of the paper, is referred to at least once in the body of the paper. Similarly, ensure that the exhibits are presented and numbered in the order in which they appear in the article.

Peer-Critiquing

There is plenty of apocryphal and research evidence in support of the value of peer-critiquing in improving student writing even when the peer reviewers are novices. See, for example, Cho and Schunn (2007) and Cho, Schunn and Charney (2006) for recent evidence, specifically related to peer-review of writing, and Topping (1998) for the first comprehensive review of peer evaluation studies.

That peer review should help writers refine and improve their writing is not at all surprising. As you are familiar with every aspect of your story, you may unwittingly jump from one subplot to another without taking your potential reader along. In other words, you may leave large gaps in your story, making it difficult for your readers to reconstruct it or interpret your message. When someone reads and comments on your writing, she helps you identify any gaps you need to fill. When a reader says she cannot make sense of what you have written, it can be annoying; but remember, *Reader is King*. You have to do everything possible to make your meaning clear and interesting to your anticipated readers.

The value of others critiquing your writing is also evident from the practice of blind peer reviewing that all good academic journals follow. The peer reviewers have to base their judgement exclusively on the written text because they are not told who has written the text that they review. As a result of this, even experienced contributors to journals and highly regarded thought-leaders are asked to revise and resubmit their papers, as we have already noted.

What kind of reviewers should you look for? It will be good if you can get an expert in the content area of your document and a non-expert. They contribute differently, but equally valuably, to the process of revision. The expert can quickly spot any gaps or weaknesses in your story; the non-expert can tell you if the document makes sense. Critiquing by a combination of experts and non-experts will help you identify and avoid most of the weaknesses in your document.

Just as you ask some of your peers to critique your documents, you should be prepared to critique others' documents when asked. Critiquing others' documents will benefit you too. You will realize the kind of problems writers fail to notice in their own writing. These insights will feed into your self-critiquing. The critical reading ability that you develop will help you treat your text also somewhat objectively and refine it for readers.

When you critique someone else's text, you can ask the questions mentioned in the section above on self-critiquing. You should go beyond answering 'yes' or 'no;' you should be able to suggest ways of recasting parts of the text, if you believe that you have figured out the writer's meaning in spite of bad gaps or poor articulation.

We shall examine two extracts from student papers critiqued by the writers' fellow students.

Peer-critiquing: Sample 1

Sample 1 is an extract from a graduate student paper entitled "Public Private Partnership in Water Management: A Public Misery or a Public Good?". The objective of the paper, according to the introduction, is "to evaluate PPP [Public Private Partnership] as a feasible solution to the water problems in India, and critically review the Tirupur project from inception to the implementation stage." The extract given below comes immediately after the introduction and before a longish Section 2, which gives a detailed description of the Tirupur Water Supply and Sewerage Project, a PPP project.

Six peers from the writer's class commented on the paper as part of a double blind peer feedback exercise. Two of them did not make any comments on this part of the paper. The comments made by the other four peers are given in square brackets. Although all the peer comments are incorporated here, no student knew who else critiqued the same paper and what their comments were.

Some words/phrases/sentences have been underlined to indicate that the comments following them refer to them.

1. The case for Public Private Partnership in water management

In India, water management function has largely been under the purview of the Government and even today, water is not accessible to 12% (see exhibit 1) [*Peer 1. Exhibit 1 would suffice, omit "see"*] of the total population. [*Peer 2: Not clear whether you are trying to connect the two facts.*] Public water utilities have not always been efficient and there are some regions where <u>leaky and broken pipes</u> [*Peer 2: A bit inappropriate phrase for such an article.*], un-metered taps and illegal connections account for a significant loss in water revenue.

Add to this, the energy cost of pumping all that extra water and the inefficiencies only increase [*Peer 3: "decrease in efficiency of water utilization" can be put in instead of "inefficiencies only increase"*]. These inefficiencies can be attributed to a number of reasons [*Peer 2: a couple of reasons*]. One, the government is playing multiple roles – that of an owner, a manager and a regulator at the same time. [*Peer 1: How does this make the system inefficient?*] [*Peer 4: How does this in itself lead to inefficiency? Is this the basis of the case for PPP?*] Two, there are lack of funds to manage the system effectively. [*Peer 2: Government does not have lack of funds. It's basically the lack of interest and appropriate policy I believe.*]

To make the system more efficient, a number of attempts were made to privatize water supply during the last decade. However private sector experiences with Sheonath river project in Chattisgarh, Chandrapur water supply project in Maharashtra, Sonia Vihar water treatment project in Delhi etc. were not very successful, either (http://www.hinduonnet.com). [*Peer 4: Wrong referencing style – there is no way I can look up this article easily based on the information given here.*] The failures in the above mentioned projects can be attributed to large scale exploitation and misuse by the private authorities. [*Peer 2: This is a very strong statement to make especially when it is not supported by data. Also should have been corroborated with an example for the benefit of readers who are not aware of this fact.*]

This theoretically makes Public Private Partnership (PPP) a more attractive option [*Peer 4: How, after previous attempts failed because of misuse by private players, does PPP become more attractive?*] as it delegates the execution and implementation part of the project to a private body which brings in technical and management expertise apart from the huge capital investments required and limits the role of the Government to [*Peer 3: word missing here*] a regulator which can concentrate on policy making and offset the negative externalities.

Different readers have noted different weaknesses in the text. It is interesting to note the wide range of questions and comments raised. Some show linguistic concerns; most deal with weak logic; some point to insufficient information and one highlights improper referencing. While the writer may choose to ignore a purely stylistic suggestion such as made by Peer 1 who wants the word "see" omitted from "see Exhibit 1," he has to address the questions raised by the readers about the soundness of his assertions. If he wants to continue making those assertions, he has to provide evidence in support. Or he may have to alter the assertions so that they are more tentative and acceptable to his readers.

Note how Peer 2 reacts to the statement, "These inefficiencies can be attributed to a number of reasons." He suggests that the writer change it to "a couple of reasons" because the writer has provided only two reasons. The writer should either give more reasons to justify the phrase "a number of reasons" or tone down the claim as suggested. Another way out would be to retain "a number of reasons" and to highlight the two most important ones. A writer is unlikely to notice such mismatches unless someone points them out.

Peer-critiquing: Sample 2

The second sample is Section 5 of a student paper entitled "R&D in Pharmaceutical Industry: Challenges and Opportunities from IPR and Globalization." The paper talks about how the R&D activities of Indian pharmaceutical industry have been shaped by the recent improvements in Intellectual Property Rights (IPRs) brought about by globalization. Section 5 deals with problems that the pharmaceutical industry has to face because of Trade Related Intellectual Property Rights (TRIPS) and globalization. It comes after Section 4, which deals with the implications of patenting and IPRs in the Indian Pharmaceutical Industry, and before the conclusion, which provides an action plan for the Indian pharmaceutical industry to make the most of the opportunities already identified in the paper.

Six peers commented on this paper also as part of the same double blind peer feedback exercise mentioned above. One of them did not make any comments on this part of the paper. The comments made by the other five peers are given in square brackets, as in the first example.

5. IMPACT OF TRIPS ON PHARMACEUTICAL INDUSTRY

"The purpose of biopharmaceutical R&D is, ultimately, to find new medicines and vaccines to make people well and keep them healthy. It is not about economics, industrial development or job creation per se although these things are essential grist to the market economy of today," <u>says Dr. Bale</u> [*Peer 1: Source of quotation??*] [*Peer 2: Who is he?*] [*Peer 3: Who is this Dr. Bale and where has he said this? Reference missing.*] [*Peer 4: Reference and source should be provided in case someone wants to read it in detail.*] Even though the WTO states a similar motto, the hidden intentions of developed countries are clear from the TRIPs agreement. [*Peer 1: Elaborate on TRIPs agreement.*]

The endorsement of product patents by TRIPS implies the following for the industry: start afresh on research, evolve a policy for innovation, develop the IT strategy and improve the novel drug delivery system (NDDS) (Ashok, 2004). [*Peer 3: So? How does this come into the picture for the Indian industry that we are discussing?*]

It also poses the following challenges:

[*Peer 4: Doesn't come well along with flow right after implications.*]

• <u>Unaffordability</u> of important drugs for the common man [*Peer 5: Unaffordability is not a proper English word. One could use "Reduce affordability" instead.*]

• Compromise <u>of</u> [*Peer 4: Compromise is followed by on in standard English.*] Indian sovereignty and public health policy. It is opined that TRIPS violates the human rights.

• Loss of job for thousands due to shutting down of small scale companies

• Stagnation of overall growth rate of the industry

[*Peer 3: How did you arrive upon these set of challenges? Conclusions not supported with any analysis.*]

India can still get away with the <u>articles 7 and 8</u> [*Peer 1: What are mentioned in these 2 articles??*] of <u>the agreement</u> [*Peer 4: Which agreement? Not coming out clearly. Needs more exclusivity.*] which in grave situations, allow it to take <u>measures</u> [*Peer 2: Mentioning of measures would have helped*] for public health and safety (Krishnan, 2001). With millions of people affected with AIDS, there is no reason why India should not consider this option.

[*Peer 3: Lack of flow. I am experiencing jerks while reading this section. One thought does not seem to lead to another. It seems more like a random set of things the author just wants to say without any underlying theme being argued for.*]

This text also has attracted a variety of comments. Four out of the six peers want to know who Dr Bale is. The writer has sprung a name and a quote on the reader without adequate preparation or citing the source. The other comments cover mainly the gaps in thinking and reasoning left by the writer indicating that the readers have difficulty jumping with the writer from one idea to another.

While five readers would like to see improvements in the content and flow of the text, the sixth reader apparently has no problem with it. We do not know if it is because he has approached peer-critiquing casually or because he is an uncritical reader.

You may find that some peer comments on your text are unfair, based on wrong perceptions, or based on a particular approach to life that you do not share. It is not at all necessary to accept all peer comments. They alert you to the problems your readers have faced in processing your message. After giving them due consideration, it is up to you to decide whether you should take them seriously or ignore them. If two or more readers have difficulty with a part of your text, you need to take their concerns seriously. Whether you accept or reject those comments, just becoming aware of them is bound to help you in revising and refining the text. If you pay attention to such reader comments, the final product is likely to be far more satisfactory than if you never sought them or ignored them when they came. That these comments are from peers rather than from teachers or scholars does not diminish their value.

TIDYING UP THE DOCUMENT

What your document looks like is important. Just as important as the way food is arranged and presented at the dining table. You should try to make your document appealing to the eyes and conforming to reader expectations. You may be proud of the insights that you have put into a paper and may rightly believe that it is worth a good read; but if the reader is put off by the document's appearance, you are the loser. Remember that you are not around to nudge the reader; the document should do all the work including the nudging and tugging. So the writing process is not over until you tidy the text up for the reader and format it in an appropriate fashion.

If you are writing for publication, the journal determines what appearance is acceptable. Editors of peer reviewed journals would expect you to submit the paper, the abstract and the author details separately to help blind refereeing. Journals may specify the font type and size for different items such as the main title, subtitle (if any), subheads and the body along with the size of the margins and the kind of line spacing required. Some journals also provide guidelines on where to place figures, tables and notes. Some, for example, will not allow footnotes; any notes will have to come at the end of the paper. Most journals are strict about these because they have to maintain consistency across different papers and different issues. If a journal does not specify these details, it is a good idea to figure them out from the style followed in its recent issues or consult the style guide that the journal follows or recommends. Such guides or handbooks give you all the relevant information regarding the formatting of documents.

For students of management, we recommend American Psychological Association's (2001) *Publication Manual* and (2007) *APA Style Guide to Electronic References.* Together these two give you comprehensive guidelines. The sixth edition of *Publication Manual,* published recently (2009), gives you the latest guidelines, especially for using electronic sources.

When you write a paper for submission to your instructor, set the first page aside for the title and related information. Present on it the title (and subtitle, if any), your name (along with all the essential identifying details such as your section number or roll number), the name of the person you are submitting the paper to, the name of the course in connection with which you are submitting the paper and the date of submission. If you are part of a small group where the instructor knows everyone very well, roll numbers may not be required. Even in such contexts, it is good to provide details such as the person to whom the paper is submitted, the date of submission and the course as part of which the paper is being submitted. This is because as a document, the paper may have a life beyond the immediate context. The document should carry enough information for a future reader also.

Let us look at the way the two writers of "Microfinance: A Boon or a Bane for Rural Entrepreneurship?" present their title page (Box 5.1). You will recall that we have already referred to this paper earlier in this chapter (see Section "Self-Critiquing") and reviewed its abstract. This is not presented as a model, but as a sample that was judged satisfactory by the instructor to whom it was submitted. There are different and equally acceptable ways of presenting the same information. This sample merely points to the kind of information that the writers should present on the title page.

Box 5.1 Title Page of Student Report "Microfinance: A Boon or a Bane for Rural Entrepreneurship?"

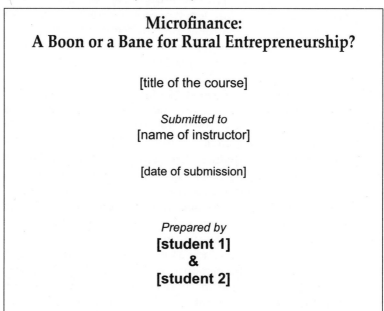

Microfinance:
A Boon or a Bane for Rural Entrepreneurship?

[title of the course]

Submitted to
[name of instructor]

[date of submission]

Prepared by
[student 1]
&
[student 2]

[NAME OF THE INSTITUTION]

Compare this with the way another group presented its report to its instructor (Box 5.2). The title, subtitle, the names of students, the contents and the introduction were squeezed into the same page. This is not at all attractive although it contains most of the required information.

The second page of the paper, "Microfinance: A Boon or a Bane for Rural Entrepreneurship?" is set aside for the abstract.

Box 5.2   Title Page of Student Report "Communicating with YYY"

Group X	Communicating with YYY Project	Course: ABC

Communicating with YYY

Building and Maintaining Corporate Reputation project submission by
Group X
[Student 1, Student 2, Student 3, Student 4, Student 5, Student 6]

Contents
1. ...
2. ...
3. ...
4. ...
Introduction

Abstract

The concept of microfinance is not new to India. But with the increasing availability of credit and development of new frameworks for microfinance, it has gained immense popularity as a contributor to self-sustainability and development at the grass-roots level. This article critically evaluates the claim of microfinance as a leading means of fuelling rural entrepreneurship in India. The essential characteristics of microfinance are outlined and the recent developments in this sector are discussed in the Indian context. The two most widely used microfinance models, the Grameen model and the Self-Help Group model, are explained. Based on data from several sources, the article analyzes in detail the pros and cons of the microfinance lending framework for rural entrepreneurs in India. The article reconciles these contradicting views and based on the various issues uncovered from the analysis it recommends what needs to be done to make microfinance more entrepreneur-friendly.

(Taken from "Microfinance: A boon or a bane for rural entrepreneurship?" student assignment, 2008)

In the original report, the writers use double spacing for the abstract and the body of the paper because that is what they are asked to do. Instructors prefer documents with double line spacing because they need plenty of space to write in their comments and suggestions for improvement. If that is what your readers want, you should provide it. You will find that journals generally insist on double line spacing even when they allow soft copy submission.

The third page provides a detailed table of contents (Box 5.3). Such detailed listing of contents is not necessary in a short paper such as this one. Journal papers never carry them. However, the writers of this paper provide a table of contents, again because their instructor wants it for pedagogical reasons. This is yet another instance of writers meeting reader expectations.

Box 5.3   Table of Contents for Student Report "Microfinance: A Boon or a Bane for Rural Entrepreneurship?"

What we find here is a simple listing of the main sections in the paper. There are, of course, different ways of numbering sections and subsections. Choose the one that best suits the development of thought in your paper. Number the pages even when you submit your paper in the digital form. Page numbers help the reader navigate more easily.

If the instructor gives no specific instructions on what fonts or font sizes to use, adopt a standard font such as Arial, Times New Roman or Calibri. The preferred size is between 10 and 12 for the body of the paper. Do not boldface or italicize words unless there is a good reason. Consult a few good journals to understand how academic writing is presented.

If you have a few exhibits and they are very small, you may insert them in the main body of the document closest to where they are referred to. If, however, the exhibits are large, present them all in a separate section called "Exhibits," at the end of the paper. If the instructor or the journal has a specific policy regarding the placement of exhibits and tables, you should, of course, follow it rather than these guidelines. In any case, sequence the exhibits in the order in which they are referred to in the text.

If you have borrowed any concepts or pieces of text from any source, you need to indicate it in the relevant part of the paper and then provide full bibliographical details in the section called "References." Do not include in this section any resources which you have not referred to in the body of your paper. Please see Chapter 6 for specific guidelines on how to acknowledge what you borrow and how to give bibliographic details.

CHAPTER SUMMARY

In this chapter we have focussed on the process of writing. We have argued that skipping any important part of the process of writing can lead to an unsatisfactory product.

Once we have done our research and developed a story that we want to share with others, the first step is to create an outline of it. The next step is to flesh it out, which should be done in cycles. The fleshing out is followed by polishing it. Polishing has two stages: self-critiquing and peer-critiquing. We have identified the questions we should ask ourselves when we critique our own draft. Peer-critiquing, we have noted, is as important as self-critiquing. The reason is that in spite of our best efforts, we may fail to spot some gaps in our story that may make it difficult for readers to make sense of it and enjoy it. The final stage of writing is tidying up the text and formatting it in such a way that it conforms to the readers' expectations and is pleasing to their eyes.

If we follow these steps in our academic writing, we are likely to come out with stories worth reading.

Part III

Acknowledging Academic Debts

6

Using and Citing Sources of Ideas

CHAPTER OVERVIEW

We noted in Chapters 3 and 5 that one of the fundamental features of academic writing is the meticulous citing of the sources from which we borrow facts or ideas and put into our text. In this chapter we shall explore that feature further. We shall explain why we should cite our sources, what failure to do so leads us to, and how scrupulous acknowledgement of sources enhances our reports and papers. We shall distinguish between the kind of sources we ought to acknowledge and the ones we need not.

We shall also illustrate how to acknowledge borrowings from different sources, including electronic. Our recommendations and illustrations are derived from our observation of practice in many journals and scholarly publications in management and behavioural sciences, our own experience of academic writing, and our understanding of the citation guidelines of a few journals and style guides of professional associations. We also introduce you to resources where you can get detailed and authoritative guidance.

THE WORLD OF CITATIONS

Here are two extracts from a discussion on how the work–family challenges faced by Indian women professionals impact their careers. Go quickly over them to get the drift.

Extract 1

Women give birth to children and still do most of the work of bringing them up. To do a demanding job and managing family and social life simultaneously is notoriously difficult. It is generally women who take the primary responsibility for childcare and who, in situations of conflict, adjust their working lives to accommodate family pressures (Wajcman, 1981; Falkenberg and Monachello, 1990). Data show that women professionals still assume the primary responsibility of home and child-care activities (Googins and Burden, 1987; Jick and Mitz, 1985; Zappert and Weinstein, 1985).

Extract 2

The growing number of educated women in India—who are now participating in the urban, organized, industrial sector in technical, professional, and managerial positions—has been accompanied by a steady growth in dual career families (Komarraju, 1997). Research on career women in India shows that work and family dilemmas are often different from those reported by women in the West (Sekaran, 1992). As compared to their counterparts in other parts of the world, Indian employees face a lot of difficulties in managing their work and life.

Research conducted by Rout, Lewis and Kagan (1999) finds that women in India experience considerable pressure, in the morning before going out to work and after work, to do all that is necessary for the family. Komarraju (1997) notes that the relative absence of an infrastructure that provides a reliable supply of electricity, water, and time-saving, modern-day kitchen and other appliances, renders the performance of domestic responsibilities a burden, particularly for women in dual career families. In addition, inflexible working hours and the absence of childcare facilities constitute impediments rather than sources of support for employed mothers (Bharat, 2001). Though in urban India, things have started improving, yet they are not adequate.

A quick glance is all you need to figure out that these extracts are from a research paper. Extract 1 is from page 33 and Extract 2 from page 34 of "Work-family Challenges and their Impact on Career Decisions: A Study of Indian Women Professionals," a paper authored by Sanghamitra Buddhapriya and published by *Vikalpa* in 2009 (Volume 34, Number 1, pages 31-45). There are 10 citations in the short text of about 250 words; they are the telltale signs of academic writing. The references given below complete the picture of citations.

References

(only those relevant to the two extracts, taken from pages 43-45)

Bharat, S (2001). "On the Periphery: The Psychology of Gender," in Pandey, J (Ed.), *Psychology in India Revisited: Developments in the Discipline*, Volume 2, New Delhi, India: Sage.

Falkenberg, L and Monachello, M (1990). "Dual Career and Dual Income Families: Do they have Different Needs?" *Journal of Business Ethics*, 9(4-5), 339-351.

Googins, B and Burden, D (1987). "Vulnerability of Working Parents: Balancing Work and Home Roles," *Social Work*, 32(4), 295-300.

Jick, T D and Mitz, L F (1985). "Sex Differences in Work Stress," *Academy of Management Review*, 10(3), 408-420.

Komarraju, M (1997). "The Work-family Interface in India," in Parasuraman, S and Greenhaus, J H (Eds.), *Integrating work and family: Challenges for a changing world*, Westport, CT: Quorum Books, 104-114.

Rout, U R; Lewis, S and Kagan, C (1999). "Work and Family Roles: Indian Career Workmen in India and the West," *Indian Journal of Gender Studies*, 6(1), 91-105.

Sekaran, U (1992). "Middle-class Dual-earner Families and their Support Systems in Urban India," in Lewis, S; Izraeli, D N and Hootsmans, H (Eds.), *Dual-earner families: International perspectives*, Newbury Park, CA: Sage, 46-61.

Wajcman, J (1981). "Work and the Family: Who gets "The Best of Both Worlds?" in *Cambridge Women's Studies Group: Women in Society*, London: Virago Press.

Zappert, L T and Weinstein, H M (1985). "Sex Differences in the Impact of Work on Physical and Psychological Health," *American Journal of Psychiatry*, 142(10), 1174-1178.

Why do scholars write like this? They want to acknowledge meticulously everything they have borrowed from other sources. What are the advantages of such citations? Don't they slow down the reader? What if writers do not acknowledge their borrowings like this? Does the reader care? How do writers indicate different kinds of borrowing? We shall answer these and similar questions on the following pages.

REWARDS OF INTELLECTUAL HONESTY

There are three major advantages in acknowledging intellectual borrowings by citing your sources honestly and accurately. The first is the satisfaction that you have done the right thing. You have complied with the ethical demands of scholarly work. If you do not do it. you will be guilty of plagiarism (more about it later in this section), a serious offence in the academic world that can lead to penalties that include disqualifications and dismissals whether you are a student or a professor. As vanLeunen (1978, p. 9) says, "Citation keeps you honest." When you have acknowledged your sources honestly, you can walk with your head held high; you do not run the risk of being caught. The feeling is quite similar to the one you get when you calculate your income tax honestly, pay it by the deadline and file your returns.

The second advantage is that it enhances your credibility as a writer without burdening you with proportionate responsibility. If, for example, you state that there has been very little research on what organizational designs lead to successful technical and organizational innovations, it is a mere statement of your opinion. Your readers may not take it seriously unless they recognize you as an expert in the field. But if you cite Khandwalla and Mehta (2004) in support of your statement, there is a fundamental difference in the way your readers perceive it. It is no more your opinion; it is based on a review of relevant literature by the authors cited. References to this and similar sources also help the reader accept your other observations more easily because it shows that you are aware of recent scholarly work in the field and that you are not reinventing the wheel. If the ideas you borrow turn out to be wrong, the responsibility belongs to the authors cited, not to you. Of course, you should go only to reliable and respectable sources, sources that provide knowledge generated through an appropriate research process. If you build your case on data collected from sources that offer merely individual opinions or findings of poorly conducted research, you will destroy your credibility as an academic. The responsibility for any error stays with the source you have borrowed the data from, but you will be guilty of poor judgement if you choose such unreliable sources. You must keep this in mind, especially when you search the mixed bag of the World Wide Web for information.

The third advantage goes to your readers. Accurate acknowledgement makes it possible for them to go to the original source and study the issue in depth if they wish to. They may do it either because they disagree with your analysis or because your statement excites them enough to want to delve deeper into the topic. If, for instance, you claim that graduate students who assess their peers as part of their courses develop several "employability skills," and cite Cassidy (2006) in support, some of your readers may be reluctant to accept it and may want to find out how that researcher came to this conclusion. Similarly, in Extract 2 above, the writer claims that Indian women's work and family dilemmas are often different from those of women in the West, and cites support from Sekaran (1992). Some readers may want to find out what the similarities and differences are. Proper citation will help them do so.

PLAGIARISM: IDEA THEFT

Most of us do not steal even when we can easily get away with it. We have learnt from early childhood that it is wrong to take other people's things without their permission. We would be embarrassed if we were caught stealing anything, even something as small as a pen from a neighbour's house. The embarrassment would be worse if others found out that something that we flaunted as our own was not ours, but stolen.

Yet some of us forget or ignore this basic tenet when we deal with easily accessible intellectual property that we find in books, journals, magazines and the Internet. Or we mistakenly assume that property rights do not apply to the fruits of intellectual or artistic efforts. We should realize that when we do not acknowledge, we let others believe that these products are our own even if we do not explicitly claim so. We deny the real owners the credit for creating them. It is nothing but stealing intellectual property and flaunting it as our own. It is wrong. It is plain cheating. It is called plagiarism.

There is nothing shameful about borrowing other people's ideas. They are a resource that, unlike material things, borrowing does not shrink. We can borrow and synthesize ideas from different sources and create new knowledge. That is how science grows. That is why Isaac Newton said in his 1676 letter to Robert Hooke: "If I have seen further it is by standing on the shoulders of giants" (Shapiro & Epstein, 2006, p. 550). But we must acknowledge the ideas we borrow. Complete and scrupulous acknowledgement of source documents helps us to comply with the ethical principles of scholarly writing which enjoin us, in the words of the American Psychological Association (2001, p. 348), "to ensure the accuracy of scientific and scholarly knowledge," and "to protect intellectual property rights."

Of course, we shouldn't take acknowledgement of sources to ridiculous extremes. There is a rich fund of common knowledge that we have inherited, we contribute to and pass on to the next generation. In most such cases we can't even figure out who discovered what. We know, for example, that *neem* (*Azadirachta indica*) has insecticidal properties; that looking directly at the sun during a total solar eclipse can damage one's eyes; and that smoking or chewing tobacco regularly can harm one's health. We have no idea who originally figured these out. Just as we don't need anyone's permission to breathe fresh air or walk on a public road (which could have started out as a private path through someone's private property), we don't need to acknowledge the source if we take ideas from that common intellectual fund for general academic purposes. If we use anything that has not passed into that common intellectual fund, however, we must acknowledge it. Otherwise we will be guilty of plagiarism.

There is often little more than a thin line separating the common intellectual fund from specific data or insights that we need to acknowledge. Take, for instance, the claim that *neem* has insecticidal properties. It is part of the common intellectual fund.

You may have heard it from a farm worker, a shopkeeper or your grandmother. You may never know who discovered it. There may be many people who discovered it independently of one another. It is virtually impossible to acknowledge the source of this kind of information; it is also unnecessary.

But assume that we are writing a paper on botanical insecticides. Assume also that we start the paper with the following statement: *Botanical insecticides derived from neem have generated more interest, investigation and commercial development than any other botanical product in the 20th century.* What would readers think of the claim in this statement? In the absence of any citation they would think that it is our idea clothed in our words. But it is neither our idea nor our words. We have lifted the entire sentence verbatim from page 33 of "Factors Limiting Commercial Success of Neem Insecticides in North America and Western Europe," a chapter written by M. B. Isman in *Neem: Today and in the new millennium,* a book edited by O. Koul and S. Wahab and published by Kluwer Academic Publishers in The Netherlands in 2004.

By not mentioning this source and the relevant page number, we let the readers assume that the claim is ours. By not putting Isman's words in quotes, we let the readers think that the words we have used are ours. Both are dishonest. We are guilty of plagiarism.

Imagine that we started our paper on botanical insecticides with the following statement: *Many botanical products have been studied and commercially developed in the last hundred years, but none of them match neem-based botanical insecticides in depth of investigation or range of commercial exploitation.* We haven't copied Isman's words; the words are our own. Are we still guilty of plagiarism? Certainly. We have paraphrased Isman's words, but we haven't given Isman the credit for studying the relevant data and coming to the conclusion that we have harvested. It is not a self-evident claim. Nor is it part of the common fund of knowledge. We can avoid plagiarism by introducing Isman in the second part of the statement: *Many botanical products have been studied and commercially developed in the last hundred years, but as Isman (2004) notes, none of them match neem-based botanical insecticides in depth of investigation or range of commercial exploitation.* Now this is an honest statement; there is no hint that it is our discovery.

Box 6.1 Additional Resources on Plagiarism

Additional resources on plagiarism

Visit www.plagiarism.org and http://www.web-miner.com/plagiarism for a
detailed discussion on various aspects of plagiarism.

There are times when you are not sure whether a piece of information pertains to the common intellectual fund or not. If in doubt, acknowledge the source when it can be traced. If you can't trace it, phrase the statement in a manner that clearly tells the reader that it is based on common belief without any supporting source. You may, for instance, start the statement with, "it is commonly known/believed that…" or "the general understanding is that…" In this case, the belief expressed through such a statement must indeed be a commonly held belief or reflect general understanding. But you must realize that it will not have the kind of authority or trustworthiness that statements supported by citations have.

How about the quote from Isaac Newton that we have reproduced a few paragraphs earlier? Suppose that we use those words without indicating them as Newton's. The quote is so well known that there is hardly any chance of readers mistaking us to have created it ourselves. Yet, according to scholarly norms, it would be wrong to leave out Newton's name. It would be plagiarism. Now, suppose that we reproduce the quote and say that it is from Isaac Newton's 1676 letter to Robert Hooke, but avoid mentioning Shapiro and Epstein (2006) as our source. We are not guilty of plagiarism, but we have not done enough to give credit to the editors of the volume we have taken it from. Nor are we helpful enough to the reader, who might want to go to that source.

THREE KINDS OF BORROWING

If you borrow Rs 500,000 from your bank, they will not only record it in their books but also insist on collateral security. If you borrow Rs 5,000 from your bank, they will record it in their books but will not ask you for any collateral security. If you borrow Rs 500 from a friend, neither you nor your friend may keep a record of it anywhere; you will remember it and return the money when you can or by a mutually agreed deadline. The kind of records kept thus depends on the kind of borrowing. Similarly, there are different levels of borrowing in the academic world. How you acknowledge your intellectual debt depends on how deep your indebtedness is.

Here are the three broad levels of borrowing in the context of academic writing:

a. You borrow an idea and the original text that the idea came packaged in.
b. You borrow an idea but package it in your own words.
c. You borrow nothing in particular, but take someone's support in general for an idea.

We hinted at these different levels of borrowing when we examined plagiarism. We shall look at each of these three levels in detail.

Borrowing Ideas along with the Original Text

When we borrow not only ideas but also the author's text in which the ideas were originally packaged, we have the heaviest scholarly indebtedness. We must indicate it by putting the borrowed words in quotation marks (inverted commas), besides pointing out the exact location from which we have taken it.

There are different ways in which another author's words can be introduced in your text. Here are three examples: (1) Furnham (2002, p. 23) observes that "few companies have courage as a core competency"; (2) "Few companies have courage as a core competency" (Furnham, 2002, p. 23); and (3) According to Furnham (2002, p. 23), "few companies have courage as a core competency." The text in quotation marks is reproduced word for word from page 23 of Furnham's paper published in 2002.

If such reproduced text contains four lines (40 to 50 words) or more, the convention is to indent it without quotation marks. That is why all the longer extracts we have reproduced in this book, such as the two at the start of this chapter, have been indented and they appear without quotation marks. When we use short or long direct quotes, we must mention which page(s) in the source document we have taken those words from.

We have to be careful when we quote others' words. They are sacred! We have no right to make any changes in them.

If we have to introduce a brief comment or explanation within a quote to enhance its clarity for our readers, use square brackets around the insertion. Here are two examples: (1) "We've spent Rs 5 crore [50 million] on advertising alone."; and (2) "Since then [1997] we have never visited a top business school for recruitment." In these two examples, we introduced the terms '50 million' and '1997' to help the reader understand the quote better.

We may not even correct spelling or grammatical errors in a direct quote. Imagine that the following is the quote you want to use: "PCC Ltd was declared bankrupt in October 2009." You cannot drop the extra 'm' from October. But if you leave the offending 'm' in, your readers might think that perhaps you made that spelling mistake while copying the original words. In such cases, you can use [sic] after the problematic word: "PCC Ltd was declared bankrupt in October [sic] 2009." *Sic* (pronounced 'sik') is a Latin word that means *thus* or *so*. It tells the reader that you have faithfully reproduced the word as you found it in the original, although there is something odd or wrong about it.

If you italicize, underline or boldface a word or phrase in the quotation to give it emphasis, you must tell the reader that you have added it. Imagine, for instance, that the original sentence says, "There is a huge fund of knowledge that belongs to everyone, rather like public roads." If you italicize 'everyone,' this is how you should tell the reader: "There is a huge fund of knowledge that belongs to *everyone* [emphasis added], rather like public roads." If the original text had a word or phrase in italics or boldface and you are worried that the readers might think it was your addition, you can mention, in square brackets, that the emphasis was the original author's: [emphasis in the original].

Similarly, if you omit words from a direct quote, you must indicate that too. The convention is to use three dots in a row.

Box 6.2   Three Levels of Academic Borrowing

Three levels of academic borrowing
(*i*) You borrow an idea and the original text that the idea came packaged in.
(*ii*) You borrow an idea but package it in your own words.
(*iii*) You borrow nothing in particular, but take someone's support in general for an idea.

Suppose you want to quote the following sentence dropping the words in italics: "There is a huge fund of knowledge *that belongs to everyone,* rather like public roads." This is what you will need to do: "There is a huge fund of knowledge… rather like public roads." Of course, you should not omit words in a way that distorts the meaning of the original text. It would, for example, be dishonest to drop the word "hardly" from "China is hardly in a position to challenge the supremacy of the American dollar" and to indicate the gap with three dots when reproducing the sentence in your text.

Use direct quotes very sparingly. Reproducing exact text, even with adequate acknowledgement, seems reasonable only when it is necessary for conveying the meaning contained in the source text without any dilution or distortion. Your readers will not respect you if your document is a collage of quotes. Besides, you may have to seek the copyright owner's permission for quoting substantially from copyrighted work. (We have, for instance, taken *Vikalpa*'s permission to reproduce a few extracts from it in this book.) Many journals will allow only up to 250 words to be quoted from a single article without express permission from the publishers. You could treat 250 words as a reasonable norm for the limits of direct quotations from a single source. If you have to borrow more words, check with the publishers concerned if they have higher limits.

You may have noticed that in the extracts reproduced at the start of this chapter, there are 10 citations but not a single direct quote. If you go to the full 8,000-word paper from which those extracts are taken, you will find 53 references to published sources, but not a single direct quote. The author has briefly paraphrased the ideas she has borrowed or merely indicated awareness of supporting evidence in other sources. That is a better way to use others' findings in one's writings. This takes us to the next level of borrowing, namely, paraphrasing others' ideas.

Paraphrasing Others' Ideas

To paraphrase others' ideas is to borrow them without the text they came in. As we have already noted, even though we use our own words, the ideas are not ours and so we need to acknowledge them.

Imagine that you find the following in a paper on change management:

Furnham (2002) singles out courage – courage to take risks, courage to deal with the emotions of co-workers, and courage to stand up for one's values and beliefs – as the most important requirement for a manager interested in initiating and managing change in his organization.

That the statement's contents are borrowed from Furnham's paper of 2002 is clear from the citation. If you check out the original paper, you will realize that this short paragraph summarizes its first part. But there is no direct quotation. The writer of the paper on change management has taken the ideas from Furnham and put them in his own words. Unlike in a direct quote, page numbers are not needed when you acknowledge the source.

There is a problem when we use our own words to present others' ideas. In the absence of quotation marks clearly indicating what we have borrowed, we at times fail to let the reader know what is borrowed and what is our own. Take, for example, the following paragraph from a student report:

A typical PPP project passes through the following steps. Public sector agency defines project scope and required parameters (capacity etc.). Then among the bids submitted by private players, technical feasibility is evaluated. Subsequently the offer is made to the most competitive bidder and a long-term contract is devised delineating the terms of project and the sharing of risks and rewards. Over the life of contract, both parties are expected to ensure that the contract is maintained and required service delivered (Krishnaswamy, 2006).

(*Taken from "Public-private partnership for bridging the infrastructure gap in India: Lessons from transportation sector", student assignment, 2008*)

The writer acknowledges his debt to Krishnaswamy's article published in 2006. But what has he borrowed? From the way he has cited the source, it is not clear whether he has borrowed the ideas in the entire paragraph or only those ideas in the last sentence. If all the main ideas in the entire paragraph have been borrowed, here is a better way to acknowledge the paraphrase:

As Krishnaswamy (2006) observes, a typical PPP project passes through the following steps. Public sector agency defines project scope and required parameters (capacity etc.). Then among the bids submitted by private players, technical feasibility is evaluated. Subsequently the offer is made to the most competitive bidder and a long-term contract is devised delineating the terms of project and the sharing of risks and rewards. Over the life of contract, adds Krishnaswamy (2006), both parties are expected to ensure that the contract is maintained and required service delivered.

"Krishnaswamy (2006)" is repeated in the last sentence of the paragraph because otherwise it will not be clear to the reader if the idea in that sentence also is Krishnaswamy's or the writer's.

If the writer has borrowed only the ideas given in the last sentence, the original paragraph can be left as it is except for the last sentence, which can be revised as follows:

According to Krishnaswamy (2006), over the life of contract, both parties are expected to ensure that the contract is maintained and required service delivered.

Our objective should be to acknowledge the source in such a way that readers can easily make out what is our own and what has been borrowed. In other words, it is not enough to give a citation at the end of a paragraph if readers cannot readily make out whether the whole paragraph or only the last sentence has been borrowed. If we intersperse our own sentences with paraphrases, we must acknowledge the source in each sentence where we use borrowed ideas or introduce the paraphrase in such a way that the reader knows where it starts and where it ends.

Let us go back to the second paragraph of the second extract from Buddhapriya (2009) reproduced at the start of this chapter. It gives us three good examples of paraphrase. The ideas in the first sentence are unambiguously credited to Rout, Lewis and Kagan (1999), and those in the second sentence to Komarraju (1997) because these citations are given either at the start of the sentence or in the middle. In the third sentence, the citation "(Bharat, 2001)" comes at the end; there, however, is no room for confusion because all the previous sentences in the paragraph have proper citations. The very last sentence of the paragraph is clearly the author's and so there is no citation.

A crisp paraphrase is generally preferred to quotes because a good paraphrase demonstrates that you have understood the ideas you have borrowed and are able to strengthen your analysis with them. When you quote a long sentence or a paragraph, the reader is not sure you have understood it.

Note that some journals may treat paraphrased text like reproduced text when specifying limits on the number of words that can be borrowed freely from a single article. The moral is clear: do not depend heavily on any single source.

Taking Someone's Support in General for an Idea

At this level of borrowing, the writer brings to the readers' notice the support that her analysis has from different sources. The writer also demonstrates to the readers her awareness of relevant work in the field. She may do this to indicate sources that take a position that contradicts or supports hers.

You will find this kind of citation illustrated in Extract 1 at the start of this chapter.

> Women give birth to children, and still do most of the work of bringing them up. To do a demanding job and managing family and social life simultaneously is notoriously difficult. It is generally women who take the primary responsibility for childcare and who, in situations of conflict, adjust their working lives to accommodate family pressures (Wajcman, 1981; Falkenberg and Monachello, 1990). Data show that women professionals still assume the primary responsibility of home and childcare activities (Googins and Burden, 1987; Jick and Mitz, 1985; Zappert and Weinstein, 1985).

The writer states that childcare is essentially women's responsibility and that if it comes in the way of work, they have to adjust their work life. She then cites two sources in support of that idea. She goes on to cite three sources in support of her claim that women professionals still have to look after their home and care for their children.

Box 6.3 Additional Resources on Paraphrasing Others' Ideas

Additional Resources

For a more detailed treatment of how to paraphrase others' ideas and how to support your ideas with those of others, read "Writing about the work of other authors" and "Writing about your own thoughts," under the feature *Research Writing Skills* on the website of the University of South Australia.
http://www.unisanet.unisa.edu.au

Here is an extract from Dadhich and Bhal (2008, p. 16). (The full bibliographical details of the citations within the extract have not been reproduced here from the original.)

> However, some have suggested that transformational and charismatic leaders can be unethical (Bass, 1985) if they are motivated by selfishness rather than altruism (Bass, 1998; Howell, 1998; Howell and Avolio, 1992), and if they use power inappropriately (House and Aditya, 1997; McClelland, 1975).

Anubha Dadhich and Kanika T. Bhal synthesize a claim from six different sources: transformational and charismatic leaders who are driven by selfishness and who use power inappropriately may do unethical things. The writers don't use any direct quotes nor do they paraphrase others' ideas. Instead, they show their awareness of the ideas developed by other writers and cite them in support of the claim that they have made. In a sense, these are one-phrase summaries of entire papers or of entire sections. While this approach is highly recommended in academic writing, we should make sure that such one-phrase summaries are fair and adequate.

Here is another example of the way brief references are made to other scholars' ideas to build up the background to one's contribution. It is from Quinn (2009, p. 254). (Here, again, the full bibliographical details of the citations within the extract have not been reproduced from the original.)

> It is apparent that the term "lifestyle" has long been used ambiguously in the marketing literature (Wells 1975), often interchangeably with the term "psychographics" (Demby 1974; Koponen 1960).

Quinn does not mention any page numbers in the citations because he is not quoting any phrases but taking the support of ideas from three earlier sources.

For a more detailed treatment of these ideas and additional illustrations, read "Writing about the work of other authors" and "Writing about your own thoughts," under the feature *Research Writing Skills* on the website of the University of South Australia (http://www.unisanet.unisa.edu.au).

THE ANATOMY OF A CITATION

The basic elements of a standard citation in the print world are the name of the idea's author, the source from which we picked up the fact or idea (for example, an article in a journal or on the Internet, a chapter in a book, an interview on radio or television), the name (and place) of the publisher and the year of publication. Let us look at each of these elements.

The author's name

The need for naming the idea's author is self-evident. We must give credit to the person who generated the idea or gathered the fact that we borrow and use.

The idea's source

Mentioning the exact location (that is, the title of the article and the name of the journal or the publication in which the idea appears) helps your reader visit it if necessary. Another reason for mentioning the location is that the credibility of the idea depends to some extent on it. It is like our residential address. The way the world looks at us may vary if our address points to a slum or an exclusive and expensive zone in the city. A highly regarded international journal (for example, *Academy of Management Journal*, or *Harvard Business Review*) and a tabloid (or a random website) are at the opposite ends of the credibility spectrum. The location thus helps readers judge the quality of the information that has been borrowed.

The publisher's name (and place of publication)

The publisher of a source of information deserves credit for making it available to the rest of the world. The credibility of the information also depends to some extent on the publisher. The reputation and quality control of some publishers are such that the reader is sure of authentic and reliable information. Nowhere is this more evident than on the Internet. We find millions of worthless and unreliable websites along with highly respected and trustworthy sites maintained by reputable organizations such as universities and research organizations. In order to judge how credible your idea is, or to order a copy, a reader may need information about the publisher.

The year of publication

The year of publication is critical in many fields of knowledge. In a fast emerging area like information technology or biotechnology, for example, there may be substantial changes in a matter of a few months. Disruptive innovations in 2009 can render worthless some claims that were well established and widely accepted in 2008. Even in a field where change is not fast, the year of publication may help us accept or question the value of the borrowed idea. Take, for example, the following sentence and citation from Extract 1 that we have already studied: "Data show that women professionals *still* [emphasis added] assume the primary responsibility of home and child-care activities (Googins and Burden, 1987; Jick and Mitz, 1985; Zappert and Weinstein, 1985)." The author is making a claim about the way women professionals 'still' behave in 2009 based on research findings from the mid-1980s. Perhaps the way they take care of home and children has changed significantly in the last 25 years. Perhaps it has not. In the absence of more recent research findings that corroborate the data from the 1980s, readers will be justified in not taking the claim very seriously.

The exploding electronic world is different from the print world in several respects, and that poses certain challenges. Publishing on the World Wide Web is so easy that information of doubtful validity sits there comfortably along with products of highly regarded scholars and research institutions. Another problem is that the host can make changes at will in the content and style of information already uploaded by him and accessed by others. Often we have no information about the author, the place of publication or the date of publication. On the positive side, we can access through databases, the electronic version of the current and back issues of a large number of international journals in a wide range of disciplines. Increasingly, there are also online journals without any print version at all. We shall take up later in this chapter ("In-text Citations and References (Electronic Sources)") how to cite electronic sources of different kinds.

Box 6.4 Parts of a Standard Citation

A standard citation consists of two parts: (i) In-text citation (in the body of the paper)   (ii) Reference (at the end of the paper)

There is a good reason why a combination of different biblio-graphical elements is used to acknowledge sources: the need for unique identification. If we say, "Payal designed a new centrifugal pump for use in farms," a question will come up: "Payal who?" There are thousands of Payals. Which one are we referring to? When we say, "Dr Payal Gupta, Associate Professor, AVS Institute of Engineering, Patna...," we are almost certain to zero in on just one individual out of thousands of Payals and perhaps hundreds of Payal Guptas. In the same way, when we use a combination of three or four bibliographical elements, we will be able to identify a source uniquely.

We have been stressing that we should acknowledge our sources meticulously when we write for academic purposes. But this advice raises a problem. If we acknowledge the source of every idea we borrow and use, we will slow our readers down and even annoy them. They may miss the woods for the trees! Some may be interested only in the facts and ideas presented rather than the details of their sources. So we have to find a way of acknowledging our sources without creating a stumbling block in the readers' path. The solution that scholars have arrived at is to have a minimal, unobtrusive acknowledgement in the text (in-text citation) right where you use the borrowed idea, and full bibliographical details (references) elsewhere. Thus, a citation can be divided into two parts, namely, *in-text citation* and *reference*. We shall take a close look at both in this section.

In-text Citation

Let us take a sample in-text citation from Extract 1 at the start of this chapter: (Sekaran, 1992). As we read, we note that the idea (the work and family dilemmas of career women in India and in the West are different) has been borrowed by author Buddhapriya from something Sekaran wrote and got published in 1992. We can continue reading the paper if we don't need any additional details. If we want to know what kind of publication it is, we can stop reading and go to "References" at the end of the paper where we find the following details: Sekaran, U. (1992). "Middle-class Dual-earner Families and their Support Systems in Urban India," in S. Lewis, D. N. Izraeli, and H. Hootsmans (Eds.), *Dual-earner families: International perspectives*, Newbury Park, CA: Sage, 46–61. Now we know that it is not a journal article but a chapter in a book edited by three scholars and published by Sage in the USA.

In this sub-section we shall focus on in-text citations. See Figure 6.1 for an illustration.

Figure 6.1 In-text Citation Examples

Author's last name	Year of publication	Location (page number)
Sekaran	1992	(not applicable)
Buddhapriya	2009	p. 37

Splitting the citation into two components—in-text citation and references—and using only the first component for giving minimal information about the idea's author and year of publication in the body of the paper is a neat solution. However, it is not always simple to identify a source using these elements of citation. There are problems with each one of these elements. Take, for example, the name(s) of the person(s) who generated the idea we want to borrow. In some cases, we may not know who the author of a document is. Most newspaper editorials fall in this category. There may not be an identifiable author for a dictionary or encyclopaedia. Similarly, the exact location from which we take a piece of information from the Internet can be difficult to specify. If our source is a book or an article in a conventional print journal, we can cite the page number. But if it is an Internet source, there may be neither page numbers nor indications about when the document was uploaded. There is obviously no publisher for any information we gather through personal communication. How do we identify the source by providing the citation elements in such cases? We shall illustrate later in this chapter ("Illustration of Citation and References") how to deal with some of these problem cases and take you to published sources that give you guidelines on a wide range of citation contexts.

Another question we need to consider is how the in-text citation should be formatted. If, for example, we borrow a few words from page 37 of Buddhapriya's 2009 paper, how should we format the in-text citation? Here are four possibilities:

Buddhapriya (2009, p. 37)
Buddhapriya (2009: 37)
(Buddhapriya, 2009, 37)
Buddhapriya[14]

We shall deal with this aspect in the next section ("Common Citation Styles") devoted to different citation styles.

List of References

As we mentioned earlier in this chapter, the full bibliographical details of all the sources you cite in the body of your document should be given in a section called "References," or "Works Cited," which comes at the end of the body of the document. Thus, for each document cited in the text, there would be one entry in the references section providing bibliographical details of that document. The entries in the references section should be arranged alphabetically according to the surnames of authors (see, for example, "References" at the end of this book). Depending on the kind of sources you use, there are different details you need to provide. See Figures 6.2 and 6.3 for the structure of three sample entries in a list of references. These are simple because all the three sources have all the standard identifying features. (We shall look at some of the more difficult ones in sections "In-text Citations and References (Print Sources)" and "In-text Citations and References (Electronic Sources)."

a. Buddhapriya, S. (2009). Work-family challenges and their impact on career decisions: A study of Indian women professionals. *Vikalpa, 34*(1), 31-45.
b. Eagleton, T. (2005). *The English Novel: An Introduction,* Oxford: Blackwell.
c. Sekaran, U. (1992). Middle-class dual-earner families and their support systems in urban India. In S. Lewis, D.N. Izraeli, and H. Hootsmans (Eds.), *Dual-earner families: International perspective* (pages 46-61). Newbury Park, CA: Sage.

Figure 6.2 Reference (to a paper in a print journal and to a book)

Author's last name + initials	Year of publication	Source 1 (title of paper)	Source 2 (title of book or journal)	Source 3 (journal's volume, issue number and page numbers, or book's place of publication and publisher)
Buddhapriya, S.	2009	Work-Family Challenges and... Professionals	*Vikalpa*	Volume 34, number 1, pages 31-45
Eagleton, T.	2005	(Not applicable)	*The English Novel: An Introduction*	Oxford, Blackwell

Figure 6.3 Reference (to a chapter in an edited book)

Author's last name + initials	Year of publication	Source 1 (title of chapter)	Source 2 (title of book)	Source 3 (page numbers)	Name of publisher, place of publication
Sekaran, U.	1992	Middle-class Dual-earner Families and their Support Systems in Urban India	*Dual-earner families: International perspectives* edited by S. Lewis, D.N. Izraeli, and H. Hootsmans.	Pages: 46-61	Sage, Newbury Park, CA.

There are formatting issues in the way we list references. Here are a few. Should the title of the book be in italics? Should all the main words in the title start with a capital letter, that is, should the title be in title case? Or is it enough to have just the first word of the title start with a capital letter, that is, should the title be in sentence case? How should the titles of journal papers appear? In single quotes? In double quotes? With no quotes? In title case? In sentence case? In what sequence should the different elements of a reference entry appear? Where, for example, should the year of publication appear? Immediately after the author's name? At the very end of the reference elements? How should we separate one element from its neighbouring ones? With a comma? With a period?

It is largely answers to these questions on punctuation and formatting that distinguish one citation style from another and one journal's citation style from those of others. We shall deal with the formatting differences in the next section ("Common Citation Styles") before we illustrate the American Psychological Association (APA) style ("Illustration of Citation and References"), which we recommend for reports and papers in management and behavioural sciences.

COMMON CITATION STYLES

While the elements identified above are the ones used extensively in academic circles to specify sources, you will notice that journals and professional associations in different disciplines have adopted different styles. This is somewhat like traffic regulations in different countries; while the objectives and basic components (for example, stopping, limiting speed, giving way, parking) are the same, there are differences in the way in which rules are framed and executed in response to local conditions. Some differences in citation styles reflect the differences in the requirements in various disciplines. The year of publication of source documents in physical and social sciences, for instance, is so important that the reader wants that information upfront in the text itself. The year of publication is often not so critical in humanities, especially Language and Literature; therefore, there is no need to burden the reader with that information in the body of the paper. This difference is reflected in the in-text citation style adopted by humanities journals and science journals.

However, most of the differences in formatting are in punctuation, not in substance if you compare some of the widely adopted styles such as APA Style, Harvard Style, Modern Language Association (MLA) Style, Chicago Style and Institute of Electrical and Electronic Engineers (IEEE) Style. You can find detailed online illustrations of these styles in *A Research Guide for Students* (2008), *Citation Style for Research Papers* (n.d.)[1] and *Citation Explained* (2005). What is presented below is intended merely to

---

[1] (n.d.) stands for No Date.

give you a taste of different citation styles. We shall illustrate the differences between citation styles by showing the way a simple direct quote from a print journal article would be handled in each of those citation styles.

Box 6.5 Additional Resources for Different Citation Styles

Additional resources

For a detailed introduction to different citation styles, visit:

A research guide for students (2008). Research, writing, and style guides (MLA, APA, Chicago/Turabian, Harvard, CGOS, CBE). Available from http://www.aresearchguide.com/styleguides.html

Citation explained. (2005). University of Maryland University College site. Available from http://www.umuc.edu/library/tutorials/citation/html/M1_whichStyle.html

Citation Style for Research Papers. (n.d.). Long Island University's B. Davis Schwartz Memorial Library site. Available from http://www.liu.edu/cwis/cwp/library/workshop/citation.htm

Purdue University Online Writing Lab (OWL) (2009). *The Purdue Online Writing Lab*. Available from http://owl.english.purdue.edu/

Before we move to the illustrations, a word of caution is due. Do not think of these styles as frozen or sacrosanct. Citation styles evolve over time. Journals and other scholarly institutions also tend to adapt these styles and, therefore, there may be variations between different journals following the *same* citation style. Compare, for example the two sample references given below. The first is from page 209 of *Journal of Transport Economics & Policy* (Vol. 43, Part 2, 2009), published by London School of Economics and the University of Bath, UK, and the second is from page 250 of *Journal of Marketing Management* (Vol. 25, No. 3-4), published by the Academy of Marketing, UK. In their guidelines for contributors both the journals claim that they follow the Harvard style of citation.

Goh, M. and J. Yong (2006): 'Impacts of Code-Share Alliances on Airline Cost Structure: A Truncated Third-order Translog Estimation', *International Journal of Industrial Organization*, 24, 835-66.
Yankelovich, D. and Meer, D. (2006), "Rediscovering Market Segmentation", *Harvard Business Review*, Vol. 84, No. 2, pp. 122-131.

While the elements and their sequence are the same in these two references, there are obvious differences in punctuation.

Similarly, if you go to the start of this chapter and examine the list of references following the two extracts reproduced there, you will find that while they are internally consistent, they do not fit neatly into any of the six citation styles we illustrate below. The conclusion is that when you format your in-text citations and references, strictly follow the current practice of the journal you want to publish in. If you are submitting written assignments to your instructors, you should follow their citation style specifications or preferences. There may be little to choose between double quotation marks and single quotation marks, but if you ignore your journal's or your instructor's style choice, you may face trouble.

APA Style

Brief description:

In-text citation: author and date of publication; list of references at the end of the document; authors' surnames arranged alphabetically. The APA style has been developed by American Psychological Association. Consult American Psychological Association's *Publication Manual of the American Psychological Association* (2001) and *APA Style Guide to Electronic References* (PDF) (2007) for an authoritative and detailed guide. The latest version of the *Publication Manual*, however, is the sixth edition, published recently (2009).

Citation in the text:

Buddhapriya (2009, p. 42) concludes that during the last two decades there has been "hardly any change in the societal perception that women are required to shoulder greater family responsibilities."

Or,

During the last two decades there has been "hardly any change in the societal perception that women are required to shoulder greater family responsibilities" (Buddhapriya, 2009, p. 42).

In the list of references:

Buddhapriya, S. (2009). Work-family challenges and their impact on career decisions: A study of Indian women professionals. *Vikalpa, 34*(1), 31-45.

Harvard style

Brief description:

In-text citation: author and date of publication; list of references at the end of the document; authors' surnames arranged alphabetically; similar in many respects to APA style. Although it originated in Harvard University and is known as the Harvard style of citation, Harvard University does not publish any citation style manuals. For illustrations of the Harvard citation style, you can consult the websites of a few universities (e.g., Bournemouth University (http://www.bournemouth.ac.uk/library/citing_references/docs/Citing_Refs.pdf)).

Citation in the text:

According to Buddhapriya (2009, p. 42), there has been "hardly any change in the societal perception that women are..."

In the list of references:

Buddhapriya, S., 2009. Work-family challenges and their impact on career decisions: A study of Indian women professionals, *Vikalpa*, 34(1), 31-45.

However, according to the websites of some other universities such as the University of Melbourne (http://www.lib.unimelb.edu.au/cite/harvard_dis/journal_dist.html), Monash University (http://www.lib.monash.edu.au/tutorials/citing/harvard.html) and Canterbury University (http://canterbury.libguides.com/content.php?pid=23624&sid=199475), the references are formatted differently:

> Buddhapriya, S 2009, 'Work-family challenges and their impact on career decisions: A study of Indian women professionals', *Vikalpa*, vol. 34, no. 1, pp. 31-45.

This highlights the need for you to study the citation style as followed by the journal in which you want to publish.

Chicago Style

Brief description:

Developed by University of Chicago; the latest available guide is *The Chicago Manual of Style*, 15th edition, published in 2003. A more recent (2007) online version is available at: http://www. chicagomanualofstyle.org/tools_citationguide.html. The Chicago Style has two versions, one for humanities and the other for sciences. In the humanities version, the citation in the text is indicated by a number (superscript); a corresponding number at the bottom of the page supplies the full bibliographical details. The scientific version is like APA and Harvard styles because the in-text citation mentions the author and date of publication; the references are given at the end of the document and the entries arranged alphabetically according to the surnames of the authors.

Humanities version

Citation in the text:

Buddhapriya[23] concludes that there has been "hardly any change in the societal perception that women are…"

At the foot of the page:

23. Sanghamitra Buddhapriya, "Work-Family Challenges and Their Impact on Career Decisions: A Study of Indian Women Professionals," *Vikalpa* 34-1(2009), 42.

In the Chicago Style, Humanities version, there is no need for a section called "References" or "Bibliography" at the end of the paper because the full bibliographical details are supplied in footnotes throughout the paper. If, however, the writer of a book or longish paper provides such a section called "Bibliography," the entries are arranged alphabetically according to author surnames.

In the list of references:

Buddhapriya, Sanghamitra. "Work-family Challenges and Their Impact on Career Decisions: A Study of Indian Women Pro-fessionals." *Vikalpa* 34(1) (2009): 31-45.

Scientific version

Citation in the text:

Buddhapriya's (2009, 42) conclusion that there has been "hardly any change in the societal perception that women are..."

In the list of references:

Buddhapriya, Sanghamitra. 2009. Work-family challenges and their impact on career decisions: A study of Indian women professionals. *Vikalpa* 34(1): 31-45.

MLA Style

Brief description:

In-text citation: author and page; list of references at the end of the document in a section titled "Works Cited"; entries in this list are arranged alphabetically by author surname; developed by Modern Language Association of the USA. It publishes two guides: The MLA Handbook for Writers of Research Papers (7th edition is the latest) and the *MLA Style Manual and Guide to Scholarly Publishing* (3rd edition is the latest). Detailed information is available at http://www.mla.org. The MLA style is widely adopted by journals in humanities, especially Language and Literature.

Citation in the text:

The view that there has been "hardly any change in the societal perception that women are..." (Buddhapriya 42).

Or,

Buddhapriya's (42) conclusion that there has been "hardly any change in the societal perception that women are..."

In both these examples, 42 is the page number. For the year of publication one has to go to the 'Works Cited' at the end of the paper. The reason for dropping the year of publication in the in-text citation may be that often it is not critical in humanities, especially Language and Literature, unlike in physical and social sciences.

In the list of references (Works cited):

Buddhapriya, Sanghamitra. "Work-family Challenges and Their Impact on Career Decisions: A Study of Indian Women Professionals." *Vikalpa* 34.1 (2009): 31-45.

IEEE Style

Brief description:

Developed by Institute of Electrical and Electronics Engineers, USA; generally found in engineering and technology journals. The feature that makes it different from the other styles is that each source used is given a number, and it is that number rather than the author's last name that appears in the in-text citation and forms the basis of sequencing in the list of references that comes at the end of the document. The sources cited are numbered in the order in which they appear first in the body of the docu-ment. Visit http://www.ieee.org/portal/cms_docs_iportals/iportalspublications/authors/transjnl/stylemanual.pdf or http://www.ecftoronto.edu/~writing/handbook-docum1b.html or http://www.lib.murdoch.edu.au/find/citation/ieee.html for detailed illustrations.

Citation in the text:

Buddhapriya [27] does not find any significant change in society's perception that women...

Or

There has not been any significant change in society's perception that women... [27].

In the list of references:

[27] S. Buddhapriya, "Work-family challenges and their impact on career decisions: A study of Indian women professionals." Vikalpa, vol. 34, no.1, pp 31-45, Jan-March 2009.

Figure 6.4 shows how in-text citations are given in six different citation styles.

Figure 6.5 summarizes the salient formatting features of the "References" or "Works Cited" in six citation styles. Some words from the title of the paper, "Work-Family Challenges and

Their Impact on Career Decisions: A Study of Indian Women Professionals," have been dropped (indicated by three dots) for the sake of brevity.

Figure 6.4 In-text Citations in Different Styles

Citation Style	Author's name/ number	Year of publication	Page number
APA	Buddhapriya	(2009,)	p. 42
Harvard	Buddhapriya	(2009,)	p42
Chicago – Humanities	Buddhapriya[23]	[Not given in text]	[Not Given in text]
Chicago – Sciences	Buddhapriya	(2009,)	42
MLA	Buddhapriya	[Not given in text]	42
IEEE	27	[Not given in text]	

Figure 6.5 Listing of Bibliographic Details (a paper in a print journal): Comparison between Styles

Citation style	Author	Year of publication	Source 1 (paper)	Source 2 (journal)	Source 3 (journal's volume, issue number, page numbers)
APA	Buddha-priya, S.	(2009).	Work-family challenges and their impact on career decisions: A study of Indian women professionals,	*Vikalpa,*	34(1), 31-45. (Volume 34 number 1 pages 31-45)
Harvard	Buddha-priya, S.	2009.	Work-family challenges … professionals,	*Vikalpa,*	34(1), 31-45.
Chicago A (humanities)	23. Buddha-priya, Sangha-mitra,	[2009, but it comes after volume and number.]	"Work-Family Challenges… Women Professionals,"	*Vikalpa*	34-1(2009), 42.

(Continued Table 6.5)

(Continued Table 6.5)

Chicago B (scientific)	Buddha-priya, Sangha-mitra.	2009.	Work-family challenges... women professionals.	*Vikalpa*	34(1): 31-45.
MLA	Buddha-priya, Sangha-mitra.	[2009, but it comes after volume and number.]	"Work-family Challenges... Women Professionals."	*Vikalpa*	34.1 (2009): 31-45.
IEEE	[27] S. Buddha-priya,	[2009, but it comes at the end of the reference.]	"Work-family challenges... women professionals."	*Vikalpa*	vol. 34 no.1, pp. 31-45, January-March 2009.

ILLUSTRATIONS OF CITATION
AND REFERENCES

There is considerable variety in the types of source documents that you can borrow from. These include books, edited books, journal articles, papers which are "in press," magazine articles, newspapers, corporate reports, government reports, working papers, conference presentations, conference proceedings, dissertations, dictionaries, encyclopaedias, translations and personal communications. Some of these may be available in print, some online and some both in print and online. The range, depth and accessibility of online resources are changing fast. It is, therefore, not practical to provide comprehensive guidelines here. We shall illustrate a few frequently occurring citation tasks and direct you to authoritative manuals for detailed guidance.

In the previous section ("Common Citation Styles"), we chose a short quote from an article in a print journal to illustrate different citation styles. That, along with single author books, is one of the simplest and commonest sources to cite. There are other sources that pose difficulties. What, for example, should we do if the author's name is not available or if the source has several authors? How do we acknowledge electronic sources that do not indicate the year of publication or even page numbers? We shall turn to those more difficult citation tasks now and illustrate them.

All our recommendations below (except the one on citing Internet documents without page numbers) regarding the citation format are derived from the current practice that we observe in a number of academic journals (such as *Journal of Organizational Behavior, Journal of Applied Behavioral Science, Business Communication Quarterly* and *Journal of Management Education*) that follow the APA citation style. We have adopted it in this book also to acknowledge our borrowings. We recommend it for management students and researchers because it is, as Harvey (2003) says, the most widely adopted citation style for academic writing in social sciences, business and management.

There, however, is a problem. The APA style is not uniform in all respects across the journals that have adopted it. As we have noted in the last section, a journal may introduce minor variations (generally in punctuation) in the format of in-text citations, or references, or both, and, therefore, some of our recommendations may differ slightly from the practice of some journals that follow the APA style. So, if you want to publish in a journal, go carefully through its citation style guidelines (which may be found in a note titled "Instructions/guidelines for authors/contributors" in some issues of that journal and/or at the journal's website); check out the papers in a few recent issues for illustrations; then follow the format meticulously. If you need additional help, we recommend that you consult American Psychological Association (2001, 2007 and 2009a) for authoritative guidelines covering almost all kinds of citation tasks involving both print and online resources. Another excellent resource is Purdue University Online Writing Lab (OWL) (2009).

Box 6.6   Additional Resources for Guidelines on APA Style

Additional resources

For detailed and authoritative guidelines on the APA style, consult:
American Psychological Association. (2001). *Publication manual of the American Psychological Association* (5th ed.). Washington, DC: Author.
American Psychological Association. (2007). *APA style guide to electronic references* (PDF). Washington, DC: Author. Available from www.apa.org/books/
American Psychological Association. (2009a). *Publication manual of the American Psychological Association* (6th ed.). Washington, DC: Author.
American Psychological Association. (2009b). *APA journals manuscript submission instructions for all authors*. Retrieved June 26, 2009, from http://www.apa.org/journals/authors/all-instructions.htm

In the following illustrations, you will find how different sources are briefly cited in the body of the paper and how their full bibliographical details are presented in the list of references at the end of the paper.

In-text Citations and References (Print Sources)

One author

Citation in the text:

Use the author's last name followed by the year of publication, and in the case of direct quotes, the exact page number. Examples:

- Hughes (2009) finds that meanings of the value clusters of Chinese…
- Although China has always valued education, traditionally women in China received no formal education (Hughes, 2009)…
- Traditionally, education in China was "neither universal nor scientific" (Hughes, 2009, p. 214).
- Kellogg's' Cereal Mates, launched with great hopes, became "a major flop" (Haig, 2003, p. 37) and had to be withdrawn.

Note:

When there is a single author, the format of the in-text citation is the same whether the source is a book or an article in a journal.

In the list of references:

Hughes, N. (2009). Changing faces: Adaptation of highly skilled Chinese workers to a high-tech multinational corporation. *The Journal of Applied Behavioral Science, 45*(2), 212-238. doi: 10.1177/0021886309334031.

Haig, M. (2003). *Brand failures: The truth about the 100 biggest branding mistakes of all time.* London: Kogan Page.

Note:

- The author's first name is reduced to initials; there is a period following the initial.

- The year of publication is in parenthesis; it is followed by a period.
- The title of the journal article is in sentence case (only the first word and proper nouns begin with a capital letter); there are no quotation marks enclosing the title.
- The title of the journal is in title case (all main words start with a capital letter); it is in italics.
- The journal's volume number (*45*) is in italics; the issue number (2) is in parenthesis. Strictly speaking, the issue number is not needed in this particular case because *The Journal of Applied Behavioral Science* numbers its pages continuously across all the four issues in a volume. You need to mention the issue number only if each issue in a volume starts with page 1. *Vikalpa,* for example, does that.
- The page numbers of the articles come at the end of the reference without the word 'pages' preceding it.
- There is a long number preceded by the acronym DOI. This is the Digital Object Identifier of this electronic document, the unique number issued by the publisher. (More about DOI at the start of "In-text Citations and References Electronic Sources.")
- In the case of the book, the title is in sentence case (only the first word in the title and in the subtitle starts with a capital letter) and in italics.
- The place of publication of the book comes before the name of the publisher; a colon (:) separates the two.

Two or more authors

Citation in the text:

Cite the same way as a single author except that all the surnames appear. Examples:

- When an individual joins a corporation, he has to adapt himself to it by abandoning something and adopting something new (Boerner & Jopp, 2007).
- Boerner and Jopp (2007) argue that...
- This point has been raised by several scholars (e.g., Miller, Fitzgerald, Murreli, Preston, & Ambaker, 2005).
- Miller, Fitzgerald, Murreli, Preston, and Ambaker (2005) support the...

Note:

- Before the last surname 'and' comes in continuous text and ampersand (&) comes in citation. While this is the most common pattern, some journals do not allow '&' in either place.
- If there are three to six authors, mention all the names in the first citation. If you cite the source again, it is enough to use the name of the first author and then, 'et al.,' the Latin expression for 'and others.' The multi-author citation above will become: Miller et al. (2006) further suggest that …
- If there are more than six authors, it is enough to use the first surname and 'et al.' even when the source is cited for the first time. Whether to use 'et al.' right from the first occurrence or only from the second occurrence onwards of a citation would depend on the style adopted by a particular journal.
- This citation format for multiple authors of books and articles applies also to working papers, dissertations, papers in conference proceedings and papers presented at conferences.

In the list of references:

Boerner, K., & Jopp, D. (2007). Improvement/maintenance and reorientation as central features of coping with major life change and loss: Contributions of three life-span theories. *Human Development, 50*, 171-195.

Miller, M.G., Fitzgerald, S.P., Murreli, K.L., Preston, J., & Ambaker, R. (2005). Appreciative inquiry in building a transcultural strategic alliance. *Journal of Applied Behavioral Science, 41*, 91-110.

Note:

- The ampersand (&) is used to link the two authors in the first reference and the first four with the last author in the second reference. Note the comma (,) before the ampersand.
- This time the issue number is not given in parenthesis immediately after the volume number (*50* in the first reference and *41* in the second) because both these journals

number their pages continuously across all the issues in a volume.

A group, committee or an organization as the author

Citation in the text:

Use the group's/organization's name in place of the author's name. Examples:

- American Psychological Association (2001) recommends that...
- An abstract can be defined as "a brief comprehensive summary of the contents of the article" American Psychological Association (2001, p. 12).

In the list of references:

American Psychological Association. (2001). *Publication manual of the American Psychological Association* (5th ed.). Washington, DC: Author.

Note:

- In the list of references, the organization's name is mentioned in the slot for the author's name.
- American Psychological Association is not only the author but also the publisher of this book; that is why the word, 'Author' is given in the slot for publisher. This is how you let the reader know that the author and the publisher are the same. This applies also to individual authors who publish their own books.

Documents without the author's name

Citation in the text:

Use the first few words of the title of the document in place of the author's name. Example:

- In the world of international finance, China certainly has clout because it has nearly $2 trillion in foreign currency reserves ("Taking the Summit," 2009, April 11).

Note:

- The example refers to an article entitled "Taking the Summit by Strategy," and published on April 11, 2009 in *The Economist*. The author's name is unknown. In its slot, the title of the document is given. To make the in-text citation brief, the first few words rather than all the words in the title have been used.
- When a work does not mention any author names, the level of credibility may be low except in the case of well-known reference books or sources such as *The Economist*, from which the idea cited above has been taken.

In the list of references:

Taking the Summit by Strategy. (2009, April 11). *The Economist, 391*(8626), 28.

Note:

The Economist mentions the volume number (*391*) and the issue number (8626). Hence, both these are given in the reference.

Several works supporting the same point

Citation in the text:

A semicolon separates a citation from the one following it. List the citations alphabetically by the last name of their first authors, not chronologically. Example:

- The main reason why students choose online courses over traditional ones appears to be convenience (Bocchi, Eastman, & Swift, 2004; Hiltz & Shea, 2005; McEwen, 2001; Moskal & Dziuban, 2001).

In the list of references:

The references related to the sources will be arranged alphabetically according to the first surname in each citation. Thus, in the list of references, Bocchi, Eastman, & Swift, 2004 comes before Hiltz & Shea, 2005, and that comes before McEwen, 2001, and so on.

Two or more works published by the same author in the same year

Citation in the text:

If, in your document, you have to refer to two or more documents of one author published in the same year, use the lowercase letters of the alphabet to distinguish one publication from the other. Examples:

- In an examination of disciplinary and course-specific effects on course outcomes of web-based courses, Arbaugh (2005a) found that...
- While it is important for students to perceive the software platform for online courses to be useful and easy to use (Arbaugh, 2005b), ...

In the list of references:

Arbaugh, J.B. (2005a). How much does "subject matter" matter? A study of disciplinary effects in online MBA courses. *Academy of Management Learning & Education, 4,* 57-73.
Arbaugh, J.B. (2005b). Is there an optimal design for online MBA courses? *Academy of Management Learning & Education, 4,* 135-149.

Sources accessed indirectly

Citation in the text:

At times you are unable to access the original work (called *primary source*). Take, for example, a Master's dissertation presented by D.M. Teekell, in 1989. You are unable to access it. But you find that an important idea from it has been quoted, paraphrased or referred to by Keith Topping in his 1998 paper, which you access. Teekell (1989) is the *primary source* and Topping (1998) the *secondary source*. In such a case, you need to indicate both the primary source and secondary source in your in-text citation. Example:

- Teekell (1989, as cited by Topping, 1998, p. 255), says that "while instructor feedback is beneficial for students at low skill levels, it can be detrimental for students at high levels of skill."

In the list of references:

Topping, K. J. (1998). Peer assessment between students in colleges and universities. *Review of Educational Research, 68*(3), 249-276.

In the list of references, the details of Teekell's 1989 document are not given because you did not consult it. In the "References" section, you need to give the full bibliographic details of only the secondary source—Topping, 1998—that you actually consulted.

Personal communication

Citation in the text:

You can cite a personal source such as e-mail or telephone conversation. In such cases, give full details in the text. Examples:

- Anil Bedi (personal communication, July 18, 2009) attributed the breakdown of the negotiation to…
- Anil Bedi (telephone conversation, July 18, 2009) attributed the breakdown of the negotiation to…
- The breakdown of negotiation has been attributed to "sheer pig-headedness of the overpaid expatriate managers" (Anil Bedi, e-mail, July 18, 2009), and…

In the list of references:

There is no need to list personal communication in the References section because it will not be accessible to anyone other than you.

In-text Citations and References (Electronic Sources)

The broad guidelines for citing print sources apply to electronic sources also. Citing an electronic source is easy when it has all the standard identifying features such as author, title, year of publication and publisher, but accessed electronically. In those cases, the in-text citation would be the same as its counterpart in the print form. In "References," you can add the Digital Object Identifier (DOI) or the PII (Publication Item Identifier) of the document, if available. DOI and PII are unique numbers that publishers have started assigning to each of the electronic documents they publish. A DOI or PII will take you directly to particular electronic document it represents.

The main principle we need to follow when dealing with electronic sources is that we must help the reader go to the source as quickly and as reliably as possible. We need to give the reader as many standard identifying details (author's name, title of the document, year of publication) as possible and the Uniform Resource Locator (URL), that is, the address of or the path to the source in cases where a DOI or PII is not available. If a document has a DOI/PII, there is no need to give the URL.

We shall illustrate a few instances of in-text citations and references when the sources are accessed electronically.

Article from a print journal, accessed through an electronic database

Citation in the text:

The in-text citation norms for comparable print sources apply to these.

In the list of references:

Examples:

> Terry, N.G., & White, P.J. (1997). The role of pension schemes in recruitment and motivation: Some survey evidence. *Employee Relations, 19*(2), 160-175. doi: 10.1108/01425459710171049.

> Mahoney, J. T. (2001). A resource-based theory of sustainable rents. *Journal of Management, 27*(6), 651-660. pii: S0149-2063(01)00116-7.

Each of these references is to a paper published in a print journal but accessed through an electronic database. The first example mentions the DOI and the second example mentions the PII of the document. Apart from the addition of these identifying numbers, the references are identical to the ones you make to their print journal counterparts. If the copy accessed is a PDF file, the original page numbers will be retained. If, however, the copy accessed is an HTML file, there may be no page numbers.

In these examples, even without the DOI/PII, the reference is adequate because the original sources are print journals; the DOI/PII number merely confirms that the paper has been accessed electronically and, therefore, lets the reader know that it is available in the electronic form.

When accessing documents through electronic databases, scholars were expected to identify the database they accessed. That is no longer necessary partly because of the unique identifying numbers, and partly because the same document may be available in more than one database. Mohoney (2001), cited above, can be accessed, for example, both through both http://www.sciencedirect.com and http://web.ebscohost.com

Given below is the electronic path to Mahoney (2001), cited above:

http://www.sciencedirect.com/science?_ob=MImg&_imagekey=
B6W59-44NM46T-3-1&_cdi=6565&_user=1009876&_orig=search&
_coverDate=12%2F31%2F2001&_sk=999729993&view=c&wchp=d
GLzVzz-zSkWA&_valck=1&md5=2193ad90e7dade6e2bc2ecc1808e
923c&ie=/sdarticle.pdf

This is obviously unwieldy. It is also unnecessary now because of powerful search facilities on the Internet. Even if the document does not have a DOI/PII, it is enough for the reader to know that this is accessible through http://www.sciencedirect.com and, hence, this URL can be given as the last element at the end of the reference entry for this document: Available from http://www.sciencedirect.com.

If there is a chance that the document we have consulted electronically may be revised (not uncommon with Internet documents), we have to indicate on what date we accessed it. In the case of the two print journal papers mentioned above, however, no revision is expected and, so, there is no need to indicate on what date we accessed the site.

Electronic version of article from a print source

Citation in the text:

Example:

- Guinier and Sturm (2009, July 10) note that many American fire departments are rejecting written tests for recruitment and opting for tests that focus on practical problem-solving.

The in-text citation is like the one for a comparable printed document, here a newspaper article.

In the list of references:

Example:

> Guinier, L., & Sturm, S. (2009, July 10). Trial by firefighters. *The New York Times.* Available from http://www.nytimes.com/2009/07/11/ opinion/11guinier.html?_r=1.

As the original is a print source published in a newspaper on a particular date, we have all the details necessary to identify the source. As this document has no DOI/PII assigned to it, we have to give the URL, which will take one directly to the electronic version of the article in *New York Times.* If the source is not accessible to non-subscribers, it is enough to give the URL of the source's homepage, here http://www.nytimes.com.

We have not mentioned the date of access because here again we do not anticipate any revision in the newspaper article we have consulted.

Document with no page numbers

Citation in the text:

Many electronic sources do not have page numbers. In such cases, American Psychological Association (2001, p. 120) recommends the use of paragraph number preceded by the symbol ¶ or by the abbreviation 'para' and the relevant number to guide the reader to the exact location. If the document has no paragraph numbers but has headings, the recommendation is to cite the appropriate heading and indicate which paragraph under that heading you are referring to. Example:

- The Indian government's pension reforms including the New Pension System (NPS) for central government employees are likely to "percolate into the private sector" (Kakar, 2008, Pension reforms in India, para. 2).

Here, "Pension reforms in India" is a subheading, and the direct quote comes from paragraph 2 in the section with that subheading. However, powerful search facilities currently available on the Internet and in databases may make such a detailed citation unnecessary. If, for example, you search for "percolate into the private sector" + Kakar, the article from which this phrase was taken will show up. Hence, we rarely see paragraph numbers of Internet documents in the in-text citations. The best course of action may be to follow the guidelines issued by the journal you wish to publish in or the supervisor you have to submit your assignments to.

In the list of references:

Kakar, G. (2008, May). Retirement in India: Pension benefits and beyond. Retrieved July 11, 2009, from http://www.mercer.com/referencecontent.htm?idContent=1303935.

Note:

- Along with the year of publication, the month (May) also is given because the version cited is the one that was updated in May 2008. It is possible that the author will revise it later in the year.
- The date on which information was retrieved from the website (July 11, 2009) is mentioned because there is a likelihood of the document being revised.

Document with no date of publication

Citation in the text:

Example:

According to an investigative report (Siedle, n.d.), many employees who have participated in defined contribution retirement plans have lost money because of the selfish practices adopted by the providers of services to these retirement plans.

Note:

The phrase "n.d." (no date) is used because the publication date of the article is not available.

In the list of references:

Siedle, E. (n.d.). *Secrets of the 401k industry: How employers and mutual fund advisers prospered as workers' dreams of retirement security evaporated.* Retrieved July 11, 2009, from http://www. benchmarkalert.com/alert.html.

Note:

As we do not know when the document was developed or uploaded, it is useful to give the date on which information was retrieved from the website.

Document with no author's name

Citation in the text:

Example:

- According to *The Economist,* the yuan is "unlikely to challenge the dollar as a reserve currency for years" (China and the dollar, 2009, July 9).

Note:

The Economist, a highly respected international news magazine, generally does not indicate the author's name in any of its analytical reports. So, here we have used the first four words of the title of the article in the slots for author's name.

In the list of references:

Example:

China and the dollar: Yuan small step. (2009, July 9). *The Economist.* Retrieved from http://www.economist.com/businessfinance/display Story.cfm?story_id=13988512&source=hptextfeature.

Note:

- We need not give the date of retrieval here because the text is unlikely to undergo changes. Moreover, the date of publication is available in the reference.
- If the content is not accessible to the general reader, it is enough to give the URL of *The Economist's* website: http:// www.economist.com.

Document in an Internet-only journal

Citation in the text:

Example:

- According to Sobrero (2004), futuring is not planning, but a first step in program development.

Note:

The citation follows the same pattern as in other print journal articles except that there may be no page numbers.

In the list of references:

Example:

> Sobrero, P. M. (2004, April). Futuring: The implementation of antici-patory excellence. *Journal of Extension, 42*(2). Retrieved June 29, 2009, from http://www.joe.org/joe/2004april/comm1.php.

Here, "42" is the volume number and "2" is the issue number. As the month and year of publication are available, they have been included in the reference entry.

An entire website

Citation in the text:

Example:

- The Internet search service, Google, has made it easy for Indians seeking information on and from India by creating a site (http://www.google.co.in/) where one can go straight to web pages from India.
- The website of the scriptwriter of the Walt Disney film, 'RememberTheTitans'(http://www.gregoryallenhoward.com) has many useful resources for classroom use.

Note:

Here, you need to cite an entire website rather than a particular document within it. The URL of the website is given within the text of the paper rather than in the reference list at the end of the paper.

In the list of references:

There is no need to mention the website in the list of references because you are not providing here any information beyond what is given in the in-text citation.

CHAPTER SUMMARY

The focus of this chapter is on the proper citing of the sources from which we borrow facts or ideas and put into our text. We explain what it means to acknowledge our sources, why we should do so and what advantages we derive from meticulously acknowledging our sources. We illustrate the three different kinds of borrowing: direct quote, paraphrase and general support, and show what leads to plagiarism.

After analysing the process of citing and showing the differences between citation styles of different journals and professional bodies we briefly illustrate in-text citation and references (both print sources and electronic sources) according to the APA style, which is the style most widely adopted in management and behavioural sciences journals.

Our illustrations cover only the most common citation tasks, easily observed in journals. For detailed and authoritative guidance, we recommend American Psychological Association (2001, 2007, 2009a and 2009b). But if you are publishing in a journal, its current practice overrides all the guidelines from all other sources.

Appendix 1

BRIEF DESCRIPTIONS OF SOME OF THE RESEARCH TERMS USED IN CHAPTER 2

Various technical terms associated with research process have been described in Chapter 1 as a part of the description of various research process steps. However, some other specific terms have been used in Chapter 2. A brief description of these additional research-related terms used in Chapter 2 is outlined below.

Reliability of a Scale/Measure

This refers to the consistency with which a scale or measure provides a measure of the aspect being measured. This is assessed through multiple methods. For example, one method is known as 'test–retest reliability' in which the same scale is administered to two groups at two different points in time. The correlation between the scores/measures obtained at two different times is taken as an indicator of test–retest reliability and reflects the stability of the scale/measure. The most common indicator of reliability is referred to as *cronobach alpha* level or *cronobach alpha coefficient*. The value of this indicator ranges from 0 to 1 and a guideline in research, based on Nunnally (1978) as cited by Hinkin (1995, p. 979), is that for a scale, the value of at least 0.7 is required. This indicator is routinely computed and reported in nearly all empirical papers to present descriptive statistics of study variables. This is presented in the results section before reporting the results of the main data analysis for hypothesis testing.

Validity of a Scale/Measure

This measures the extent to which a scale/measure actually measures the concept it has been designed to measure. In other words, this indicates the extent to which the measure taps the true meaning of the concept that it is designed to measure. There are various forms of validity, namely, content validity, criterion-related validity and construct validity (convergent validity and discriminant validity). There are methods available for assessing these different forms of validity.

Scale Items

In the behavioural areas of management, a concept is usually measured through a scale that contains multiple statements. A respondent is required to read each statement and respond to the statement. The sum of responses of an individual to all statements in the scale is taken as the total score of the individual on that scale. Each of these statements in a scale is referred to as a scale 'item.'

Response Format

For each item in a scale, a respondent is required to provide a response. Typically, these responses are recorded in a format that has a set of response options and a respondent is required to choose one response option. The response options indicate various points on a continuum and can also be referred to as anchor points. There is an anchor descriptor (for example, *strongly agree, always, sometimes*) and a score value associated with each anchor point which forms one of the response options. This collection of anchor descriptors and the associated anchor point scores arranged in an order of increasing or decreasing value of anchor point scores is referred to as the response format. While this is the description of the most common response format, sometimes a different response format (for example, ranking) may be used in a research study and for such a response format the above description of a response format will not entirely apply.

Correlation

In data analysis for a research study, sometimes the strength of association between two variables (for example, employees' calculative commitment and employees' helping behaviour) needs to be assessed. An indicator of the strength of association or relationship between two variables is correlation coefficient. Its value ranges from -1 to 1, with correlation coefficient of -1 indicating a perfect negative relationship, 1 indicating a perfect positive relationship and 0 indicating no relationship between two variables.

Regression Coefficient

In data analysis for a research study, sometimes a study variable is treated as the dependent variable and another study variable is treated as an independent variable. To assess the extent of predictive power of an independent variable in predicting the dependent variable, the dependent variable is regressed on the independent variable. The coefficient of the independent variable in the resulting regression equation is known as *regression coefficient*. When a single dependent variable is regressed on more than one independent variable, a regression coefficient is associated with each independent variable.

Test Statistics

The indicators such as correlation coefficient and regression coefficient generated from statistical analysis are referred to as *test statistics*. The magnitude of a test statistics is used to test whether the hypothesis under consideration is supported.

Significance Level

For the various indicators obtained from statistical analysis or statistical test (for example, correlation coefficient, beta coefficient), it is necessary to assess whether the indicator's magnitude is large enough. Statistical significance level, also referred to as *p value*, is used to infer how large an indicator's magnitude is. For instance, typically, significance levels of 0.001, 0.005, 0.01 and 0.05 are used in research. For each of these levels, certain magnitude of the indicator will be regarded as statistically significant at that p value or *significance* level (for example, 0.001, 0.005).

Appendix 2

RESOURCES FOR HONING ACADEMIC WRITING

Here are some resources that you might like to consult if you want more detailed guidance on various aspects of academic writing. Some of these are very useful if you want to write a dissertation or publish papers in international journals. These resources are divided into three parts. Part 1 lists books that help you do research and write it up. Part 2 consists of freely accessible online resources on citation styles. Part 3 has both print and online resources that help you make your documents free from errors in language (English) and style.

PART 1: PRINTED BOOKS—
HOW TO DO RESEARCH AND WRITE IT UP

American Psychological Association. (2001). *Publication manual of the American Psychological Association* (5th ed.). Washington, DC: Author.

An invaluable, detailed reference guide on all aspects of writing up and publishing your research. While the formatting guidelines given are specific to the American Psychological Association (APA) style, which is adopted by a large number of journals in management and behavioural sciences, you will also find help with designing and reporting research and reducing bias in language. (It has an online supplement brought out in

2007: *APA style guide to electronic references* [PDF]. Washington, DC: Author. This supplement, which gives an update on how to cite electronic sources, can be bought from www.apa.org/books/.) The sixth edition of the *Publication Manual of the American Psychological Association* (2009) is also available now.

Gibaldi, J. (2004). *MLA handbook for writers of research papers*. New Delhi: Affiliated East-West Press.

Apart from a comprehensive description and illustrations of the Modern Language Association (MLA) citation style, this book provides detailed guidelines on various aspects of research writing.

Golden-Biddle, K., & Locke, K.D. (1997). *Composing qualitative research*. Thousand Oaks, CA: Sage Publications.

This book takes you through the process of writing up your research. The most interesting aspect of this book is the use of the metaphor of story writing to describe the process of professional writing. The chapters are accordingly titled: "Crafting the story-line," "Developing the storyline," "Characterising the storyteller" and "Rewriting the story."

Kerlinger, F. N. (1988). *Foundations of behavioral research*. New York: Hold, Rinehart, and Winston, Inc.

While this book is on research methodology, the early pages discuss aspects pertaining to knowledge, research, science and theory. Very useful!

Lunenburg, F. C., & Irby, B. J. (2008). *Writing a successful thesis or dissertation*. Thousand Oaks, CA: Sage Publications.

This book gives tips and strategies for students in social and behavioural sciences. It covers the whole process starting from planning research, writing it up and getting it ready for a publication.

Rubens, P. (Ed.). (2004) *Science & technical writing: A manual of style* (2nd ed.) New York: Routledge.

This is a comprehensive book on writing in science and technology. Especially useful are its chapters on grammar, punctuation, numbers and symbols, illustrations and displays. The chapter on using quotations, citations and references provides valuable illustrations.

Rudestam, K. E., & Newton, R. R. (2001). *Surviving your dissertation* (2nd ed.). Thousand Oaks, CA: Sage.

The authors take you through the research process and the writing process. The style is easy on the eyes. The chapter on writing is very useful. Especially noteworthy is the section, "Twelve tricks to keep you going when you write" (pages 218–221).

PART 2: FREELY ACCESSIBLE ONLINE RESOURCES ON CITATION STYLES

Academy of Management Journal. (2008). Style guide for authors. *51*(1), 197-200. Available from http://aom.pace.edu/amjnew/style_guide.html.

American Psychological Association. (2009). APA journals manuscript submission instructions for all authors. Available from http://www.apa.org/journals/authors/all-instructions.html.

APA Formatting and Style Guide. (2009). Purdue University Online Writing Lab (OWL), Purdue University, USA. Available from http://owl.english.purdue.edu/owl/resource/560/01.

Coates Library, Trinity University (n.d.). Available from http://lib.trinity.edu/research/citing/APAelectronicsources.pdf.

Harvey, G. (2008). *Writing with sources: A guide for Harvard students* (2nd edition). Indianapolis/Cambridge: Hackett Publishing Company, Inc. Available from http://isites.harvard.edu/fs/docs/icb.topic273248.files/WritingSourcesHarvard.pdf.

Journal of Organizational Behavior. (2009). Instructions to authors. Available from http://www3.interscience.wiley.com/journal/4691/home/ForAuthors.html.

Journal of Organizational Change Management. (n.d.). Author guidelines. Available from http://info.emeraldinsight.com/products/journals/author_guidelines.htm?id=jocm.

MLA Formatting and Style Guide. (2009). Purdue University Online Writing Lab (OWL), Purdue University, USA. Available from http://owl.english.purdue.edu/owl/resource/557/01.

University of Maryland University College (2005). APA Citation Explained. Available from http://www.umuc.edu/library/tutorials/citation/html.

PART 3: PRINT AND ONLINE RESOURCES FOR IMPROVING ENGLISH

Eastwood, J. (2005). *Oxford learner's grammar: Grammar builder.* Oxford: OUP.

This book is an English grammar resource pack of reference and practice material for intermediate and advanced students. *The Grammar Builder* has a range of meaningful exercises on the grammar areas explained in the *Grammar Finder* (which incidentally has a *Grammar Checker* CD-ROM), also published by OUP. *Grammar Builder* is suitable for self-study and can be used independently of the *Finder.*

Purdue University (2009). The Online Writing Lab (OWL). Available from http://owl.english.purdue.edu/owl.

Purdue University's Online Writing Lab (OWL) is an excellent source of free writing resources that will interest teachers and students alike. It is useful also for students who need to refine their English grammar and style. The website is regularly updated.

Raimes, A. (2004). *Grammar troublespots: A guide for student editors* (3rd ed.). Cambridge: CUP.

This book covers word order, important areas of grammar and punctuation. It includes interesting exercises that deal specifically with problem areas in grammatical accuracy.

Strunk, W. Jr., & White, E. B. (1959). *The elements of style.* New York: Macmillan.

A very short and very popular guide for those who want to write simple, clear and correct English. Originally published in 1918, it has been revised and republished several times because of its popularity. The latest version (2005) is *The elements of style illustrated* published by Penguin Books. The current online publisher of the 1999 version is Bartleby.com. You can freely access the online version of the whole book from http://www.bartleby.com/141/

Wehmeier, S. (Ed.). (2008). *Oxford advanced learner's dictionary* (7th ed.). Oxford: OUP.

This is highly recommended because besides giving meanings of words, it also illustrates how those words are used. The book has a short but very useful reference section on grammar and punctuation.

Yule, G. (2006). *Oxford practice grammar (advanced).* Oxford: OUP.

Each unit begins with a detailed explanation of the grammar area concerned. It is followed by a set of awareness-raising exercises. There are very useful self-assessment tests at the end of the units. A Practice-Boost CD-ROM comes with the book.

References

American Psychological Association. (2001). *Publication manual of the American Psychological Association* (5th ed.). Washington, DC: Author.

American Psychological Association. (2007). *APA style guide to electronic references* (PDF). Available from http://books.apa.org/books.cfm?id=4210509

American Psychological Association. (2009a). *Publication manual of the American Psychological Association* (6th ed.). Washington, DC: Author.

—— (2009b). *APA journals manuscript submission instructions for all authors.* Retrieved June 26, 2009, from http://www.apa.org/journals/authors/all-instructions.html

Bacharach, S. B. (1989). Organizational theories: Some criteria for evaluation. *Academy of Management Review, 14,* 496-515.

Baronov, D. (2004). *Conceptual foundations of social research methods.* London: Paradigm.

Barrass, R. (2002). *Scientists must write: A guide to better writing for scientists, engineers and students.* London: Routledge.

Bhal, K. T., & Gulati, N. (2007). Pay satisfaction of software professionals in India. *Vikalpa, 32*(3), 9-21.

Buddhapriya, S. (2009). Work-family challenges and their impact on career decisions: A study of Indian women professionals. *Vikalpa, 34*(1), 31-45.

Cassidy, S. (2006). Developing employability skills: Peer assessment in higher education. *Education + Training, 48*(7), 508-517.

Cho, K., & Schunn, C. D. (2007). Scaffolded writing and rewriting in the discipline: A web-based reciprocal peer review system. *Computers & Education, 48*(3), 409-426.

Cho, K., Schunn, C. D., & Charney, D. (2006). Commenting on writing: Typology and perceived helpfulness of comments from novice peer reviewers and subject matter experts. *Written Communication, 23*(3), 260-294.

Citation explained. (2005). University of Maryland University College site. Retrieved June 17, 2009, from http://www.umuc.edu/library/tutorials/citation/html/M1_whichStyle.html

Citation style for research papers. (n.d.). Long Island University's B. Davis Schwartz Memorial Library site. Retrieved June 17, 2009, from http://www.liu. edu/cwis/cwp/library/workshop/citation.htm

Cooper, D. R., & Schindler, P. S. (2003). *Business research methods*. New Delhi: Tata McGraw-Hill.

Daft, R. L. (1983). Learning the craft of organizational research. *Academy of Management Review, 8,* 539-546.

Dadhich, A., & Bhal, K. T. (2008). Ethical leader behaviour and Leader-Member Exchange as predictors of subordinate behaviours, *Vikalpa, 33*(4), 15-25.

Dubin, R. (1969). *Theory building*. New York: Free Press.

Feynman, R. P. (2003). *Don't you have any time to think?* London: Penguin Books.

Furnham, A. (2002). Managers as change agents. *Journal of Change Management, 3*(1), 21-29.

Golden-Biddle, K., & Locke, K. D. (1997). *Composing qualitative research*. Thousand Oaks, CA: Sage.

Gopen, G. D., & Swan, J. A. (1990). The science of scientific writing. *American Scientist, 78,* 550-558. Retrieved from http://www.americanscientist.org/issues/ feature/the-science-of-scientific-writing/1

Gupta, M. P., Kanungo, S., Kumar, R., & Sahu, G. P. (2007). A study of information technology effectiveness in and government organisations in India. *Vikalpa, 32*(2), 7-21.

Harvey, M. (2003). *The nuts and bolts of college writing*. Retrieved June 17, 2009, from http://nutsandbolts.washcoll.edu/apa.html

Hessler, R. M. (1992). *Social research methods*. St Paul: West Publishing Company.

Hinkin, T. R. (1995). A review of scale development practices in the study of organizations. *Journal of Management, 21,* 967-988.

Isman, M. B. (2004). Factors limiting commercial success of neem insecticides in North America and Western Europe. In O. Koul and S. Wahab (Eds.), *Neem: Today and in the new millennium* (pp 33-41). The Netherlands: Kluwer Academic Publishers.

Jauch, L. R., & Wall, J. L. (1989). What they do when they get your manuscript: A survey of Academy of Management reviewer practices. *Academy of Management Journal, 32,* 157-173.

Kerlinger, F. N. (1988). *Foundations of behavioral research*. New York: Hold, Rinehart, and Winston.

Khandwalla, P.N., & Mehta, K. (2004). Design of corporate creativity. *Vikalpa, 29*(1), 13-28.

Klein, L. R. (1965). Writing problems in the social sciences. *Journal of Business Communication, 2,* 1-9.

Lee, A. S. (1991). Integrating positivist and interpretive approaches to organizational research. *Organization Science, 4,* 342-365.

vanLeunen, M-C. (1978). *A handbook for scholars*. New York: Alfred A. Knoph.

Lewin, T. (2003, April 26). Writing in schools is found both dismal and neglected. *The New York Times*. Available from http://www.nytimes.com

Mitchell, T. R. (1985). An evaluation of the validity of correlational research conducted in organizations. *Academy of Management Review, 10*, 192-205.

Murdick, R. G., & Cooper, D. R. (1982). *Business research: Concepts and guides.* Columbus, OH: Grid.

Needleman, M. H. (1968). *Handbook for practical composition.* New York: McGraw-Hill.

Ogburn, W. (1947). On scientific writing. *The American Journal of Sociology, 52*(5), 383-388.

Paul, R., & Elder, L. (2007). *How to write a paragraph: The art of substantive writing.* Retrieved July 21, 2009 from www.criticalthinking.org

Purdue University Online Writing Lab (OWL) (2009). *APA formatting and style guide.* Available from http://owl.english.purdue.edu/owl/resource/560/01/

Quinn, L. (2009). Market segmentation in managerial practice: A qualitative examination. *Journal of Marketing Management, 25*(3-4), 253-272.

A research guide for students (2008). Research, writing, and style guides (MLA, APA, Chicago/Turabian, Harvard, CGOS, CBE). Retrieved June 17, 2009, from http://www.aresearchguide.com/styleguides.html

Rahul, N. (2009, January 25). Two Price Waterhouse auditors held. *The Hindu,* Retrieved January 25, 2009, from www.hindu.com/2009/01/25/stories/2009012557960100.htm

Ritchie, J., & Lewis, J. (2004). *Qualitative research practice: Guide for social science students and researchers.* London: Sage Publications.

Rogers, P. S., & Rymer, J. (1995). What is the relevance of the GMAT analytical writing assessment for management education? A critical analysis, Part 1. *Management Communication Quarterly, 8*(3), 347-367.

Shapiro, F. R., & Epstein, J. (2006). *The Yale book of quotations.* Yale: Yale University Press.

Stone, E. F. (1978). *Research methods in organizational behavior.* Glenview, IL: Scott, Foresman.

Subramaniam, K. (2007). *Mahabharata* (14th ed.). Mumbai: Bhartiya Vidya Bhavan.

Topping, K. (1998). Peer assessment between students in colleges and universities. *Review of Educational Research, 68*(3), 249-276.

Tripathi, S. N., & Siddiqui, M. H. (2008). Effectiveness of mobile advertising: The Indian scenario. *Vikalpa.* 33(4), 48-59.

Turk, C., & Kirkman, J. (1989). *Effective writing: Improving scientific, technical and business communication* (2nd ed.). London: Spon Press.

UNESCO (1999). *Guidelines on gender-neutral language.* Available from http://unesdoc.unesco.org/images/0011/001149/114950Mo.pdf

Whetten, D. A. (1989). What constitutes a theoretical contribution? *Academy of Management Review, 14*, 490-495.

Williams, J. M. (1990). *Style: Toward clarity and grace.* Chicago: The University of Chicago Press.

Zelazny, G. (2007). *The say it with charts complete toolkit.* New Delhi: Tata McGraw-Hill.

Index